# The Mughal Aviary
## Women's Writings in Pre-Modern India

Sabiha Huq

Series in Literary Studies

VERNON PRESS

Copyright © 2022 by the author.

All rights reserved. No part of this publication may be reproduced, stored in a retrieval system, or transmitted in any form or by any means, electronic, mechanical, photocopying, recording, or otherwise, without the prior permission of Vernon Art and Science Inc.
www.vernonpress.com

*In the Americas:*
Vernon Press
1000 N West Street, Suite 1200,
Wilmington, Delaware 19801
United States

*In the rest of the world:*
Vernon Press
C/Sancti Espiritu 17,
Malaga, 29006
Spain

Series in Literary Studies

Library of Congress Control Number: 2021950202

ISBN: 978-1-64889-484-8

Also available: 978-1-62273-852-6 [Hardback]; 978-1-64889-427-5 [PDF, E-Book]

Product and company names mentioned in this work are the trademarks of their respective owners. While every care has been taken in preparing this work, neither the authors nor Vernon Art and Science Inc. may be held responsible for any loss or damage caused or alleged to be caused directly or indirectly by the information contained in it.

Every effort has been made to trace all copyright holders, but if any have been inadvertently overlooked the publisher will be pleased to include any necessary credits in any subsequent reprint or edition.

Cover design by Vernon Press.

Cover image: *The Quintessential Woman* (2019, oil on canvas) by Abu Kalam Shamsuddin, Bangladesh

I am no muse

I am a maker

If you love me, be my accomplice…

This book is dedicated to all women writers
whose memory has been erased from the annals of history

# Table of Contents

| | |
|---|---|
| Acknowledgements | vii |
| Introduction | xi |
| 1 The Mughal Aviary and Women In/Out | 1 |
| 2 Humayun's Biographer Gulbadan Begam: A Quiet Observer of the Aviary | 23 |
| 3 Jahanara's Hagiographies: The Mind of a Matriarch | 61 |
| 4 Dissenting Songbird in the Aviary: The Poetry of Zeb-un-Nissa | 103 |
| 5 The Plaintive Songbird beyond the Aviary: Habba Khatoon's Lol | 135 |
| 6 Where to Conclude? | 159 |
| Bibliography | 167 |
| Index | 175 |

# Acknowledgements

*The Mughal Aviary* is a labor of love. The book was conceived of at a stage in 2019 when my life unfolded untracked avenues both in literary and personal domains. Kathryn Lasky's fictional diary of Princess Jahanara Begam[1] came to me as a sudden delight; alongside the pleasure of reading into the past, Jahanara's sharp comments on Noor Jahan in the book made me apprehensive of the politics of representation that have put the pre-modern period in India in a state of confusion today. "There goes another of those Orientalist texts!", I said to myself. Lasky visualized the Mughal *harem* as a domestic space where women exercised all kinds of pleasure experiments without much thoughts on self and subjecthood. Several other fictional works on the Mughal women by Ruchir Gupta, Ira Mukhoty and Subhadra Sengupta gradually revealed to me how women become the object of exoticized representation if they are considered 'Others' where time, gender and religion become deciding factors. I am indebted to these authors for initiating my earliest thoughts.

While digging into the history of the Mughal women, I simultaneously learned about their literary merits and their politico-social turbulences. An avid reader of world literature as I am, I could sense the distinctive nature of these pre-modern women's writings in India. My understanding of the Mughal princesses' lives initiated the aviary metaphor, and I coincidentally discovered the existence of Habba Khatoon within that framework. S. N. Wakhlu's fictional biography of Khatoon enlightened me. To that connection, I came across films and media productions too, the existence of which created the possibility of a cultural study of the time through the existing documents on these women. Vernon Press's call for book proposal was an opportune moment, as this motivated the work with all the urgency of research and necessary communications. I would like to thank Vernon Press and many beautiful people like James McGovern, Argiris Legatos, Javier Rodriguez, Victoria Echegaray and Ellisa Anslow for their patience with my many queries and demands.

Professor Sonia Nishat Amin of Dhaka University and Srideep Mukherjee of Netaji Subhas Open University in Kolkata have been instrumental in the making of the book. Among ourselves, we shared initial ideas, conceptualized the structure, and re-read drafts with critical insight. The perspectives of a historian and a literature scholar, though not fundamentally different, complement each other in

---

[1] Lasky uses 'Begum' in her book, but here the modernized version 'Begam' has been used. Only in quotes the older version has been retained.

numerous ways. The book is about women's literary contributions, and much of the work demands a lot of historical reading and deeper understanding into the women's issues, both of which needed someone like Professor Amin, a renowned historian, and the author of *The World of Muslim Women in Colonial Bengal, 1876-1939*, to affirm that the book is a timely contribution to Indology and women's writings. I am grateful to her for the general introduction she has written. Srideep commented and helped in copy editing, without which I could never have made it this way. I have no words to express my gratitude to him.

I must mention Professor Sunil Sharma of Boston University, who has been incredibly generous in sharing with me the draft of his translation of *Risala-i-Sahibiya*. Without his help, my book would not have come this far. I am also indebted to Afshan Bokhari for her responses to my e-mails and her writings on Jahanara that enlightened this study.

I must acknowledge my debt to the anonymous peer reviewer of the manuscript; whose constructive suggestions helped me find lacunae in my first draft. I have tried to address the gaps as per my abilities, and the rest lies to the reader's judgment.

This book is blessed by scholars and colleagues across the globe. Several senior scholars including Fakrul Alam and Syed Manzoorul Islam from Bangladesh, my mentors, have encouraged the work. They have read and suggested important edits. I do not have words to thank them enough. Syed Foyez Ahmed helped me connect with Nadeem Jahangir Bhat of the University of Kashmir, and I am truly thankful to Foyez for the efforts he made to connect me to people and collect books for me. In the same breath, I express my gratitude to Nadeem Bhat for his suggestion on the translation of Kashmiri poetry, the useful links, and documents he sent me. Critical essays on the writings of pre-modern Indian women are scarce. Debamitra Kar sent me her Bangla article on Zeb-un-Nissa and she also read my chapter on Zeb-un-Nissa thoroughly. I am indebted to her.

Shariful Islam of Dhaka University helped me access a few rare books in the confined section of the Central Library of Dhaka University; thanks are due to Sharif and the librarian for their generous support. For the pandemic I could not visit the libraries in India and UK; but as books were necessary, my colleagues A B M Monirul Huq and Firoz Mahmud Ahsan, who have been staying in Hong Kong for their PhD research, took the pain of borrowing books from their library, and scanning and sending those whenever I demanded. I am indebted to these two young scholars. M Rezaul Haque of St John's University in Queens, New York, also sent a vital book borrowed from the library of his institution for my reference. I thank him from the core of my heart. My sister and mentor, Professor Fayeza Hasanat of Central Florida University, must be acknowledged for her guidance and last-minute support preparing the indexes.

*Acknowledgements*

My institution granted me a sabbatical leave for writing the book. The extensive research travels planned between the months of April-June 2020 had to be shelved because of COVID-19 that spread around the world in March, but I acknowledge the gracious gesture of Khulna University, Bangladesh, and the colleagues who wished me luck for the success of my project.

My parents and children have been a constant source of support and inspiration. My children's questions on why I was working on this project helped me understand my passion for women of the past with literary talent that also served as a soul searching. I once again realized the uncertainties of women's fate as writers, and for women how difficult it was and still is, to make space in the publication industry. My little daughter Shanita needs to be acknowledged because she was the one who kept faith in me. She would repeatedly remind me of the mammoth task of completing this manuscript, since she needed me to write a children's story book for her after I am done with it. I hope when Shanita will grow into a fine young woman, she will read the book and come to know of these Indian women writers. I wish she and all other girls get all those that they rightfully deserve in life.

Sabiha Huq

# Introduction

> Notions of "loss" and "exclusion", for instance – lost women writers, lost classics, exclusion from the canon – are always underwritten by a dream of wholeness or completeness.
> – (Tharu and Lalita, 1991, 23)[1]

Women of the Mughal Age in India (1526-1707/1858)[2] have been the subject of a sensuous, demeaning and damaging fantasy, originating in but not always confined to, the West, and comprising part of what is known as the Orientalist Gaze. Among the irrevocable harm this has wreaked on the destiny of the 'Oriental' races, is the adverse effect on the medieval/precolonial historiography of the region. Denigration of the colonized was a common epistemological tool of all colonial powers in the play of domination and control. Proving that 'native' peoples were debased, and immoral, a condition manifest in the oppression of their women, enabled the colonizing power to assume what Gauri Viswanathan terms the 'Masks of Conquest' (Viswanathan, 2014). This provided the basis for the hegemonic accompaniment to the brutal, military subjugation of subject races. For the colonist's notorious "civilizing mission" to hold water, there had to be a people that 'needed' civilization. As one British civil servant put it – "The natives must either be kept down by a sense of our power or they must willingly submit from a conviction that we are wiser, more just, more humane and more anxious to improve their condition than any other rulers they could have" (Farish, 1938, cited in Tharu and Lalita, 1991, 9)[3]

A key feature in the negative representation of oriental women (from the upper and middle strata of society) was the concept of the *harem*[4] as the sole site where women's lives were lived. The harem was the eroticized domestic terrain where men went for pleasure, rest, and recuperation. It is a pity that

---

[1] Source: *Women Writing in India: 600 BC to Early Twentieth Century* by Susie J Tharu and K. Lalita, Feminist Press. CUNY, 1991. Pg. 23.
[2] The Mughal Empire in India, according to some historians, ended with Aurangzeb who reigned till 1707; though the Mughal progeny was officially in power till 1858.
[3] Minute of J. Farish, 28.8.1938. Cited in Susie Tharu and K. Lalita (eds) *Women Writing in India*, ref. note 1.
[4] *Harem* or haram is usually the domestic part of a Muslim household where a man's wives, concubines, and female servants live. In the western Orientalist iconography, it is a world of sexual subjugation where women are portrayed in lascivious and evocative poses that have influenced many paintings, literary works, stage productions and films.

what became popular among Europeans at the time were pictures of women reclining in languorous, eroticized poses inside the imagined harems. We could have had instead the "Portrait of a young lady"- reading from a book in front of her in a garden, recently identified as Jahanara and attributed to the painter Lalchand (c. 1631-3, Losty and Roy, 2013, 132). However, the matter of the orientalist gaze is complicated by the fact that women's activities were considered inferior and unworthy of being recorded by the *indigenous* population of *contemporary* times as well. As such, their lives had to bear the double burden of being erased from the historical record and remaining unrepresented, save in patriarchal terms and being denied the opportunity to record it for themselves. Thus, women were excluded from the process of knowledge production both by the colonial power and their own indigenous contemporaries.

What amazes us more is that even today, the practice of erasing women from history and/or the trope of mythologizing them continues. This is evinced from the plentiful crop of fictionalized accounts on Mughal women in bookstores to the present day. But soon, there was a change in the air, especially in academia, due in part to diligent efforts of 20th-century feminist activists and scholars. The winds of change dictated that it was time to come out of the fog and take a sober look at the activities of these 'other/oriental' women of the harem and set the record straight. What greatly facilitated this process was the move to discover and compile women's writings. As Tharu and Lalita inform, "By the 1970s three major book-length studies that set up women's writing as a new disciplinary field had appeared" (Tharu and Lalita, 1991, 16). These were: *Literary Women* by Ellen Moers (1976), *A Literature of Their Own* by Elaine Showalter (1977)[5] and *The Mad Woman in the Attic* by Sandra Gilbert and Susan Gubar (1979). Tharu and Lalita in a groundbreaking work hails the movement: "Feminist criticism has actually shaped a new discipline and in the process created, as the object of its study, a new field: women's writing" (Tharu and Lalita, 1991, 22). Following Elaine Showalter, one of the terms used for this new discipline as pointed out in Tharu and Lalita is *Gynocritics*. They note further that this plays a crucial role in the new scholarship "concerned with woman as the producer of textual meaning with the history, themes, genres and structures of literature by women" (Tharu and Lalita, 1991, 18). It is however worth noting that while the two volumes edited by Tharu and Lalita cover an extensive span of time from 600 BC to the early twentieth century, they hardly include any of the texts by the Mughal women discussed in Sabiha Huq's work. Extracts from Gulbadan's *Humayun-Nama* has been given a short space in the book, and the other three are not mentioned at all. This is an omission that not only needs

---

[5] Sources: Elaine Showalter's *A Literature of Their Own: British Women Novelists from Bronte to Lessing,* Princeton: PUP, 1977 and *The New Feminist Criticism,* London Virago, 1986.

redressal, but also poses an intriguing question in the domain of gynocriticism, the politics of which merits interrogation, as a perusal of Huq's book will testify.

Sabiha Huq's *The Mughal Aviary: Women's Writings in Pre-Modern India* (henceforth *The Mughal Aviary*) seeks to set the record straight by – a) a discussion of past actions of women contained in almost forgotten and unevaluated writings by them, b) restoring to whatever extent possible, the rightful place to women who had played a role in the production of meaning by chronicling contemporary times and interpreting them through their own lens. Being out of the empire's vortex or at the margins so to say, they were able to do this without the usual constraints of fear, favor, power, or privilege. However, as women of the Mughal royal family or members of the aristocracy (a minority within a minority), there were other compelling constraints within which they lived and worked. The workings of power equations in the case of the authors discussed by Huq assume seminal importance in this context.

At the very outset, *The Mughal Aviary* challenges existing patriarchal use of language by replacing certain words, the most obvious of them being aviary for harem. An aviary is a large enclosure for keeping birds in human habitats. Unlike a cage, it allows birds a more extended living space where they can fly, though such flight is of a qualified kind and not limitless as in nature. Often trees and shrubberies are planted to simulate natural surroundings. This makes the term an inherently loaded one, where it becomes a far cry from the assumptions of harem and turns our eyes to the activities of the women rather than the activities conjured by the male imagination. (The word harem is a part of the English language now and divested of its sensuous implications, it was used to refer to "the separate quarter of a Muslim household reserved for wives, concubines, and female servants"). Most prevalent in Arab countries, Persia, Turkey and Mughal India, its function was to preserve the modesty and protection of women in well to do Muslim households. As the remaining part of the title suggests, Huq's objective in undertaking this work is twofold. She wishes to discover the seeds strewn in women's writings from the 15th to the 16th centuries C.E. that later gave birth to the phenomenon of modernity in defining selfhood. In other words, hers is a quest for the selfhood that predates modernity – the premodern self. In South Asia, the Modern Period starts around the mid-18th century with the decline of the Mughal Empire and the coming of the Europeans, unlike the west where the onset of the Renaissance in the 14th century ushered in a 300-year long process of modernization. In India, this liminal stage was reached around the middle of the 18th century, when the political, economic, and social contours of India began to change drastically. Any period prior to that is termed pre-modern by scholars engaged with South Asia.

Huq recreates the Mughal aviary by discussing four authors writing over a period of about 200 years starting with Gulbadan Begam and ending with Habba Khatoon. Some of their texts already exist in translation, but it would not be an exaggeration to say they are overlooked and find no place in the canon. To Huq goes the credit of (a) bringing to center-stage from an obscure periphery, the literary output of these nearly forgotten women; and, (b) throwing into sharp relief the unique, extraordinary nature of these writings by analyzing their *contents*. The author's contribution is thus two-fold.

The first text discussed is by Gulbadan Begam (1523-1603), the youngest daughter of Emperor Babur – founder of the Mughal dynasty in India. She (the Rose-body Princess) wrote a biography of her half-brother, Emperor Humayun, who succeeded Babur. The second text is by Princess Jahanara (1614-1681), also known as the Sufi princess, the eldest daughter of Emperor Shah Jahan, the fifth and one of the most remarkable Mughal emperors. Jahanara wrote the biographies of two Sufi saints – Moinuddin Chishti of the Chishti order in India and Mullah Shah Badakhshi, her guide and mentor. The third writer Huq dwells on, is about Zeb-un-Nissa (1638-1702), eldest daughter of Aurangzeb, sixth Mughal ruler of India. She was a poet who wrote under the pseudonym of 'Makhfi'. While the first three belong to the *zenana*[6] of the royal court and their literary output exists as discursive records from a position of gendered subalternity, the case of the fourth writer Habba Khatoon (1554-1609) is an interesting example of a lady not born into the royal family, but aristocratic in character and lifestyle. Famously known as the 'Nightingale of Kashmir', she was an extraordinary poet of passion and longing.

## I

After an introductory chapter where the author depicts the historical and social context in which the four women lived and worked, Huq presents the first of the writers under discussion in the chapter titled "Humayun's Biographer Gulbadan Begam: A Quiet Observer of the Mughal Aviary." Princess Gulbadan Begam wrote the *Humayun-Nama*, an account of the life and reign of her half-brother Humayun, second Mughal Emperor of India, at the request of her nephew Emperor Akbar the Great. It is highly significant that Akbar had great regard and trust in the character and *intellect* of his much-loved aunt Gulbadan, to the extent that he requested her to write the biography of his predecessor and father Humayun. This was meant to provide the basis and background to his own biography *Akbarnama* (Book of Akbar) soon to be

---

[6] *Zenana* (in India and Iran) in Persian means the part of a household that is reserved for women.

commissioned to his illustrious court scholar and historian Abul Fazl. Akbar asked his aunt to write whatever she remembered of the reigns of Humayun, knowing full well, in her he had an astute, impartial, and erudite first-hand witness to the tumultuous and tragic events surrounding the life of the second Mughal ruler.

Gulbadan borrowed the style of the *Baburnama*[7], the autobiography of Emperor Babur and wrote in simple yet elegant Persian following the literary genre of the Nama much in favor then in the Perso-Arabic-Turkic world she inhabited. Unlike some of her contemporaries, Gulbadan penned a factual account of what she saw and remembered. She chronicled the trials and tribulations, wars, triumphs, and losses of Humayun; but the book is also replete with pictures of domestic activities, life in encampments and on the road. For one thing, the Mughals (their women included) were an itinerant lot, traveling from place to place for purposes of warfare, empire-building and administration. So much for the idea of the harem and Mughal ladies' lives therein!

Though ostensibly a biography, Gulbadan inserts parts of her own life into the *Humayun-Nama*. From the book, we get to know of her marriage and subsequent life in Kabul, Lahore, Agra and Mecca. Educated, pious, cultured and loved, she was a keen observer of war and diplomacy. It is a pity that in subsequent times, the book which Akbar had commissioned so that it could be a guide for Abul Fazl, was lost for generations and sank into obscurity. A battered copy now rests in the British Library and was translated into English by Annette Akroyd Beveridge in 1901. According to the historian of medieval India Dr. Rieu, it was one of the most remarkable manuscripts in the possession of Colonel Hamilton, a collector of 1000 manuscripts!

The neglect accorded the text is lamentable given the fact that the *Humayun-Nama* must have served as a primary source for the *Akbarnama* by Abul Fazl. This brings us back to the point that (male) authors who produced the canon and were entrusted with the production of knowledge, chose to obfuscate the work of women authors, even though they might have drawn heavily from such texts.

Huq's third Chapter "Jahanara's Hagiographies: The Mind of a Matriarch" discusses the work of Princess Jahanara Begam, daughter of Emperor Shah Jahan. She has been immortalized later not so much by her own treatises but by Abanindranath Tagore's painting 'The Passing of Shah Jahan'. In the famous

---

[7] *Baburnama* is the title for the English translation published by Penguin Classics series. However, the hardcover version published by Penguin Random House has *The Babur Nama* as its title.

painting, the emperor is shown on his death bed with his daughter, companion, and caretaker, Jahanara who had accepted confinement along with her father at the order of Aurangzeb, grieving at his feet.

Jahanara has been the subject of several fictionalized narratives, as the author rightly states at the beginning of the chapter. This favorite daughter of Shah Jahan, his constant companion, caregiver and advisor after his consort Mumtaz Mahal died, has constantly captivated the popular imagination in contemporary and later times. Huq mentions in Chapter 3,

> Jahanara Begam is, perhaps, the most striking of all the Mughal princesses. This statement stands not on speculations; the plethora of fictional writings on this royal woman confirms the fact that her captivating persona became the subject of imagination for writers of later generations. There are at least half a dozen historical novels written on Jahanara's life in recent times, most of which focus on her participation in harem politics; some concentrate on her charismatic leadership with respect to the strong patriarchy of the Mughal empire; and the rest capitalize on her supposed romantic liaisons with men. (87)

These writings as well as rumors about Jahanara's incestuous relation with her father, point to the fact that the power, learning and capability, of extraordinary women in history have been subjected to the lurid (male) imagination till their lives become erased from history, and what is more lamentable, misrepresented. For as Huq points out in the chapter,

> ...It remains a question why all of Jahanara's fictional biographies voyeuristically dote on a speculated life of romance instead of dwelling upon the specifics of a life that she actually led. Is it so because our subversive taste in reading is not satiated with a purely mystic and ordinary life of a woman? Sometimes it becomes difficult to discover the 'real' Jahanara from the palimpsest that her persona has become in these writings. She is a victim of fictional romance without which historical fiction or fictional biography can hardly thrive in today's publication industry where the search for novelty gets obsessive to the point of inaccuracy. (97-98)

On the contrary, Jahanara's life and work testify to the radical roles women could and did play in two patriarchal domains considered the sole preserve of men: religion and scholarship (the pulpit and academy in modern feminist parlance). Women were expected to be religious in the sense of observance of the rules and regulations set down; they could, if they were fortunate enough and belonged to the upper class, write. But the domains of shaping religious practice, writing commentaries or hagiographies, i.e., the act of defining reality through epistemological means and media (texts), were deemed forbidden

Introduction  xvii

territory. Yet it is in these spheres that Jahanara chose to leave her imprint. As Huq adequately enunciates in the chapter, Jahanara had a spiritual bent of mind and began her search for God from an early age. Encouraged by crown Prince Dara Shikoh her brother, when she was in her thirties, she set out on the mystical journey of seeking God as a Sufi. Her first entry was as a follower of the Chishtiyah Order established by the late Saint Moinuddin Chishti who died in Ajmer, India in 1236 long before Jahanara was born. She then became a disciple of her lifelong mentor and guide Mullah Shah Badakhshi of the Qadiriya Order. Her mentor Mullah Shah had great admiration for Saint Rabi'a Basri of Baghdad, one of the very few female saints acknowledged in Islam.

According to Huq, "Mullah Shah was very impressed with Jahanara's progress in the Sufi line and would have nominated her his successor in the Qadiriya, but the rules of the order did not allow a woman to be a leader in the path" (106). The chapter also describes Jahanara's life in Mullah Shah's *khanka* or seminary in Kashmir where she stayed for a vital six months, her significant position in the fold and her subsequent recounting of the lives of two Sufi Saints. Her praxis was in itself a radical departure for women who were enjoined to pray and observe the rituals of purity rather than be active describers/definers of religious reality.

It must be borne in mind that at the time the Princess was writing the biographies, the Mughal Empire was undergoing a process of northward expansion. Much like the eastward expansion of Aryans in the *Mahabharata*, Jahanara's *Sahibiya* depicts the eastward expansion of the Mughals, e.g., the Annexation of Kashmir. The Mughal empire, like its other Asian (Ottoman, Safavid) and European counterparts, sought legitimization through the tenets of religion –enunciated in a right to kingship divinely bestowed. The Mughals cleverly and strategically deployed the forces of military prowess and spiritual and scriptural power to reinforce the foundations of empire. The Sufi Order tracing a lineage back to the holy Prophet of Islam was especially instrumental in this project. It provided the bond between the Creator, the Prophet, the King and the Commoner. The author of *The Mughal Aviary*, meticulously shows the connections between the two biographies of Gulbadan Begam and Jahanara Begam by highlighting the complex 'interactions' between the princesses' works and statist objectives. In the case of the latter, the political objectives are more pronounced in her two biographies *Munis-al-Arwah*, and *Risala-i-Sahibiya*, the biographies of Moinuddin Chishti and Mullah Shah Badakshi respectively. Here Huq echoes the contention of historian Afshan Bokhari who wrote a seminal book on Jahanara and her life and times. After acknowledging the religious nature of Jahanara's career, Bokhari studies the biographer's oeuvre against the background of the politics of Empire building. In her groundbreaking book (2015) *Imperial Women in Mughal India: The Piety and Patronage of Jahanara*

*Begam* and an essay "Masculine Modes of Female Subjectivity: The Case of Jahanara Begam", (in Malhotra and Lambert-Hurley, 2015) Bokhari highlights Jahanara's participation in and promotion of the imperial agenda of the Mughal dynasty in its heyday (under Shah Jahan). In the essay which presents her arguments in the book Bokhari contends "Mughals propagated imperial ideology through sustained patronage of history writing and utilized historiography as a means to legitimize and sustain empire" (Bokhari in Malhotra and Lambert-Hurley, 2015, 177).

It is easy to gauge that the women biographers who also acted as historians, were part and parcel of this ideology maintenance. What amazes us is that two women were chosen and (chose) to be part of this important historical project. As Bokhari states that Jahanara was not allowed to marry, she was also deprived of the advantages of a matrimonial alliance with a royal or noble family. She was not even strengthened by a line of dynastic reproduction. Thus, the primary and probably the only means for "projecting" or "perpetuating" her authority was through "concepts of kingship" in the sacred and secular milieu. Bokhari comments, "Jahanara's imperial "semantics" to convey her subjectivity and objectify her persona are her Sufi treatises, *Munis*, an anthology of Sufi saints, and the autobiographical *Risalah*…" (Bokhari in Malhotra and Lambert-Hurley, 2015, 184). Thus, the Sufi treatises of Jahanara are her contribution to the male agenda of the Mughal empire and she legitimized her position by participating in the historical texts of sovereignty (and her buildings). Hers was a mission to uphold the Mughals as the champions of Islam (manifest in the imperial India of the Mughals through Sufi Islam).

Sabiha Huq adds Gulbadan to the cause as well. Both biographers operated under the shadow of a towering father/brother/ mentor figure. Both women enjoyed a high degree of respect, intellectual trust and power, but in the end, they had to live according to the patriarchal dictates of the day. They were in an enclosure, true, but they chose the kind of enclosure it would be and exercised very considerable agency within its parameters. For both Jahanara and Gulbadan – their engagement with Sufism was part of a personal and imperial agenda. Huq examines the conflict between the "authorial subject position and a rigid regulatory frame" which she likens to a Mughal Panopticon or "a broad aviary that allowed qualified freedom" as she mentioned in her proposition.

How much of the two biographies, are "palimpsestic"? That is how much did the princesses write in their own life experiences/selves into biographies of an emperor and a saint, in an age that discouraged women's reading themselves? Through biographies it is safe to assume sometimes the boundaries between narration and self-narration, are blurred. As Malhotra and Lambert-Hurley point out in the 'Introduction' to their book *Fashioning a Self*, biographical elements are found woven in and out (Malhotra and Lambert-Hurley 2015,

Introduction). And if individuality, a sense of the self and subjectivity are ingredients of pre-modern selfhood, then these women were certainly in possession of traits that can be termed pre-modern. In discussing these texts, Huq brings to the forefront the rich tradition of biographical and autobiographical writing in the medieval 'Orient'. A careful perusal of her book leads the reader to locate the women writers in the male autobiographical and biographical literary canon of the time, and thus restore them to their rightful place. In doing so Huq also helps to disprove another Orientalist myth: autobiographical writing of depiction of self is a recent *western* phenomenon.

A sweeping glance at contemporary centers of imperial power in, for instance, Western Asia (Ottoman and Safavid empires) or Europe (France, Germany, England etc.) and royal families that ruled there, reveal that the 15$^{th}$ and 16$^{th}$ centuries witnessed some aristocratic women taking up the pen. In England, the Elizabethan age was in full swing when Gulbadan was penning her *Humayun-Nama*, but we hear of few biographies and histories. Venice-born Christine de Pizan of France (1364-1430) was an exception, however. She was an extraordinary scholar and writer of the medieval Europe who transcended her age and went down in history as a prolific writer on socio-historical and "feminist" issues. For, in actuality, one had to wait a few hundred years till the 18$^{th}$ century to get a writer like Mary Wollstonecraft who has been hailed as the originator of a genre. Although there were many writers in early modern times in Europe, it was the 15$^{th}$ century that saw an efflorescence of women writers. However, unlike the writers described in *The Mughal Aviary*, they were not of the royal family, nor commissioned to write historical biographies. Viewed from this perspective alone, the women writers discussed in the first half of Huq's book provide new material to rethink history and the position of women in pre-modern India.

## II

Chapters 4 and 5 dwell on two Mughal women who made a name as poets. In chapter 4, "Dissenting Songbird in the Aviary: The Poetry of Zeb-un-Nissa", the author discusses the tragic, turbulent life of the worthy successor of Jahanara's intellectual and artistic legacy, her talented and erudite niece Zeb-un-Nissa (1638-1702). Born 34 years after Jahanara to the last of the "great" Mughals, the orthodox Sunni emperor Aurangzeb, Zeb-un-Nissa was chosen by Bengal's greatest Renaissance novelist Bankim Chandra Chatterjee to be the heroine of his novel *Durgesh Nandini*. But the mythologizing can be traced far back in time. As Huq quotes Jadunath Sarkar in her chapter,

> The India of the Mughals attracted the attention of post-renaissance Europeans, and its bazars thronged with men of every description from beyond the Mediterranean: traders, travelers, and free-lance adventurers,

who roamed with eyes and ears wide open to inform themselves about everything odious. For, the East was "mysterious" and its institutions "barbarous". With a frankly dehumanized attitude, it was not surprising if scandals concerning lives of Mughal ladies found free entry into their writings. Nor could Zeb-un-Nissa be an exception. A sordid episode of her carnal romance with Aqil Khan Razi and his death inside a hot cauldron with burning fire under it, gained wider currency and was eagerly picked up by the vulgar populace. Nothing could be more absurd. 'Aqil Khan lived long as an imperial servant and died a natural death. It was too late when a modern historian took stock of facts and data and wrote his vehement denunciation. (Jadunath Sarkar quoted in Chapter 3; Hadi, 1995, 639)

Little is known about this beautiful and accomplished woman who was the darling of her father's eyes, but fell from grace on account of her non-conformist lifestyle and passion for the poetic vocation. Though Aurangzeb who was an Orthodox adherent of Sunni Islam, did not much like the poet's calling, he initially listened to the counsel of Zeb-un-Nissa's eminent mentors and invited poets and scholars from Persia and Kashmir to congregate in literary circles where his daughter could cultivate her talent. Zeb-un-Nissa spent a large part of her handsome allowance on her libraries, manuscripts and scholarly projects. Adept in Persian, Arabic and Urdu, she had many Arabic and Sanskrit texts translated into Persian. This last action depicts a multicultural bent of mind (for Sanskrit was the language of the Hindu scriptures) and denotes a liberal, secular mode of thinking.

But Zeb-un-Nissa fell out of the emperor's favor in later years and spent the greater part of her life as his royal prisoner. Huq summarizes the various versions of her life - her girlhood and youth; her education and accomplishments, passion for poetry, the rumored love affairs, the displeasure of the monarch, her abiding commitment to the Muse of Poetry, and fall from grace on account of her refusal to conform to patriarchal norms of marriage, wifehood and domesticity, and perhaps the rigid tenets of Sunni Islam as well. Like her illustrious predecessors, Zeb-un-Nissa had great trust placed upon her by the most powerful man in the realm – the emperor, only to be reduced to the state of a royal prisoner in later years. Nonetheless, here we have time and again the cases of princesses who were advisors to the monarch on matters of the state and chroniclers and artist-scholars.

Zeb-un-Nissa was undoubtedly a challenger; she was close to power but spent most of her adult life in imprisonment because she did not learn to submit to patriarchy. Once adored by her orthodox father, as mentioned above, Zeb-un-Nissa's imprisonment and banishment from the public sphere could be read as tragic were it not for the fact that nothing could stop her pen. Her verses or Ruba'i translated by Paul Smith are published in a volume titled *Makhfi the Princess Sufi Poet Zeb-un-Nissa: A selection of Poems from her Divan* by New Humanity Books in 2012. The author of the *Aviary* describes her poetry, its pathos and passion bordering on sexuality. She was a thinker and poet before her times. A few hundred years had passed since the quiet and gentle observer Gulbadan Begam had taken up the pen. Zeb-un-Nissa did not cloak her passion as religious sentiment and spiritual utterances. They were candid admissions of a woman's response to love, its pangs, and bodily and emotional manifestations.

Zeb-un-Nissa's poetry is reminiscent of European women poets of the $15^{th}$ and $16^{th}$ centuries. A few of the notable women writers (poets, novelist, essayist) included Veronica Franco (1546-1591) the Venetian Courtesan whose poetry was an expression of love, desire and sexuality; the $16^{th}$ century Parisienne Marguerite de Briet who wrote a novel on the dangers of love not tempered by reason; and Louis Labe, a commoner, who wrote poems about the debate between Love and Madness. Zeb-un-Nissa's poetry is redolent with similar themes.

It will not be out of context to draw a comparison here between the Mughal princesses Jahanara and Zeb-un-Nissa and their contemporaries in England; the poet, playwright and translator – Aphra Behn (1640-1689) and Margaret Cavendish (1623-1673) – poet, scientist, philosopher and playwright. Cavendish, Duchess of Newcastle upon Tyne came from the aristocracy though Behn rose from obscurity. While Zeb-un-Nissa was penning verses in her gilded prison (after enjoying a life of unusual liberty), Aphra Behn was writing plays for the London stage in the 1670s, the height of the English Renaissance. This points to Europe in general, and England in particular, that had ushered in the age when women writers grew in numbers, gained popularity and were beginning to gain acceptance into the literary fold. It is significant that Aphra Behn (like Christine de Pizan, centuries before her) earned money through writing, something women in India had to wait for some more centuries to even visualize. Cavendish's work was remarkable in that they ranged from poetry, plays, to essays on natural philosophy and social and political issues. The London of Aphra Behn and Margaret Lucas Cavendish experienced a different socio-economic and political reality from the one in the Delhi of Jahanara and Zeb-un-Nissa. England was already witnessing the rise of its middle class, which was a forerunner to the modern middle class or bourgeoisie created by the Industrial Revolution. Conversely, India sadly was just about to enter in 50 years' time its age of decline and colonization by the English exploitative power. This, if anything marks the economic and socio-cultural differences between Renaissance or Restoration England and Mughal India, and this difference did not really keep its mark on the women's intellectual sphere, if judged from an Occidental perspective.

The last chapter before the conclusion is an account of the life and work of poet Habba Khatoon (1554-1609), known as the Nightingale of Kashmir. Chronologically she is a contemporary of Gulbadan Begam, but her position outside of the Mughal fold makes her inclusion a unique aspect of Huq's work. Habba's rise and fall took place in the 'Paradise of India'- Kashmir, hence technically beyond the central theatre of the Mughal empire, nevertheless an important province in its northward expansion during the lifetime of Habba Khatoon – "The point behind including Khatoon in this selection is to underscore the evidence that on or off royalty, Indian women especially from the Muslim aristocracy, were developing a literary sense during the 16th and 17th centuries" as Huq points out in chapter 5.

Huq recreates the enigmatic life of Habba from the scant sources available. The poet's life reads like a fairy tale. The author traces the various versions of Habba's origins, beauty, education, rise from obscurity in a failed first marriage to becoming the royal consort while pursuing her literary path throughout. Her modest birth and an unhappy first marriage paved the way for her writing as she uttered her first songs; in that sense, fictionalized art becomes a mirror for the self. Parts of her life read like a fairy tale, the most significant being Habba's meeting the King of Kashmir Yusuf Shah on the banks of the river, their subsequent attachment, and its culmination in marriage. S. N. Wakhlu, Habba's biographer, narrates her happy conjugal life with Yusuf Shah Chak as his Queen consort, which however was short lived as Akbar's army marched northwards and her husband was caught in the tentacles of war, captured, separated, and exiled. This, according to Huq propelled her to the pinnacle of her poetic calling.

The Mughal empire infringed upon and dismantled not just her public position but also her personal life, as she found herself desolate a second time when she was torn from her loving husband. She had to leave the palace, and she chose to live, according to S. N. Wakhlu, at Panda Chok, in a small cottage on the bank of Jhelum. Khatoon was offered an opportunity to reunite with her husband in secret, but she refused to do that for Yusuf's safety. Her biographer states that she burned all written copies of her poetry and renounced worldly life. Finally, she breathed her last in 1605 at Panda Chok.

The chapter presents excerpts from her poetry to a literary readership mostly unfamiliar with Habba's exquisite work. Romanticism, sensuousness, audacity, secularism, are articulated through her timeless verses. The love theme is no longer camouflaged or expressed in spiritual, mystic terms – the longing and desire of a disciple for a union with God. Huq reads a 'feminist' voice in this –as the poet emerges a true harbinger of a modern consciousness. Referring to Khatoon's lines,

> "I read the Koran in one attempt
> I didn't make a single mistake
> But I could not read the text of love
> What will you gain from my death?"

Huq writes in chapter 5, "The woman who dared to ask her creator this audacious question was not built in a day, nor was she moulded from one single form". S. L. Sadhu's book *Haba Khatoon* in the "Makers of Indian Literature" series published by Sahitya Akademi from India is a dedicated English text on her life and poetry. Habba's poetry has been translated by Mattoo, and Huq relies upon this version for its lucidity and simplicity. Huq exemplifies how Sadhu as a male translator connects the poet's emotion with her husband Aziz Lone, whereas there is no mention of a proper in a particular poem that Sadhu translated. On the other hand, Matto has provided a lexically more authentic translation that also preserves the expression of female sexuality that was the feature of Habba's poetry. Such minute observation leads the present author to a strong point to bestow a "feminist" voice to Habba.

It is ironic that Gulbadan Begam was watching over the expanse of the empire known as Kashmir while sitting among the women of the Mughal zenana in Delhi, enjoying the love and trust of the mighty Emperor Akbar. The aviary was extended to the boundaries of Kashmir, but on its northward journey following the turbulent line of imperial expansion, the aviary had indeed become less airy and more oppressive.

Sabiha Huq's *The Mughal Aviary* seeks to restore balance to not just the literary canon, but also Orientalist and male-centric historiography by initiating an excavation and discussion of overlooked texts. Susie Tharu and K. Lalita articulated the matter very succinctly,

> If we ask the questions… who has lost these writers, or rather to what cause have they been lost, several answers suggest themselves. At one level, they are lost to feminists today, lost to a tradition of women's writing, lost to literary studies, lost to the reader's experience. But more significantly, they are missing from another more deeply embedded cultural institution. […] These writers, the unstated argument is, are lost to the select company of great (male) writers whose works were charged with the task of providing post-Enlightenment society in general, and the nation in particular, with its ethical capital. (Tharu and Lalita, 1993, 24)

These words from Tharu and Lalita provide a befitting mainframe to justify Sabiha Huq's conceptualization of *The Mughal Aviary* as we stand at the threshold of the third decade of this 21$^{st}$ century. As a scholar of history, I understand the challenges involved in extricating strangulated portions of historical perception from any grand narrative. It goes without saying that the present monograph attempts to resurrect through cultural documents a gyno-history that is avowedly liminal. This liminality inheres in not just the perception of aristocratic Mughal/ Muslim women within the given time frames, it is also perceptible in later historiography as the preceding sections have pointed out. I have no qualms in saying that these preliminary thoughts had first traversed my mind when the author broached her topic about a year back. As the manuscript stands, I am happy she has lived up to its possibilities within understandable constraints of the time that have restricted the amount of research she had initially planned. In my understanding, it is not just a happy coincidence that here is an enterprising female academic from Bangladesh casting a literary-historical glance on pre-modern women writers. It is rather my belief that Huq's insistent questions on the position of women within Islamic cultures in South Asia at large have encouraged her to take up this detailed study which is located within a rich period of South Asian history and fills a void in the contemporary historiography on the time. The task of writing this 'Introduction' has been a pleasurable one and I look forward to much discussion on this book once it sees the light of day.

Sonia Nishat Amin
University of Dhaka
Author of *The World of Muslim Women in Colonial Bengal, 1876-1939*,
Brill Academic Publishers Inc., 1996

# 1
# The Mughal Aviary and Women In/Out

> I shall marry someone; but he shall be a man whose collar my hand can touch, and not one whose skirt it does not reach.
> – (Hamida Banu quoted in Begam, 2018, 151)[1]

This statement by Hamida Banu Begam (1527-1604), Emperor Humayun's wife and the mother the third Mughal Emperor Akbar, borrowed from *Edicts from the Mughal Harem* (1979) by S. A. I. Tirmizi, was made at a time when domestic enclosures of royal households swarmed with slaves and concubines. This is not the only statement of this kind made by women in the Indian Subcontinent across late fifteenth to early nineteenth centuries. The idea of this book springs from an urge to search such voices that never surfaced through mainstream history because, history, like men in general, has kept women beneath its pedestal more often than letting them reach its lapel! A discursive history of pre-modern women in India through cultural studies is necessary, as both mainstream history and the autotopographical research (through examining the intimate objects the women possessed) done so far, fall short in understanding these women's life. Writings by women of the period become significant cultural artifacts in that sense, as writings, in Afshan Bokhari's words, "narrate and weave" (Bokhari, 2015, 166)[2] the persona of the women.

Gulbadan Begam, Jahanara, Zen-un-Nissa and Habba Khatoon– four forward-thinking women from the period who left their cohorts far behind, are the protagonists of this book. The first three were Mughal princesses and the fourth was a Kashmiri queen. While reading some recent historical novels on women of Mughal aristocracy, the idea of studying the women writers of early modern (European classification) or late medieval (preferred term by the Indian historians) or the pre-modern age in India was triggered by several simple questions: Why are today's fiction writers resurrecting these women's lives after

---

[1] Hamida Banu Begam was an avid reader, collector of books, and she also helped Abul Fazl while he wrote the *Akbarnama* by remembering events of the emperor's life.

[2] Afshan Bokhari's research on the Mughal princess Jahanara is a substantial work in the field. She comments that Jahanara's architectural as well as biographical writings are also self-fashioning in the sense these expose much her own persona. This comment is applicable to all four writes in general, who mostly wrote in a subjective way.

so many years? Why are they stereotyping their female protagonists as sensual and arbitrary beings while there is scope for looking at their intellectual advancements? If the Muslim identity of these women is a major factor that needs to be counted vis-à-vis their thoughts and action recorded in history, why are these historical novels deviating from facts and taking refuge in fantasy? Most importantly, some of these women were writers themselves, and while their writings could be used as significant sources of information for such recent fictional works, unfortunately, these do not even mention their works. In this age of open-access information and resources floating on the web, lack of research on the women of pre-modern India signals a deliberate amnesia that has engulfed the historic-literary studies of our time. While these semi-historical or pseudo-historical fiction have become a popular genre, the recent works are none other than products of that intellectual bias that held women's writings as insignificant and valueless, against which Hélène Cixous had to coin the term *Écriture féminine*[3] in 1975. Exclusivist approach of mainstream history, mostly written by male historians, neglected the documents produced by women; and portrayed women's life somewhat arbitrarily depending on speculated deliberations. These questions spring from a stark demand of the time to look back at that phase of history that can be termed as deliberately obfuscated. Pre-modern Muslim women writers in India seem to have been the most neglected female literati till date, and it is possible to attribute various sociopolitical reasons to this. Before going into that analysis, we need to learn about progress and modernity (attributed majorly to European classification) that loom large in the background of this work. Early modernity seems to be a significant phase in history when there was a major shift in the global scenario. The shifted political and cultural geography naturally demanded new adjustments, and this asked for new self-fashioning for both men and women. Twenty-first-century female readers need to explore the lives of women of the early phase of modernity to perceive how they self-fashioned.

As women's writings are potential sources for understanding the women's social condition and intellectual progress, the book's parameter is defined by new historicism and subaltern studies, and the rubric of exegesis of women's literary writings vis-à-vis the idea of modernity is adopted in the study. Historical documents have been found inadequate and biased, for which these 'other' sources have been explored as alternative and more intimate sources

---

[3]*Écriture féminine*, simply meaning 'women's writings' was coined by Hélène Cixous in her essay 'The Laugh of the Medusa' (1975), in which she comments that women's writings are the antithesis of masculine writing, and through writing women would be able to respond properly to the male dominated faculty of writing.

through which one could reach out to the distant and forgotten women of pre-modern times.

## European modernity and the Indian Subcontinent: challenges for women writers

History evidences that the most advanced human societies were affected by several worldwide processes of change that began to be visible since the fifteenth century, and are now taken as popular signifiers of modernity. The economic and political order of the world was under transition because of the establishment and expansion of empires. The world was much advanced in creating a global link between these empires via road and sea passages, and adventurous travelers used these links, and sometimes accepted physical challenges too, to reach out to different parts of the world. Thus, we have acquired an intercultural and comparative dimension of historical narratives through a negotiation between historians established in academia and the pedestrian travelers. Western historians were always Eurocentric while periodizing history and marking 'modernity' only in the context of changes occurring in Europe. Even within Europe, there is an east-west disparity in history. For instance, Edward Gibbon, whom Pocock calls the "most sophisticated of Enlightened historians" (Pocock, 2007, 56), identifies modernity with certain events that happened in Western Europe while he ignored much of its east. Pocock harshly remarks, "This is not only, though it is importantly, a product of western arrogance; it is also a product of the divided western culture's deep need to understand itself" (Pocock, 2007, 56).

Culture is an incredibly complex proposition, and a much more nuanced one at that when Europe and Asia are in an interface. The Asian, specifically South Asian part has not come into limelight in the global modernity narrative of most European historians. Their narrative of South Asia roughly sketches the regime changes and political history from the viewpoints of foreign academics. The fifteenth century in India was counted by Indian historians as late Medieval period, and Irfan Habib presents an interesting analysis in this regard. He claims that the British historians "turned to the history of India preceding the British conquest with the avowed purpose of showing that all governments previous to the British had been despotic, intolerant and monstrously cruel, and that the Indian people, ever divided, were fit only to be conquered and should be grateful that their last conquerors were so just and merciful" (Habib, 1961, 350). Both British and Mughals were conquerors, but Indian historiography by British writers presented Mughals as aggressive empire-builders and Muslim oppressive rulers of their Hindu subjects; and Indian historians followed suit. Mughal females were not part of this colonial trickery though they were treated most unjustly by the historians. They were never allowed to emerge as subjects per se, and when they did on rare occasions, the historians mostly depended on the records by travelers from Europe. Due to their lack of admittance into the secluded-domestic spaces of palaces and even of ordinary households, those renowned travelers, who in turn were the favorite references of historians, often gave superficial and rather imagined and exoticized versions of women's lives in the pre-modern times in the southern region of Asia. Consequently, Mughal women of the period were recognized more as backward, ignorant, sluggish, sexually charged, and licentious than being enlightened entities. Women's writings of the era that have been included in this book bring a fresh approach in this regard. These serve as the voice of the 'represented' females that was so far excluded in history, and more significantly, these can offer a scope to triangulate those politicized representations of history.

This particular approach leads to the obvious question on women's global situation – an East-West, or may be a global North-South dialogue in which one ponders on the fact that when Queen Elizabeth I (1533-1603) of England succeeded her half-sister Queen Mary I (1516-1558) in 1558, the Mughals, who roughly ruled India from sixteenth to nineteenth centuries, were still struggling to sustain in their new empire in Hindustan, that is now distributed among several national states in the Indian Subcontinent. We are dealing with an age that European historians demarcated as early modern – a time when the Ottomans occupied Constantinople, and Renaissance approached Europe and Central Asia. Indian historians usually mark the beginning of Modernity from 1800, and perhaps the establishment of Fort William College[4] in West Bengal is a cultural signifier of that. Irfan Habib and historians of his school draw back to the Neolithic period while talking about pre-modern technological and economical modes of production, and so 'pre-modern' may not be an appropriate term for determining the age we are discussing. However, using 'early modern' for the period is also inappropriate as it goes against all established periodization by South Asian historians. Due to the substantial differences between the modes of political and philosophical modernity that appeared in Renaissance Europe, and the changes that accrued due to restructuring the modes of governance in southern Asia under Mughal rule, 'pre-modern' may be a safer term chosen by South Asian historians. They

---

[4] Fort William College was founded on 10 July 1800 by Lord Wellesley, the then Governor General of British India. It was located within the Fort William complex in Calcutta (Kolkata). It was an academy of Oriental Studies and a centre of learning to train the British officials in Indian and Oriental languages as Sanskrit, Bengali, Urdu, Arabic, Persian. This institution acted as a seat of teaching and learning for the eminent Bengalis like Ishwar Chandra Vidyasagar (1820–1891) and Ram Mohan Roy (1772-1833) and Madan Mohan Tarkalankar (1817–1858), and became the center of the Bengali Renaissance.

believe that Indian Subcontinent did not so far enter the modern cartography drawn by European standards. Literary historians of this region clearly identify 1800 as the beginning of modernity, which may look like a colonial hangover to many as it legitimizes the colonial claim of enlightening and modernizing the otherwise backward Indians. One possible reason for calling the literature of the age 'late medieval literature' is perhaps because it was missing the anthropocentric, secular, and individualistic writings that Europeans produced at that time. Much of Europe was influenced by the German and French writers who advocated humanism; Heinrich Cornelius Agrippa spread his wings on Christopher Marlowe; William Shakespeare's marvelous tragic heroes expanded the horizon of human understanding, John Donne was dominating English verse with his new kind of understanding of the world and beyond–their writings developed around man's strive for knowledge and power. Indian literature was mostly influenced by divinity and spirituality. Even then, the women of this study were exceptional. Their writings are centered around diverse topics – family, history, kingship, love, sufferings – all with an abiding sense of the personal that offered a new undertone to the contemporary literary scene. However, the book looks for a new historicist understanding of the time, and that too through a subaltern perspective. It is rather difficult to call these royal women subalterns, compared to the less privileged women living among the common millions whose history we might never come across. Nonetheless, with their limited freedom and subordinate existence, they showcased pseudo autonomy under which lay an oppressed existence. Women writers of the period coming from the secluded domestic space of the harems of Muslim rulers, who were neglected by historians and literary scholars till date, are taken up as objects of study with a view to reassess their time from their points of view. What then were their points of view, and would those be much different from that of the history narratives or travel writings? One needs to read these women's writings to know the answers.

What are the essential features of these women's writings? Why are they important? Hiuen Tsang, the Chinese traveler from the seventh century, met some regnant-queens in the women's kingdoms in the southern parts of Asia; he mentions western women's country that was near Baluchistan and eastern women's country to the north of Brahmaputra in the Kumaon region. It shows that matriarchy was prevalent in these parts as in many other parts of the globe.[5] After eight hundred years, in the Mughal era it was not only unimaginable that a woman would be coronated as the monarch, it was almost impossible to have a woman exposed in public, because the Mughals were harbingers of Islamic rule in the region.

---

[5] Tirmizi mentions this in his book *Edicts from the Mughal Harem*, page IV.

It was popularly counted as a time when beautiful women moved under their garbs in their palanquins or on elephant backs, exquisitely ornamented and richly attired. They were seen as relentlessly following their male masters because the Timurid and Chingizid tribes[6] would take their harem with them while they were fighting in battlefields all over central and south Asia. Harem is the space typically specified for the womenfolk of the nobility; its inmates were the nobleman's female family members and relatives. The Mughal harem consisted of the emperor's mothers, sisters, wives, daughters, slaves and concubines. Tirmizi vividly narrates the Mughal harem with its hierarchies. The enclosed lodgings were well guarded by chaste women or eunuchs, typically showing the distrust the males had for their females. These guards were called *daroghas*, which usually meant matrons, a gender-neutral term popularly connected with the police department in the Subcontinent at present. Apart from the generous gifts presented by the emperor occasionally, the inmates used to get liberal salaries. If a member of the harem wanted anything within the limits of her salary, she would apply to a cash keeper, and the application would be granted by the palace accountant. From this description, the harem looks like a disciplined space with formal regulations. In return, the women would be expected to stay pretty and happy, and keep peace, even though there were co-wives and concubines competing for the attention of the male master. Does it mean that these women only provided sexual pleasure and were responsible for producing heirs? Were they only sensual beings devoid of intellectual and spiritual propensity? Did they ever have serious thoughts? How did they assess the decisions of the monarch who was their owner? Did they have any romantic life? How did they express themselves? The questions are intriguing, and their view is undoubtedly important to have a complete picture of royal living, as it would complement the essentially male narratives of mainstream history.

Some women of the time wrote, and their writings are obviously a sign of self-proclamation. It is important to note that understanding their life and time through their writings is a completely different method from that of the historian. Literary and cultural studies offer a different approach, though resources from historians properly offer the point of departure. The historian deals with a historical entity, be it a person, a pompous palace or a bloody battle. While the historian goes for causality influencing the effect, the literary

---

[6] The Timurid dynasty was named after Timur Lang or Tamerlane (1336-1405) who came from the Barlas clan of Turkicised Mongols. Timur acquired the title 'royal son-in-law' because of his marriage to a Chingizid princess. The Chingizid dynasty was established by Chingiz Khan (1158-1227). The Mughals of India who were direct descendants of Tamerlane were related to both dynasties in that way.

scholar goes for the effect (read result or production) first and eventually looks for the causal connections. When asked to comment on a book, the historian would suggest looking at its time of production, and see why and how the book came of existence as a historical product. Conversely, the literary scholar would have a discursive reading through its pages to see if and how the book reflects on its time or means of production. However, turning towards historians is important for any literary study for two reasons: first, to know from the historian what pieces of evidence are there to comment that a particular literary production is causally connected to its time; and second, to assess how the lacunae of major historical documents can be filled with the literary productions of a period that remained uncharted in mainstream history. Literary writings sometimes provide alternative sources needed for triangulation of historical claims as history is always biased. A literary piece dealing with an event of history provides the essential subjective and close reading of the event needed to understand the less mechanical and more humane understanding of history. A new historical critical approach thus demands our reading of these women writers.

As such, no dedicated women's history compendium exists that can explain women's physical-mental conditions, which could illuminate the journey of discovering and restoring whatever writings their pens have produced. The four pre-modern women writers who are now lost in the dominion of oblivion are vitally important at the present juncture of post-modern historical phase of Indian civilization. The Subcontinent is going through a resurgence of revivalist politics in which both Muslims and Kashmiris are entangled. Contemporary Indian polity is in a denial mode and refuses to accept Mughal India as a period of cultural evolution in the positive sense; and Mughal era is more and more visualized as mired in darkness of cruelty and communal hatred. The three Mughal women's writings are needed to understand that if the Mughals were just like other empire-builders whose cruelty and bloodthirsty nature was one side of the coin; on the other side of it, there was love for spouses and children, respect for elders, reverence for mentors, thirst for knowledge, penchant for art and literature. It is felt that a renewed understanding of this comprehensiveness can be a way to regain general sympathy for the mighty rulers, which seems to be vitally important for re-establishing the cultural syncretism on which the secular Indian state is to be essentially understood.

Kashmir was always an attraction for colonialists because of its natural beauty and richness of soil. Habba Khatoon's Kashmir was a sovereign state; but soon, her Kashmir was persecuted by Mughal colonial expansionists. Habba Khatoon's life and work resurrects the history of an otherwise peaceful Kashmir valley that contested for its freedom and sovereignty centuries ago under the Mughal rule. Today Kashmir has become a new colonial enterprise for the Indian government since the abrogation of Article 370 of the country's constitution in 2019,[7] and ever since Kashmiris are trying to resurrect their autonomy. Understanding the essential spirit of this community is perhaps the secret of good governance that has become indispensable for Indian polity. However, political strategies derive from social and philosophical understanding, and this book is not envisioned as a dissection of political India, rather it is intended to draw upon the fact that when political forces engage in conflicts, it is the common mass including the women and children who become the ultimate sufferers. The four women's writings including those of the Kashmiri queen poet, will testify to this fact; and reading through that untold saga of empire-building from a parallel historical perspective ignites the idea of this book.

Nonetheless, what established historians wrote about the women of Mughal aristocracy and the Kashmiri queen is vital, as it serves as a point of departure for this study. Here the Mughals and the Kashmiri are to be put under one metaphor of aviary, as there has been no previous attempt at bringing them under one rubric of a particular period; and as such, scholarly discussions on them as a unified whole are not to be found in the entire corpus of Indian history.

Ruby Lal, who has written a seminal book on Mughal harem titled *Domesticity and Power in the Early Mughal World* (Lal, 2005) that is a treasure for this study, is also unhappy about history books on the subject. She comments that most of the books including *The Private Life of the Mughals* (Nath, 1994, 2013)[8] sweepingly remark that the harem was a place of retreat and pleasure. Such books are written in the manner of listing – of attire, ornaments, kitchen, food, festivals, sports, modes of travelling, mannerism, and so on, that are sure to strike the reader as ahistorical (Lal, 2005, 8). Lal describes the harem of the first three Mughal emperors elaborately and with efficacy in her book, in which she claims that Mughal domesticity is significantly different from what we get from

---

[7] Indian constitution's "Article 370. Temporary provisions with respect to the State of Jammu and Kashmir" granted an autonomous status to the state of Jammu and Kashmir, and the power of the Indian Parliament to make laws for the state was limited. The supreme authority of the state was a President who would act on the advice of the Council of Ministers. It was included in the Indian constitution under the Maharaja of Kashmir's Proclamation on 5 March, 1948. The article was abrogated from August 6, 2019, and since then Kashmir has been under strict and oppressive surveillance of the central government. Source: https://legislative.gov.in/sites/default/files/COI_1.pdf

[8] In this book the 2013 edition of R Nath's book has been consulted. Ruby Lal obviously refers to the 1994 edition in her book.

the description by male authors. That kind of 'flattened' (Lal, 2005, 4) description of the harem is the product of the imagination guided by 'the pleasure principle'.[9] She claims that there was no separate domain for domesticity before the third Mughal ruler Akbar's reign, and since his time, the harem became a much more regulated space. She writes, "My proposition is that the very coming into being of a more institutionalized and a regulated form of Mughal domestic world was a part of the making of a new Mughal monarchy" (Lal, 2005, 5). Bestowing different titles on women and ascribing roles to them according to their station were part of those regulations. Lal, of course, mentions a few exceptional history volumes and articles by male authors that investigated into Mughal social life and culture. Tapan Raychaudhuri's *Bengal under Akbar and Jahangir: An Introductory Study in Social History* (1969), Stephen P. Blake's *Shahjahanabad: The Sovereign City in Mughal India* 1639-1739 (1990), Muzaffar Alam's essay "The Pursuit of Persian: Language in Mughal Politics" (in *Modern Asian Studies*, Vol. 32, No. 2, 1998), and Stephen F. Dale's article on Babur's poetry in "The Poetry and Autobiography of the *Babur-Nama*" (in *The Journal of Asian Studies* Vol. 55, No. 3, 1996). These writings have certainly opened new avenues of Mughal history, but none of these concentrated on the writings of Mughal women.

That being the status of Mughal women's history by male authors, what happened to the few women who wrote about the Mughals? These were mostly "biographies of women worthies" on which Lal offers her comments, "studies of this kind focus upon the visibility of imperial women and their power" (Lal, 2005, 8) which the male historians considered "sufficient to its subject (that is women)" (ibid). Thus, Mughal history in the form of biographical accounts by women was never a serious matter for mainstream male historians, and what is worse – that these biographers also limited their analyses to replicating the previous books written by men. There was no new question about men-women dichotomy regarding social activities, responsibilities, and practices of power. Lal exemplifies this trend of female historiographers by referring to a handful of titles like *Women in Mughal India: 1526-1748 A.D.* (1967) by Rekha Misra and *Notable Mughal and Hindu Women in the 16th and 17th Centuries* (1990) by

---

[9] 'Pleasure Principle' is a term popularized the founder of psychoanalysis, Sigmund Freud (1856–1939), who borrowed the concept from the German psychologist and philosopher Gustav Theodor Fechner (1801–87). Fechner introduced the term in his article published in the journal *Zeitschrift für Philosophie und philosophische Kritik* in 1848. By this he meant that human psychological processes and actions are usually governed by tendencies ofreleasing unpleasurable tension and gratification of needs; and motives underlying such actions can be unconscious. Freud introduced the concept in his book *The Interpretation of Dreams* (1900), in which he called it 'the unpleasure principle', but later he changed it into 'pleasure-pain principle' in *Two Principles of Mental Functioning* (1911).

Renuka Nath. Misra illustrates the political, commercial, architectural engagements of royal women borrowing from imperial records and European travelers, and Nath produces nothing new except for "a few more characters" (Lal, 2005, 9). Ellison Banks Findly's *Nur Jahan: Empress of Mughal India* (1993) was expected to shed some new light on the powerful Mughal queen's character because around the same time Leslie P. Peirce's *The Imperial Harem: Women and Sovereignty in the Ottoman Empire* (1993) was published with which women's historiography certainly took a new turn. Peirce's is an interesting study of the Muslim women's political power in the 15th and 16th centuries. She shows how women sought sovereignty in a crammed self-estimation ordained by religion and family pressure. In a traditional Islamic society, women were to play the role of a subordinate within the harem. On the other hand, practically women were expected to work for dynastic image-making through charitable activities and cultural patronage. Peirce comments. "Indeed, there were times when women of the dynasty were more publicly visible or built on a grander scale than the sultan himself" (1993, X). This happened in the cases of Nur Jahan and Jahanara, as they created parallel public images with Jahangir and Shah Jahan, monarchs reigning in their lifetime.

It is, however, difficult to accept the fact that literary merit of these women never surfaced in public imagination as did gossips regarding their private life. If we look at monographs on Nur Jahan, the idea becomes clear. She was not a literary person, but her sketchy rise from an ordinary courtier's daughter to the Empress of India received much attention among historians of the later ages. Lal perhaps wrote a second book on Nur Jahan to fill the lacunae of Findly's writings. Her *Empress: The Astonishing Reign of Nur Jahan* (2018) testifies to the fact Nur Jahan's ascent to the court of Jahangir was not a bolt from the blue, rather it was made possible due to of her ambition, will power and skills that are equally necessary for any male sovereign. Rosalind O'Hanlon, therefore, rightly points out that imperial masculinity was being constructed through the traditional history narratives, and there is a necessity to revisit the gender dimension of society and politics of the Mughals today. She has studied the development of patriarchal power under the third emperor Akbar in her essay "Kingdom, Household and Body: History, Gender and Imperial Service under Akbar" (in *Modern Asian Studies*, 41(5), 2007). Her study of the regulation of the men's physical and spiritual spheres for having a right to governance and regulation of the home is interesting, because in all three princesses' writings we see a tendency to respect the male members for their moral uprightness even though sometimes the men are younger in age. This fact becomes clear when Gulbadan writes about her brother Mirza Hindal or nephew Emperor Akbar with reverence, or Jahanara writes about her brother Dara Shikoh in inflated language, or Zeb-un-Nissa puts her trust on her brother Akbar against her father. Lal finds O'Hanlon's study inadequate as it remains 'Emperor-centered' and does not pay attention to how the inmates of the household negotiated the prescribed regulations. Indeed, while finding weaknesses and limitations in studies by scholars of history in the introduction to her 2005 book, Lal herself was repeating much of what she had written in 2004 in an article on Gulbadan's memoir without acknowledging the previous source.[10] Therefore, one cannot rebuff repetition as something outdated and against the rules, but one needs to add something new to the existing scholarship, which has been the intent of all these writings. However, out of this literature one fact is exposed, that is, compared to women's literary merit, their sexual appeal, power and will to ambition are much more visible in today's public sphere. Historians across nations have attempted contested biographies of Nur Jahan, whereas there is not a single scholarly analytical book on the literary writings of Jahanara or Zeb-un-Nissa.

As the English empire succeeded the Mughals in the Indian Subcontinent, English writings of and on the period are extremely important for this study. There is no substantial history anthology that provides within its folds a detailed history of the wonderful women who were both politically powerful and intellectually productive. As the British East India Company reached the region around 1600, one may naturally ask what relation between England and the Mughals existed at that time, and how the Mughals figured in English literary imagination. Of course, not to mention our great romantic poet S. T. Coleridge's preoccupation with Kubla Khan, the great Mongol who was distantly connected with the Mughals. Much before Coleridge wrote this because of his interest in the past as a glorious time, literary historians of the fifteenth century had written on the interest of the English in other empires. Why so? Bernadette Andrea's study gives the answer. In the fifteenth and sixteenth centuries, England was excluded from Catholic Europe because of its turn to Protestantism, and its economic, diplomatic, and military ties with the Ottoman empire stretched across Asia, parts of Europe, the Arabian Peninsula, and North Africa (Andrea, 2007, 1). Andrea refers to several writings that fall short in depicting the Ottoman royal women's lives in English historiography and literary studies. She claims of an "effacement of women's agency in recent studies on Anglo-Ottoman relations, most of which focus on gendered representations in male-authored travel narratives and dramas to the exclusion of sustained attention to women's cultural productions" (Andrea, 2007, 2). As a consequence of these ties, there came in the seventeenth century a plethora of "Renaissance romance

---

[10] Lal wrote an article for *Feminist Studies*, 30(3) in Fall 2004 titled "Historicizing the Harem: The Challenge of a Princess's Memoir". In her book *Domesticity and Power in the Early Mighal World* published in 2005, she has repeated much from her her 2004 article evidently existent in pages 7-9.

and sonnet sequences, the first generation of Quaker women missionaries and polemicists, the first female playwrights for the English stage, and the first English woman to compose a travelogue of her "embassy" to the Ottoman empire" (Andrea, 2007, 1). In the same breath, Andrea admits that the involvement of the English with the Islamic empire of the Mughals was minimal. She also points out that literary and cultural studies of the Islamic tradition in the Early modern era in England derives from the false dichotomy between a constantly powerful West and a correspondingly subordinate East resulting from anachronistic applications of Edward Said's *Orientalism* (1978). Her position as a Western female critique of the Orientalist notion of the East is commendable, but it is also a pity that though she thoroughly reads several writings by early modern English female authors such as Mary Wroth, Delarivier Manley, Mary Wortley Montagu in addition to the early Quaker missionary women's narratives, she does not account for any of the Ottoman women's literary merit. She must be credited partially for commenting that these English authors often "aligned themselves with patriarchal Anglocentric discourses casting them as superior to "the 'Other' woman of empire," even if that empire was "more imaginary than real in the early modern period" (2007, 11), and charting how firsthand experience of the Muslim women's lives was recounted in these writings partially making Muslim women part of English literary history.

What about the literary history of these 'other' women of other empires? Anglophone history remains silent here. Despite strong commercial and political English-Ottoman ties, Ottoman women writers did not get entry into any literary history written in English; it is no wonder Mughal women would be completely out of focus in English literary imagination. As English historians dominated the field of history writing in British and post-colonial India, Indian historians also wrote history in their tradition, the result is the list of books either on the too glorious Mughal regimes written by Muslim historians or on the too bloodthirsty parochial Muslim regimes written by Hindu historians, about which historians like Irfan Habib fretted. Mughal women were nowhere in this tug of war; For that matter, there will be no significant hits if one searches for proper history of royal women's writing of the pre-modern era in India, while there are plenty of speculative writings about the women literati of the time. What we get in those writings are stories about those women's lives in which there is hardly any analysis of their work or passion for creative writing.

Afshan Bokhari's research on princess Jahanara's work is substantially important for this book. In her chapter "Masculine Modes of Female Subjectivity: The Case of Jahanara Begam"[11] she comments that in the detailed biographies of Shah Jahan, the description of Jahanara and other women are rather mechanical and brief (2015, 165). Accordingly, the two personal treatises of Jahanara that have been analyzed thoroughly in this book, become important to stress how she and some of the royal women employed the "male-only" creative practices to articulate and perpetuate Mughal ideology (2015, 166). Bokhari initiates this enquiry by partially quoting a few extracts from Jahanara's writings, though she did not translate Jahanara's complete works written in Persian. As a historian, it was neither on her agenda, nor was it necessary or possible for her to do so within the parameter of the context in which she was reading Jahanara. Translation of the texts is an important issue in this study, and that discussion involves the politics of our translation industry.

The two poets in this book need our special attention. Poetry is a subjective genre, and given the restrictions of Mughal domesticity, Zeb-un-Nissa's emotional utterances are considered revolutionary. Some of her forefathers were practitioners of poetry, as Sufi poetry was a popular genre among the Mughals. However, writing poetry in the male tradition adopting the first-person of the speaker, and that too against the monarch's strict orders, Zeb-un-Nissa decidedly moved ahead of her time and society. Habba Khatoon's life and work bring in a new dimension to this study. There are several books on women poets of the *Bhakti* tradition in South Asia, which emerged around the seventh century under the influence of Buddhism and Jainism. In this tradition, both the supremacy of Brahmins in religious matters and preference of Sanskrit in religious writings were questioned, as vernacular languages started being adopted in literary practices by the masses. Therefore, this poetic genre came as a fresh subaltern assertion. However, gender discrimination was a fresh challenge in this tradition as the practitioners of the Bhakti movement considered women as objects of desire that had to be rejected for ultimate salvation of the soul. Women had to struggle much to get accepted in this movement. The pioneer women in this had to reject traditional women's roles and at times leave their home and society as wandering devotees. Khatoon is a much later addition to these poets, and her status as a commoner by birth and a queen by marriage gives her writings a new identity. Her travails as a Kashmiri poet writing in a local language vis-à-vis the royal language of the Mughals is also to be considered from the peripheral or subaltern's perspective.

---

[11] Bokhari's chapter is published in the volume *Speaking of the Self: Gender, Performance, and Autobiography in South Asia* edited by Anshu Malhotra and Siobhan Lambert-Hurley (Duke University Press, 2015, pp 165-204).

## The book's parameters and the aviary metaphor

At this point, it must be reiterated that the lacunae in several scholarly history books and the lack of any full-length study on pre-modern Indian female literati have intrigued the idea of this volume. Afshan Bokhari, Leslie P. Pierce, Bernadette Andrea, Ruby Lal, and others have touched upon several issues connected with women's lives, especially historically important perspectives surrounding women of medieval aristocracy, travel writings and western literature that reflected on palace culture; but there is hardly any attempt at connecting the crossroads of European early modernity through a scholarly analysis of the writings of the Mughal princesses and other royal women of pre-modern India. This connection is important to get a complete picture of women's history and to refute the Orientalist gaze of global history produced in the west.

The original and copied manuscripts by these writers are preserved in different libraries of the world including the Bodleian libraries at Oxford University, the National Library of Paris, the Library of the British Museum, the Library of Tübingen University in Germany and in the Mota Library in India. Original writings have come from various linguistic backgrounds; and as the writers are not contemporary, the present form of their languages differ much from what they used in the texts. It would be difficult for any single person to cover what lies within the folds of the book unless there had been the English translations. Translations by well-informed and leading researchers in the languages have been consulted to ensure the quality. Despite the shocking negligence shown towards these writers, it is a significant factor that English translations of these texts do exist, no matter what the quality of those translations are, or in whatever form they have been consulted for this study. It is a pity that these writings did not get enough attention from translators and publishers that could have ensured wider dissemination, which as this monograph will show, was well deserved of their literary merit.

Several reasons must have worked behind this. The span from the late fifteenth to the late seventeenth century is a time of linguistic evolution for the Mughals in India. They brought their pure Persian or Turkish mother tongues with them, and Persian became the court language. Persian thrived in the Subcontinent during the period, and many Hindu educated people learned Persian for professional benefits. The Mughals also started patronizing Indian languages and local writers; Hindi and Braj languages were fondly appreciated by the third Mughal emperor Akbar. The inmates of Mughal harem adopted some of these languages too. Gulbadan's memoir, Jahanara's auto-hagiographies, and Zeb-un-Nissa's poetry are written in Persian; Gulbadan used Turkish words with Persian as Turkish was her mother tongue; Zeb-un-Nissa used Hindustani images as she was more of a Hindustani nurturance. Persian in India remained the language of the royal people and writers migrating from the Persianate regions. Since the decline of the empire and the beginning of English colonial period, Persian lost its previous importance, and hence these Persian texts got lost in the realm of antiquity. Only a handful of scholars from India are interested in Persian language and literature nowadays.

Conversely, Habba Khatoon's poetry is in the Kashmiri language, which is spoken and written by only the people living in the valley; and Urdu, Hindi and English being equally in use by the communities living there, not many remarkable scholarly works are produced in the language. Khatoon's poetry and songs survived mainly in the oral form. Only a few writers taking an interest in the Bhakti movement included Khatoon with other poets in the tradition. Therefore, it is not wrong to assume that Persian and Kashmiri languages as source languages of the texts were never lucrative for today's global translation industry.

Lawrence Venuti's research on translation informs us that in the last decades of the 20th century, when publication industry flourished in the West, translation was a significant part of this, but only translation from English texts into other languages that dominated the field, not vice versa (Venuti, 1995, 12). Thus, it is no wonder that only a selected number of researchers who incidentally referred to these writings as part of their broader research interest, attempted translations of these texts, and publication of some of these significant translations are pending. *The History of Humayun: Humayun-Nama* is the first and only standard English translation of Gulbadan's memoir by Annette S. Beveridge. *The Master of Pure Souls* is the translation of Jahanara's anthology of biography of Sufi saints including that of Moinuddin Chishti by Dr. Valiur Rahaman and Dr. Mohammed Adil. Professor Sunil Sharma has translated *Risala-i-Sahibiya* that is yet to be published. Afshan Bokhari's translation of the same text will come out in a forthcoming book titled *Mughals & Mystics A Sufi Princess: Jahan Ara Begam (1614-1681)*. Zeb-un-Nissa's poetry has been translated by several English scholars including Paul Smith and Jessie Duncan Westbrook (in collaboration with Magan Lal). These English texts are thoroughly interpreted and analyzed in the chapters of the book spread across genres to evaluate the thinking faculty of the women writers of the pre-modern times. These give an understanding to women's self-fashioning in a variety of ways that were missing in the trajectory of historical writing.

Coming to the content, the more one thinks of looking at the early modern juncture of history through these women's writings, the more one gets entangled in the labyrinth of events that continue to spring surprises anew. Gulbadan's *Humayun-Nama*, is obviously one of those surprises. The cursory mention of Haram Begam[12] of Badakhshan in the book exemplifies the presence of strong women who operated in public space, but she was one of a kind. Nur Jahan, the wife of the fourth Mughal Emperor Jahangir, was a worthwhile model for the world regarding women's sovereignty and power in court matters. She was indeed an unparalleled woman with a declared agency of power and austerity, but would yield only through her husband whom she was exploiting as her shield. Even though Mumtaz Mahal and Jahanara also shared a similar influence at the Mughal court, women's struggle for power in public space could not be generalized.

While historians in the main have never quite prioritized this specific field for analysis, women's writings of this period have been equally neglected by literary anthologists. While there are some significant women writers in this period, women's writing, and particularly Muslim women's writing, did not get any attention as such. A seminal anthology like *Women Writing in India: 600 B.C. to the Present, V: 600 B.C. to the Early Twentieth Century* edited by Tharu and Lalita has included only a few extracts of *Humayun-Nama* among these amazingly brilliant women's writings. Vernon's initiative to launch a book series under the category created an opening for the Indian women writers, and in this book, four of the most prominent writers from mid-16th century to early-18th century are chosen.

The Mughal empire is compared with an aviary in this book. An aviary is clearly an enclosed space with a semblance of mobility that is but finite, and given the fact that the Mughal empire roughly had four million square kilometers of land under it, it is rather technically difficult to call it an aviary. Stretching from the borders of the Indus basin in the west and keeping northern Afghanistan in its northwest and Kashmir in the north, the empire stretched to the highlands of Assam and Bangladesh in the east to end up in the Deccan plateau in south India. It is obviously a huge stretch of land. Interestingly, *Haram,* the Arabic form of the westernized *Harem* originally meant a "sanctuary" (Tirmizi 2009, I) and the term aviary comes as a qualitative symbol that substitutes *Harem* or *Zenana*, which is an enigmatic liminal space of qualified autonomy and complex power equations that literally define these women's lives. Three inhabitants of the Mughal *zenana* have left indelible imprints of their literary merit in early modern India. The first, Gul-Badan Begam (1523-1603), the youngest daughter of Emperor Babur, founder of the Mughal dynasty in India, wrote a biography of her half-brother, Emperor Humayun, who

---

[12] Haram Begam was the daughter of Sultan Wais Kulabi Qibchaq Mughal and wife of Sulaiman Mirza Miran-shahi, son of Khan Mirza (Wais), who was the Governor of Qandahar. Annette S. Beveridge refers to her military prowess. Chapter 2 has the details about her.

succeeded Babur. Her text *Humayun-Nama* reflects upon the lives of Babur's wives and daughters as well as numerous experiences of royal life, showing how the destinies of these women recoil around the monarch who is the absolute decision-maker of their fates. The second, Jahanara (1614-1681), a Sufi princess who was the eldest daughter of Emperor Shah Jahan, the fifth and one of the most remarkable Mughal Emperors, wrote the biography of Moinuddin Chishti of the Chishti order in India. The third, Zeb-un-Nissa (1638-1702), the eldest daughter of Aurangzeb, the sixth Mughal ruler of India who was known for his strict religious principles, was a poet who wrote under the pseudonym of 'Makhfi.' Zeb-un-Nissa was imprisoned by her father for long twenty years for her free spirit that inspired her writings as well as made her support her father's rivals.

While the first three belong to the *zenana* of the royal court and their literary output exists as discursive records from a position of gendered subalternity, the case of the fourth woman writer Habba Khatoon (1554-1609) is an interesting (counter) point of study. Famously known as the 'Nightingale of Kashmir,' Khatoon's (earlier known as Zoon) rise and fall happened within Mughal India, which the present book visualizes as a broad aviary that allowed qualified freedom to women. Habba Khatoon's husband, who became ruler of Kashmir, was treacherously exiled by Emperor Akbar, and her pangs of separation culminated in pure experimental poetry that still resonates in the valley. The point behind including Khatoon in this selection is to underscore the evidence that on or off royalty, Indian women, especially from the Muslim aristocracy, were developing a literary sense during the 16$^{th}$ and 17$^{th}$ centuries.

Taking these earliest records of Mughal women's writings from India, the book deconstructs negotiations between the political consciousness of their authors and statist interventions upon their lives, to decipher authorial understanding of women's responsibilities in state affairs. Being royal women who wielded power to influence the great Emperors of India, their writings are piquant with the carnival of palace life amidst all its intrigues. Thus, the prose texts are replete with perceptions of conspiracies, intrigues, selfishness, emotion, love, hatred, anger, and jealousy – all from the overtly censured but covertly existent alterity of gendered power positions. Conversely, the poetic texts by both a Mughal and a common woman whose rise to eminence and subsequent self-exilic predicament have the makings of a rebel, express the emotion of love and pangs of rejection, oppression, and dissention, all of which culminate in the innermost self of the poet-creator. These writings reveal the incipient tensions of intelligent women who were capable of free thought, and whose lives were hence circumscribed by the great Mughal monarchs they lived under/with. The book problematizes the implicit conflict between authorial subject positions and the "highly rigid regulatory frame" (Butler, 2006, 45) that made for limited freedom under hegemonic patriarchal rule, but never allowed a life beyond the panopticon. Thus, while the romantic lives of these women never surfaced under rigid conventions; their indomitable understanding of the 'home-world' antinomy determinedly emerges from their works. The primary texts unfailingly expose the political imagination of these Mughal women that was constructed through statist interactions of their royal fathers and brothers, and how such knowledge percolated through the relatively cloistered communal life of the *zenana*. The centrality of position accorded to the brother/father figure(s) as Emperor in these intimate writings is barely a rhetorical trope; the modern reader must locate the equally cryptic text of gendered assertion that is subterranean. Handicapped by the lack of imminent agency to negotiate their ideas in public, these women have never captured the time-warped historians' imagination; while lack of circulation has divested their writings of deserved critical attention. Subjected to New Historicist perspectives, these writings gain importance both in tracing the evolution of women's literacy and consequent empowerment in India, and in exploring the political geography from an alternative perspective. Placed in a milieu that has mostly been regarded as retrogressive from the point of view of female self-fashioning, and still far from Western colonial impact with its claim of a rubric of Renaissance-driven modernism, forays into these authors carry a historic-literary potential of re-reading the seeds of feminist modernity in India.

Four authors are knit together in this book with a single string – the power of female writing; the feminine aspects of these writings not only serve as alternate reading of history, the writings come as redemption of the feminine self. Several other factors also serve as grounds for bringing them together. Religion, for example, is a qualifying category; for within the rubric of Muslim aristocracy, these women find their liberal space of creativity. Mughal princesses were born into this aristocracy and power equation; conversely, Khatoon was born into a Kashmiri regional sovereign as her maternal grandfather was a tribal chieftain from Gurez. She had an inborn drive for cultural progressiveness and a natural inclination towards learning, for which she acquiesced to embrace the scope to upgrade her faculty. Marrying Yusuf Shah Chak is her moment of passage into the vicious nexus of Mughal power. She entered as a stranger, and hence, was banished from it. Islam did not remain a category that could incite the Muslim ruler's sympathy, rather on the pretext that she could upset the religious emotion of the people, her poetry was criticized and she was treated most cruelly by Emperor Akbar. Thus, while the aviary was a secured space for Gulbadan, it became a tangible threat to the very existence of Khatoon.

There are similarities between the women's vocabularies as well as the way they dared to challenge the norms and categories of classification. The variety of language they use in the different genres they have written in, is noticeable.

Gulbadan has written a biography or a memoir of a blood relation, Jahanara has written biographies of men who were not blood relations, but were bound by spirit and soul; Zeb-un-Nissa's forte is intimate and private poetic expression in which the enemy is a blood-bond foe and the beloved is divine. Habba Khatoon's subjective poetry talks of love, loneliness, passion, and pain – cumulatively, these women create an infinite variety, indeed. Gulbadan pioneered the genre of self-writing with the first-ever biography by any woman; Jahanara was the first Padshah Begam who adopted the Sufi philosophy against the more steadfast Sunni Islam; Zeb-un-Nissa dared to challenge the normative values of religion by questioning the altars of faith and pillars of society and state; and Habba Khatoon was a seeker of refuge in poetry to evade the wrath of empire builders, and thus, she subverted the power equations. This book tries to read the women's oeuvre with a New Historicist perspective, considering the women's sociopolitical positions and natural bent of minds. Their progressiveness in thoughts and innovative literary expressions betray their inclination towards modernity, and it would not be wrong to say that these women were much ahead of the early modern age that they lived in.

## Modernity and Islam

Modernity is primarily to conceive of one society as more advanced than its immediate predecessors, and India was semi-modern in many aspects under Mughals who shaped the large empire and changed the earlier model of small territories governed by tribal chieftains. Eurocentric definitions of modernity obviously refer to the emergence of several new trends in global history that originated in Europe, but that does not apply to Mughals and their kind of modernity. Considering the span of early modern that is also termed as late medieval or pre-modern period in India, it must be noted that the Mughals inaugurated architectural and infrastructural development that changed Indian art and architecture; but that also brought revolutionary changes in their own lifestyle. They turned into a dynamic settler Timurid clan from a nomadic race, and new developments in statecraft and governance marked them as a much progressive group of people. Were they as progressive and modern while their women were concerned? The possible twist here is brought by historians who posit Islam as antithesis of modernity. Western concepts of governance and modernity are not consistent with Islam, according to most Western philosophers; and although Islamic societies welcomed modern technologies quite early in history, monarchs of Islamic dynasties were not recognized as civilized enough by western social standards because of their polygamy and autocratic practices. Though the Mughals do not figure in English literary imagination, there are plenty of English texts of early modern time that portray Muslims in a way that confirms Edward Said's claim in *Orientalism* (1978) that the West needed the East as its Other for self-assertion. Shakespeare's plays set in the Mediterranean, Christopher Marlowe's plays (especially the 1587 play *Tamburlaine*, 1999), Fulke Greville's *The Tragedy of Mustapha* (1596, 2010), George Peele's *The Battle of Alcazar* (1589, 1965)[13] are some of the most prominent examples of English literary imagination that outlined the identity of Muslims. The influence of such English predecessors seems to have pervaded by and large the imagination of the Indian writers who have taken stereotypical liberties in presenting the Mughal rulers as deeply religious on one hand, and on the other, as bloodthirsty, anti-democratic and largely tyrannical in their adventurous expansion of empires. Narratives of history too have largely failed to portray the essence of the philosophical enlightenment in these rulers. A monarch looks like a chimera when Babur orders his womenfolk in Hindustan to build houses according to their choice with the help of royal architects, and the same Babur orders to erect a tower with his enemies' skulls following the defeat of Rana Sanga's Rajput clans. Historical fiction only exaggerates and exoticizes such narration that aligns with the present attempt at rewriting Indian history to the erasure of Muslim rule. How these royal men perceived the arrival of modernity could have been measured if their interest in expanding commercial ties with the outer world, their democratic governance and inclination towards freedom of spirit, in whatever amount these were present in them, could be discussed. Unfortunately, such an approach is missing in literature – both historical and fictional.

Women's situation is worse in this case, as their life was not even of serious interest of any history writer. Additionally, the possibility of their possessing any modern philosophical attribute in Western standard is logically doubted, as religion and patriarchy both suppressed their feminine self. Paria Gashtili, for instance, writes that "as a worldview, Islam provides a fixed identity of women and men that is irreconcilable with any liberating theory" (2013, 121). To accord with her, it is mandatory to say that there is no way to homogenize how Islam is practiced in countries that have Muslim majority or are governed by Islamic laws. In the pre-modern times, the newly formed Islamic dynasty in India established by the Timurid pioneers, was guided by both Islamic rules and their Timurid-Mongol cultural traditions; and there must have been new necessities for which some of those rules needed to be relaxed and traditions were modified. Gradually they left their tent castles and opted for brick-built palaces, allowed marriage with the non-Muslims, adopted new culinary, modified their attires, and learned new languages for the sake of governance.

---

[13] George Peele's play *The battle of Alcazar* was first produced in 1589. This book refers to the comments on the play by Irving Ribner in the 1965 edition of *The English History Play in the Age of Shakespeare*.

They also always adapted to new ways of warfare, used new weapons and gunpowder, encouraged science and technology, and patronized arts and architecture. Modernization of the philosophical realm alongside these physical developments could not be traced due to lack of records; but there are written records of the Mughal monarchs who wrote autobiographies and poetry that mirror their philosophical worlds. It is expected that changes in the outer world affected the domestic realm too; and this book traces the modernization of those women through their writings.

This book envisions individualism as the most important modern trait in these women, and their writings are considered as their self-assertion. In addition to negating any Western claim that these women in pre-modern India were mere puppets in the hands of royal patriarchs, it emphasizes on the autonomy and power these women exercised. Catherine R. Larson's book *Early Modern Women in Conversation* (2011) is a model for this understanding, as in her introductory chapter "Beyond the Humanist Dialogue: The Textual Conversations of Early Modern Women" Larson explains why she studies writings in a variety of genres by five women writers from Sydney and Cavendish families as "conversations"; because according to her these women writers "writing out of very different circumstances in the late sixteenth and early seventeenth centuries constructed authoritative speaking positions for themselves and their female protagonists and used language to mediate relationships within and through their literary works" (2011, 4). They "negotiated the gendered interrelationship between conversation and the spatial boundaries delimiting conversational encounters to create opportunities for authoritative and socially transformative utterance within their texts" (2011, 2). If so, such conversational engagements and authoritative utterances are even more strongly evinced in the writings of the four women in the book, whose seclusion was socially sanctioned. Princess Gulbadan's memoir is a direct negotiation with her own lived life; in which she is in continuous conversation with the people of her past and present; and she re-enacts each event from the authorial-directorial vantage point. As such, she as a woman who did not have much of a choice to make in life, and followed orders of her royal father, brother and nephew all her life; but she negotiated through her silent self-assertion as the narrator of her memoir. Jahanara did the same when she chose the genre of writing hagiographies in which she could converse with her inner self. She had to promote the Mughal preoccupations in India through her own physical and spiritual engagements, but she also used the opportunity to expose her desires and desolation in a subjective way. The objective often becomes subjective, especially in *Risala i Sahibiya*, and according to Bokhari, Jahanara might have used the first-person in both of her sacred and secular autobiographical narratives to "align her authorial self" (2015, 197) with the other imperial counterparts or Mughal historiographers who were male.

The poets discussed in the book have undoubtedly produced the boldest utterances. Their entry into the male world of Sufi and Bhakti poetry are their first stepping out of the boundary drawn by patriarchy, and when they questioned marriage, love, society, monarchy, and even faith and religion, they moved way forward from their societal roots. If the act of breaking away from tradition marks modernity, they were much more modern than the pre-modern times they historically belonged to.

# 2
# Humayun's Biographer Gulbadan Begam: A Quiet Observer of the Aviary

> Woman's awareness of herself is not defined exclusively by her sexuality: it reflects a situation that depends upon the economic organization of society, which in turn indicates what stage of technical evolution mankind has attained.
> – (Beauvoir, 1997, 84)[1]

Once upon a time, there was a mighty ruler in India and he had a little princess whose complexion was like a Persian rose, and so she was called the rose-body princess. While that would be the making of a fairy tale, Gulbadan Begam's (Princess Rose-body) life was nothing like that. Born in the house of a nomadic ruler, whose fate was bound with his many adventures, defeats, and tales of perseverance, she never lived in a bed of roses. She saw the establishment of her father's empire in the faraway land called *Hindustan* that once probably existed in the fairy tales she heard from the women in the nursery; and a keen observer as she was, wrote the first history book by any woman. The great historian Abul Fazl[2] who became famous for his biography of the great Mughal Emperor Akbar, used her historical treatise *Humayun-Nama* as a sourcebook, albeit without ever acknowledging his debt, and she was lost into oblivion. Gulbadan's writing is nonetheless a piquant narrative of the Mughal adventure in India, its importance emerging from the position of alterity she inscribes into a nuanced history that stands to complement existing mainstream historical narratives of the time. Her gendered vision opens a completely new perspective of historical narration, which in the modern times has become insightful as parallel or alternate history.

The significance of a woman's looking at power equations from the proximity of great monarchs hardly needs much clarification; rather, it is the ability to do so that demands attention. If one learns about the peculiarities of a monarch's

---

[1] Quoted from *The Second Sex* (1949) translated by H. M. Parshley and published by Vintage in its 1997 classics series.
[2] Abul Fazl aka Abu'l-Fazl ibn Mubarak (1551-1602) was the grand vizier of the Mughal Emperor Akbar. He wrote the *Akbarnama*, the official biography of Akbar including the *Ain-i-Akbari*. He was one of the *Navaratnas* or the Nine Jewels of Akbar's royal court.

character, it often sheds new light on a phase of history, giving new directions to comprehend the time from a neo-historicist perspective. Gulbadan was a close observer of three great Mughal emperors in succession – her father Babur, her brother Humayun, and finally her nephew Akbar; hence her observations on the early years of the Mughal empire are of utmost importance. She observed the cruelty, polygamy, compromising of ethicality and liberties taken with religious observances, especially during Akbar's reign, but never showed disapprobation. However, there are pieces of evidence of her influence at the Mughal court, but in *Humayun-Nama* she is reticent about this. In *Daughters of the Sun: Empresses, Queens and Begams of the Mughal Empire* (2018), Ira Mukhoty mentions some fifteen women who were influential at the Mughal court, Gulbadan being one of them. While the title of *Humayun-Nama* literally translates as "the history of Humayun", its textualities offer much more than either panegyric or just the history of the second Mughal ruler. It is Gulbadan's memoir that gives a full record of the peaceful and settled palace life of the first two Mughal rulers vis-à-vis a comparatively unsettled camp life of their nomadic days. It also introduces the culinary habits of the Mughals, the valor and cruelty of rulers, the nuanced womanly habits of the *zenana* women, the interactions between people and cultures – what not! 'God's plenty' that usually describes the panorama of characters in Chaucer's *The Canterbury Tales* is what comes to the readers' mind while reading this treatise that is history, memoir, literature, and chronicle in one.

Through her memoir, Gulbadan also invites the readers to investigate her own persona that was otherwise obfuscated within the folds of history. Her efforts at making visible the palace life in its thousand intimate moments with the monarchs offer a humane side of expansive imperialism. Today, several Mughal architectures in the Indian Subcontinent are reminiscent of the Mughal history; and several canonical texts of medieval Indian history wax eloquent on the bloody battles of the period; the cumulative thrust being the ambitions of royal men and the suffering of common people. This drift of history maintains a significant silence on the perspective of royal women as well as that of the subaltern classes, both of whose fates have been acted upon by the rulers.

It is however common knowledge that no empire can sustain in a new territory for over two hundred years unless it has had an inclusive and humanitarian story to tell. *Humayun-Nama* is one of those stories that needs to be analyzed with a view to unearthing the otherwise subsumed humane aspects of the Mughal empire in India, more so in the present time when this phase of Indian history is posited to be at odds with a new nationalist narrative.

## Life of a silent witness

Gulbadan was probably born sometime in 1523 in Kabul as the daughter of Emperor Babur, already the able ruler of Kabul for 19 years. Her mother was Dildar Begam (the Heart-holding princess), who was the fifth of many wives of Babur. Dildar was perhaps from a noble family but not quite a princess; and her husband Babur became the ruler of Kabul and Qandahar after acquiring Kunduz, Badakhshan, Bajaur and Swat[3] by that time. Her lineage is neither mentioned in Babur's Persian memoir *Babur Nama*, nor in Gulbadan's *Humayun-Nama*. In the Turkish text of Babur's memoir, she finds a single passing mention as "aghacha" which would mean "concubine" in English; but taken in context it would perhaps not imply a derogatory appellation in Turkish. *Akbar-Nama* mentions her as Dildar *Aghacha* Begam, which historicizes the fact that she was one of the four remaining wives of Babur, since his first three wives (Ayisha, Zainab and Masuma) except for Maham Begam were either dead or divorced. Gulbadan's English translator Annette S. Beveridge feels that "If Babur held the view four wives were a lawful number, Dildar, of whatever parentage, may be counted amongst them" (Beveridge, 2018, 225). She gave birth to five children – Gulrang Begam (the rose-hued princess), Gulchihra Begam (the rosy-cheeked princess), Abu-n-Nasir Muhammad (popularly known as Mirza Hindal), Gulbadan Begam and Mirza Alwar. Babur's first wife among the living lawful wives, Maham Begam, adopted Gulbadan from her biological mother Dildar Begam when she was two years old. She also took Hindal Mirza since he was six days old. It was however not a custom among the royal members to adopt one another's children. Maham Begam's children had died very early, one after another, and she was perhaps given this privilege of adopting Dildar Begam's children for that reason. Gulbadan's biographer Rumer Godden writes, "Now and again a childless royal wife has adopted a child, usually from a good but middle-class woman, but never from within the haram[4], especially not from one of her husband's own wives, but Babur gave way, to Dildar's deep resentment" (Godden, 1981, 29). Godden again writes, "Maham was powerful, moody and spoilt and it seems Babur denied her

---

[3] Cities and provinces now spread in Afghanistan, parts of Pakistan, Tajikistan, and parts of China. Evidently, we can map Babur's movement from the north west of the region towards Hindustan.

[4] Haram literally means 'forbidden'. While Rumer Godden uses 'haram' and Ira Mukhoty uses 'haraman', a more familiar term is 'harem', which is widely used in English, It is usually the inner part of a Muslim household where a man's wives, concubines, and female servants live. The Mughal harem is usually large because the Emperors were polygamous, and used to keep large number of concubines. The wives and concubines had their female servants. They also used to keep hermaphrodites as servants.

nothing" (1981, 28-29). Dildar Begam must have suffered pain for this, though nothing is clearly mentioned anywhere. Nonetheless, the children remained in front of Dildar's eyes as they were part of the same harem of Babur, and the children knew who their biological mother was. After Maham's death, they were restored to their own mother.

So, the rose-body princess had, if not a troubled childhood, a complicated guardianship in the Mughal harem. Therefore, she learned adapting to shifting situations very early in life. That a Mughal woman's life in the early phase of the empire was of adjustment to hardships in the new Hindustani clime is what Gulabadan's memoir informs us.

Very little is concretely known about Gulbadan's education except that she was two years old when she was taken from her biological mother to Maham Begam's custody, who was responsible for her upbringing and education. It is obvious that the women in the royal family were given religious education under a *maulavi* or a teacher specialized in Islamic scriptures. Godden writes that Gulbadan was deeply religious, "The backbone or core of Muslim school teaching is the *Quran* and the children of that sixteenth-century royal schoolroom were as obliged to learn it as boys and girls are now in all Muslim schools..." (1981, 37-38). Whatever message of the *Quran* she received, according to Godden "with Gulbadan, every word of the Message sank deep" (1981, 38).

As the women could meet outsiders with their *niqab* or *hizab*,[5] it was possible that they could be guided by a male teacher. The fact that the royal women also got education in their mother tongue becomes obvious as Gulbadan writes *Humayun-Nama* in Persian. The women in the Mughal zenana were learned, powerful and some of them even had their personal libraries, as is evidenced in the case of Hamida Banu Begam (Humayun's wife) and princess Jahanara (Shahjahan's daughter). Ira Mukhoty writes that the Mughal women were the most educated of their age. According to her,

> Timurid[6] girls were given the same rigorous education, in mathematics, history, physics, poetry, astronomy, etc., as boys because the Timurids

---

[5] A hijab is a veil worn by Muslim women in public to maintain purdah or separation from unrelated males, according to the Islamic culture. A niqab is also a veil but it covers all the face apart from the eyes. Sometimes they are synonymous.

[6] Descendants of Timur or Tamerlane, the world-famous conqueror who was the most influential sovereign of the Timurid Empire (1370-1507) in Persia. The Mughals of India were direct descendants of Mongol-Timurid blood. Tamerlane married Saray Mulk Khanum, a descendant of the great Mongol Genghis Khan (1162-1227), the founder of the Mongol empire

placed a very high value on calligraphy, writing and erudition. The Mughals were also memory-keepers par excellence of all Indian kings. They wrote memoirs and appointed court historians in enthusiastic numbers. As for the physical evidence of Mughal ambition and glory, India is fairly studded with examples of their vision, in sandstone and in marble. (Mukhoty, 2018, xii)

Even though many of the sandstone and marble structures in India witness the Mughal glory, Mughal women's history often loses its way in the labyrinthine grand narratives as historians hardly care to speak much about them. The fact that Gulbadan never wrote anything about her own education may be understood perhaps as part of the larger trend of women not voicing their private selves. All Mughal women writers were shy about revealing their secluded inner space, and were quiet about their nurturance. Conversely, Abul Fazl, the other great biographer of the Mughals and the writer of *Akbar-Nama*, records the fact of his having received education under renowned teachers of the region. Abul Fazl was initially tutored by his own father, Nagul Fazl and eventually pursued higher education at renowned centers of contemporary learning. Gulbadan's fate was either not as favorable, or she might have been so groomed as to suppress any flamboyant expressions of her academic pursuit. According to Godden, boys and girls in the court of Kabul seem to have been educated together; her speculations possibly being sourced from miniatures showing the girls sitting on cushions at the master's feet attended by elderly women.

### Influence at the Mughal Court

Gulbadan's memoir is testimony to her father Babur's love for her, the admiration her half-brother Humayun accorded her, and the reverence her nephew Akbar offered her at the royal court. Sunita Sharma writes,

> Amongst Babur's daughters, Gulbadan enjoys a place of eminence in this fourth generation of Babur's time. Her historiographical insight makes her the only woman historian of the time in Asian history. Her *Humayun-Nama* provided an authentic source for Abul Fazl's magnum opus, *Akbar-Nama*. The work is a valuable source of information for the social and cultural aspects of the reigns of Babur and Humayun, as she was an eye-witness to many of the events that she narrated, and therefore, her account is more trustworthy. (2012, 365)

---

(thirteen and fourteen centuries) that was the largest contiguous land empire in world history. However, the Mughals were closer to the Timurid clans by blood and consciously held on to Timurid cultural legacy, but their honorific is derived from the Mongols.

Indeed, Gulbadan was a favorite of all in Babur's family. Regarding the adoption of Gulbadan by Maham Begam, Rumer Godden writes that as a child, Gulbadan was fascinating and attracted the seniors. Godden's observation about the chubbiness, whiteness of the skin and cheery nature of children of the 'high Asian' countries is interesting. She also envisages similarity between Babar and his daughter. Godden does not give the credit for Gulbadan's good looks to her biological mother Dildar, who according to her, "had beauty" but "that this most loved of Babur's 'rose' princesses should have looked, not like her mother, but him" (1981, 30). These traces of chauvinism and Orientalism in Godden's remarks make the readers uneasy, but perhaps a lot of it could be true. Physical features with sweetness of temperament might have been the probable reasons for Gulbadan's popularity in the harem. She was modest enough to call herself 'the insignificant one', which is a suitable phrase for any daughter among any emperor's eighteen children, but she was not actually insignificant. Babur must have noticed her when she traveled with Babur's most influential wife, Maham, to Hindustan for the first time. She was a favorite of Humayun too. It becomes clear when Humayun paid her regular visits after Maham Begam's death. Upon his return from Gaur (Bengal) Humayun once told her that he would often think of her but at the time of the disaster he was thankful he had not (Godden, 1981, 79). While Humayun was bringing back his harem by boat, Sher Khan fell upon them and all women got lost including Humayun's six-year-old daughter Aqiqa; and Humayun's sigh of relief clearly evidences how much he loved his sister.

Another half-brother, Mirza Kamran, was also fond of Gulbadan. Her importance to Humayun may have been Kamran's reason for craving Gulbadan's company. Humayun went to annex Gaur, leaving Agra in the custody of this half-brother; and in Humayun's absence when Kamran decided to move to the safer place in Lahore, he seized upon Gulbadan and made her go with him. Perhaps he wanted to have her as a hostage, or wanted the service of Khizr Khwaja Khan who was Gulbadan's husband. Again, when he went to Kabul, he took Gulbadan with him. In these times, Kamran received the service of Gulbadan's husband. Finally, when Humayun recovered Kabul from Kamran, Khizr Khan managed to ally with the Emperor and received his forgiveness. When Kamran renewed the siege of Kabul during the illness of Humayun, he wanted Khizr Khan in his service again. Getting to know of this, Gulbadan intervened and wrote to her husband not to separate himself from the service of Humayun, and he acquiesced. This sequence of events irrefutably shows both Gulbadan's preference for Humayun over Kamran, and the influence she wielded over her husband.

## ***Humayun-Nama*** **and perception of women's literary merit**

Literature or literary culture was part of the Mughal family tradition. An instance from Gulbadan's memoir may testify to that. Gulbadan and some of Babur's wives were taken to Dholpur to visit a newly built tank. In the Sikri Garden of Dholpur, Babur used to sit and write his book *Babur Nama*, a fond memory that baby Gulbadan etched in her mind. Ira Mukhoty comments that such a memory must have affected child Gulbadan deeply,

> That Gulbadan sees her father writing a book in the middle of the convulsion of empire formation, must have affected her deeply. She herself grows up to be a highly educated woman, writing in both Persian and Turkish. She owns an impressive library and is considered a scholar. It is because of her reputation as a learned woman that her grandson Akbar, many years later, will ask her to write down her memories of Babur and Humayun. That biography will be a unique document. The first biography by a Muslim woman in India, with an insight into the lives of the first generation of the women of the great Mughals. (Mukhoty, 2018, 23)

Mukhoty mistakenly writes that Akbar is Gulbadan's 'grandson', but her observation that Gulbadan would become the inspiration of many future generations of Mughal women writers, theologians and poets is obviously accurate. She must have been influenced by Babur's love for books. When Babur captured the fort of Milwat[7] and found several valuable books in the library he was greatly excited. He gave some of those books to Humayun and sent some to Kamran in Kabul and Gulbadan must have come across those in Kabul. Godden guesses that this incident might have been the beginning of Gulbadan's love for books. Babur wanted his sons to be skilled in the art of writing and there are instances when he chided Humayun for flawed writing.

Whether the Mughal women were less fortunate than their English counterparts could be a lucrative topic of a new study. Queen Elizabeth I (1533-1603) was under tutors who taught her grammar, theology, history, rhetoric, logic, philosophy, math, and literature. She also learned to speak six languages

---

[7] Fort of Milwat was in the north of Lahore. Around 1523, Babur was invited by Daulat Khan Lodi, the governor of Lahore who was an enemy of Ibrahim Khan Lodi, the last sovereign of the Lodi dynasty. Daulat Khan offered Babur his allegiance in exchange for assistance against the Emperor. However, Daulat Khan Lodi was disappointed when Babur, after seizing Lahore and Dipalpur, did not give him Lahore. He fled with his son Ghazi Khan to Milwat, while his other son Dilwar Khan accepted Sultanpur and paid his allegiance to Babur. Eventually, Babur seized the fort of Milwat.

fluently. *The Washington Post* reports that she learned Latin at the age of 5.[8] Gulbadan did not acquire proficiency in any of the Indian languages, but was conversant with Turkish and Persian. *Humayun-Nama*, as a memoir of the outstanding quality, claims that these royal women from Asia were in no way intellectually inferior to the European royal class. It shows that history as a discursive field of knowledge has been unnecessarily Orientalist while judging women from the global south.

The treatise written by Gulbadan displays all the necessary qualities of formal writing. Gulbadan commences her account in the customary religious manner, by starting "In the name of Allah, the Merciful, the Compassionate!" This was the style of invocation by any religious Muslim author of the time. In its Europeanized translation, Beveridge writes "in the name of God". Gulbadan was perhaps not familiar with the Western epic tradition. In ancient Greece, the authors used to invoke the nine muses of poetry. In the Christian epic *Paradise Lost*, Milton invokes the "Heavenly Muse" and "the Spirit". So, it is obvious she was following the Muslim and Persian traditions, which anyways correspond with the established practice of attempting a major work of writing.

Gulbadan's first expression in the text, "There had been an order issued, 'Write down whatever you know of the doings of *Firdaus-makani* and *Jannat-ashyani*'" (2018, 83) needs our attention. 'Firdaus-makani' meaning 'dwelling in paradise' was the posthumous title for Babur. Similarly, 'Jannat-ashyani' was the posthumous title of Humayun, which means 'nesting in Paradise.' Beveridge in her notes writes that such custom of naming after death sometimes suppressed the name borne by one during her/his lifetime, especially among some savage tribes. In this case, these names simply glorify the Mughals, and show that they venerated their creator even though they were emperors of great strength. Indeed, these first two Mughal rulers never dared to indulge in any skirmishes with religion, unlike the third, Akbar the great, who tried to amalgamate several religions of the region. This is specifically important, since the Mughal history is parallelly a history of Islamic expansion in South Asia. The more one reads into the Mughal women's writings, the more one agrees with Afshan Bokhari's claims that the Mughal women aligned their authorial selves with their imperial male counterparts, serving as 'major subsets' within "the broader category of historical writing that conveys a nuanced and textured understanding of the imperial and spiritual landscape and the place of women in this male-dominated category" (Bokhari, 2015, 197).

---

[8] Who is the most educated English queen?" by Valerie Strauss. *The Washington Post*. April 29, 2011. https://www.washingtonpost.com/blogs/answer-sheet/post/who-is-the-most-educated-english-queen/2011/04/28/AF78i49E_blog.html. Accessed 24 April 2020.

Gulbadan refers to Emperor Jalaluddin Akbar's order asking her and other members of the family to recall whatever they could of his father and grandfather so that his own biographer Abul Fazl could get some information that would help him write Akbar's biography. It is evident that members of the royal family were literate, and could write under imperial instructions, if not willingly, but on several occasions, Gulbadan makes it a point to clarify that she was compliant not because she was afraid of the monarch. She was Akbar's paternal aunt, and she proclaims her subjectivity. It is understandable that she wrote under instruction and imperial order; but her unfinished memoir has little to do with Akbar. Only a few events regarding Akbar's birth, childhood, abduction, and upbringing are delineated by his aunt in it. However, she never sacrifices her modesty in her self-proclamation. She writes,

> At the time when his Majesty Firdaus-makani passed from this perishable world to the everlasting home, I, this lowly one, was eight years old, so it may well be that I do not remember much. However, in obedience to the royal command, I set down whatever there is that I have heard and remember. (2018, 83)

The minute details she remembers can be exemplified on two occasions. The minutiae of Gulbadan's description of the gifts sent by Babur from Hindustan through his close friend, Khwaza Kilan, for the women of the royal family is one of the first instances of the brilliance of her memory. The second is the name and narration of guests at the wedding feasts of Humayun and Mirza Hindal. She sequentially remembers who sits on which side of the grooms perfectly. However, Beveridge in a note warns her readers not to take the dates and numerical statements mentioned by Gulbadan too seriously, she was considering Gulbadan's old age when memories start fading.

Beveridge's warning appears unfounded when we see Gulbadan narrating her childhood vividly and flawlessly. However, remembrance is a subjective process. When memory makes oneself proud on one hand, and legitimizes the action of ancestors on the other, memory making itself takes on a political course. Some of Gulbadan's memories are also borrowed from elders, orally carried forward to the next generation. For example, when in Babur's praise Gulbadan writes that since the days of Timur, from whom Babur was fifth in descent, there was no prince who labored as he did, and that her pen is too feeble to record the long years of Babur's struggles, one realizes that intention of glorifying her ancestry. This is reinforced by the fact that there is hardly any record of a single lapse of Babur in her memoir though, there are several accounts of Humayun's shortcomings. She writes,

> The toils and perils which in the ruling of kingdoms befell our prince, have been measured out to few, and of few have been recorded the

manliness, courage, and endurance which he showed in battlefields and dangers. Twice he took Samarqand by force of the sword. The first time my royal father was twelve years old, the second nineteen, the third time he was nearly twenty-two. (2018, 84)

Why was she so full of hero worship? Is it because her own identity as Babur's daughter depended on how she presented her father to readers? Was it because the bloodshed and massacre through which Babur conquered Hindustan needed some moral and ethical defense? Whatever her reasons were, Gulbadan caricatured Babur as a mortal man, whose defeats also had a humane side. Babur's paternal and maternal uncles abandoned him in Samarqand around 1505, and to save himself from Shahi Beg Khan, he had to marry off his sister Khanzada Begam to him. Babur remained ever grateful to Khanzada Begam, and allowed her supreme authority in his empire. The description of the hero is not that inspiring in the following lines, "With 200 followers on foot, wearing long frocks on their shoulders and peasants' brogues on their feet, and carrying clubs in their hands, – in this plight, unarmed, and relying on God, he went towards the lands of Badakhshan (Badakhshanat) and Kabul" (2018, 85).

In this and elsewhere in *Humayun-Nama* it is informed that women were accustomed to visiting new places with Babur, and they also accompanied him in his wars. In the Qandahar expedition, Babur's sister Khanzada Begam was with him; thus, he could make a truce with Shahi Beg Khan by giving Khanzada to him. So, the readers become well aware that apart from accompanying the warlord, there are instances of Mughal women being pawned. Their lives were thus not as pleasing and as gratifying as one may speculate from grand narratives of history.

Gulbadan is ingenious in depicting scenes of war and truce, with a tone of equanimity in both. On the one hand, Babur is shown as trading his sister, and on the other, he is showing benevolence to his enemies. He killed Bayasanghar Mirza and blinded Sultan Masud Mirza, both his paternal cousins. After moving out of Samarqand and reaching Badakhshan, when another cousin Khusrau Shah comes and pays respect, Babur forgives him. This Babur is someone the common readers must love and revere, for he has this ability to surprise. However, Gulbadan often narrates episodes of history from hearsay. For example, the whole episode of Babur's liberating Kabul from Muhammad Muqim's aggression is written depending on what she had heard, because the women did not accompany Babur on this expedition. The intimacy and the exchanges between Babur and others must have been heard by the child Gulbadan because Babur marched towards Khurasan in 1506 when she was not even born. Her narration of such unseen episodes of history shows that she had an apt imagination with which she imbibed the cult of bravery, attentive mind, and power of narration, that gave her memoir the uniqueness of recreated history.

Gulbadan's memoir is historiography, literature, a first glimpse of feminism, and much more. Her memoir brings in images of women who were larger than life. For example, she records the death of Babur's mother Qutluq Nigar. The record of the death mentions how Babur revered his mother, and not without reason. Qutluq Nigar was one of the most illustrious women in the Chingizid dynasty who influenced in the making of Babur as a man of perseverance. Gulbadan mentions her grandmother as "the Khanam"[9] without using her proper name, as was the custom of the time, and she does not usually mention any of the proper names of her elders except for those of the princesses and mirzas.[10] She had a natural deference to age and rank. The Khanam's death is mentioned here to highlight one special aspect of Babur's rule: Babur never usurped anything from any of his subjects. Gulbadan makes it a point to inform her readers that the land that was used to bury Babur's mother, was procured from its actual owner. Fairness in conduct and behavior was a hallmark of Babur's reign that has been praised by many historians. Gulbadan adds a personal dimension to it.

Another important trait of Babur that has been highlighted by Gulbadan was his faith in divine signs, so much so that he would always look for one before commencing any new adventure. Babur's wishful death in exchange of his son Humayun's life is a great example of his ultimate ascetic temperament that *Humayun-Nama* presents in detail. Thus, Gulbadan's writing of history gives a homely feel, and it becomes easy for lay readers to find a semblance with the Mughal patriarchs.

Gulbadan's characterization of Babur has a comparative approach; she pitted his sense of responsibility against the lack of it in other princes of the surrounding states. After the death of his father, a young Babur instantly filled the empty space and started taking necessary decisions. The same did not however happen in the case of the princes of Khurasan. While Babur waited with these princes (sons of Sultan Husain Mirza) for months to fight against the Uzbegs, they could not decide whether to fight because they lacked their father's confidence. She writes, "Eighty years long had Sultan Husain Mirza kept Khurasan safe and sound, but the mirzas could not fill their father's place for six months" (2018, 88). Gulbadan's deep religiosity is another important dimension of her treatise. She mentions the generosity of her father along with God's special favor for him. She mentions how the seizure of Kabul was a lucky

---

[9] Khanam (also Khanum, Khanom, Khanoum) literally means 'rich wife' or 'princess.' It is a royal honorific, or a feminine equivalent of the title *Khan* that was used by a sovereign or military ruler among the Mongol tribes.

[10] Mirza is a title denoting the rank of a prince or nobleman. It is of Persian origin and was used mostly by royal youth, distinguished military commander, or occasionally, bya scholar.

incidence for Babur. Unless he seized upon the capital, she would not be able to spend some peaceful years to see the birth of his eighteen children. All except two of Babur's daughters were born in Kabul. Like a historian proper, Gulbadan mentions their names in chronological order. The first among these children was Humayun who was born on Thursday 6$^{th}$ of March 1508, when the sun was in the sign of Pisces. Mention of the sun's position in the astrological signs means that the royal family believed in the signs. Gulbadan looks upon Humayun's birth as a blessing, because the title of *padshah*[11] or Emperor was conferred upon Babur around the same time. This way, Gulbadan not only establishes Babur as God's chosen, but at the same time, legitimizes Humayun as Babur's heir. This technique has been followed by Jahanara in her Sufi treatises in which she approves the monarchy of her father Shah Jahan as well as legitimizes her elder sibling Dara Shikoh's claim for the crown.

While Babur's passion for conquering Hindustan has found repeated and celebrated mention in historical accounts of the Mughal empire, it is Gulbadan alone who must be credited for her dispassionate but faithful historicizing of his many misadventures and the reasons for failure thereof. She writes that after some years' stay in Kabul, her father set out for Samarqand with his wives and five children and conquered it, but he lost Mawarau-n-Nahr (Transoxiana)[12]. Then he got back to Badakhshan and Kabul before he thought of Hindustan again. She comments that he had always desired to conquer Hindustan but could not fulfill his aspirations largely because of the rivalry of his brothers and ill counselling of his *amirs*.[13]

A weakness in Gulbadan's narration is her deliberate glossing over of polygamy that her father and other Mughal males practiced. Around the time Babur received the news of the birth of his youngest son Hindal in Kabul, he was entering matrimony with Malik Mansur Yousufzai's daughter in Bajaur after a general massacre in the province. This is interesting. Women were sometimes deliberately given to rulers by their custodians and sometimes their hands were asked for, as had happened with Babur's sister Khanzada. In what seems to be an act of political correctness of the treatise, Gulbadan's focus is solely on Hindal's birth which was considered a good sign for conquest of Hind, and the

---

[11] Padshah or Padishah is a word of Persian origin. It means 'great king'. This title was quite popular among the Muslim monarchs.

[12] Mawarau-n-Nahr is the ancient Arabic name used for the portion of Central Asia that is now divided into Uzbekistan, Tajikistan, southern parts of Kyrgyzstan, and southwest Kazakhstan. The area is mentioned as Turan in the Persian epic *Shahnameh*, and the Romans know it as Transoxania.

[13] Amirs or chiefs of surrounding provinces supported Humayun with funds and army during the wars.

simultaneous episode of yet another of Babur's marriages fades into forgetfulness. It was not a time when women could think liberally; and women's commodification remains a blind spot in Gulbadan's Mughal historiography. We would need to wait for another century to hear the the dissenting voice of Zeb-un-Nissa, who boldly spoke against the limited liberty in the aviary.

Gulbadan supports the Mughal patriarchy in numerous ways. She equally emphasizes Babur's role as a righteous father as well as a benevolent ruler. To exemplify this, she narrates the troubles in Badakhshan that delayed Babur's venture to Hindustan. History witnesses that Babur did not conquer any territory without some measure of trouble, and this time it was the death of Mirza Khan who was the nominated ruler of the province under Babur's rule. There was the risk of losing Badakhshan to the Uzbegs, and the deceased's wife came to Babur to ask for his help in support of her immature son. After much thought, Babur gave Badakhshan to Humayun, and assigned the land and inheritance of Mirza Khan to Mirza Khan's son Mirza Sulaiman. Babur risked the safety of his own son who was quite young at that time, but did not usurp the property of the deceased governor of Badakhshan. The father's part in the episode has two important propositions. Babur could think of saving Humayun who was very young, but he did not. To support him, Babur and Maham Begam just stayed with their son for a few days in Badakhshan. He wanted to see in his son the resilience he himself had in his early youth. On the other hand, he did not rest assured until he could give his other sons provinces and wealth of equal amount. He set out for Qilat and Qandahar, and after conquering both, bestowed Qandahar on his second son Mirza Kamran. These episodes of history bear witness to Babur's inclusive political philosophy as well as his sense of righteousness. Unfortunately, however, none of his sons could live up to that philosophy, as Gulbadan rightly points out in her treatise. So, this narrative serves two purposes. It provides a detailed background to Babur's Hindustan expedition, while logically analyzes his failures and successes that a regular historian often falls short of doing.

The best part of Gulbadan's narration of Babur's adventures to Hindustan is that it takes the form of storytelling and that of a journal regularly kept. Her narration has the authenticity of a first person; it seems as if she had been with Babur all this while and witnessed his advances then and there, while in reality, some of these were recorded from what she heard afterwards from other royal ladies who accompanied Babur in those expeditions. Her emotions are suppressed in the silent writings, yet her excitement is understandable when she writes,

> In the seven or eight years since 925 H. (1519) the royal army had several times renewed the attempt on Hindustan. Each time it used to conquer lands and districts, such as Bhira, Bajaur, Sialkut, Dipalpur, Lahor(e),

etc., up to the fifth time, when on Safar 1st, 932 H., his Majesty went, march by march, from his glorious encamping in Din-i-ya'qub towards Hindustan. He conquered Lahor(e) and Sirhind, and every country that lay on his path.

[...]

By God's grace he was victorious, and Sultan Ibrahim was killed in the fight. (2018, 93-94)

Babur's victory against Ibrahim Lodi at Panipat[14] was miraculous as he had only 12,000 soldiers against Ibrahim's 1,80,000 horses and 1500 head of fierce elephants, according to Gulbadan's account. So, the spirit of war touched Gulbadan, and she, like a victorious soldier, also exults in the booty when she writes that Babur confiscated a lot of treasure in this battle. She writes that the treasure of five kings fell into Babur's hand, but he gave everything away. Babur defied the suggestions of the amirs of Hind who thought it would be scandalous to fully disburse the spoils of the war emptying the royal treasury. So, she is doubly serving the empire by highlighting both the bravery and generosity of her father.

Here one needs to wonder at the account of the treasures Babur sent to Kabul for his family and friends. It was obvious that the climate of Hindustan did not suit the Turks, but Babur wanted his people to stay. His close friend Khwaja Kilan returned to Kabul after many prayers and through him Babur sent the gifts for his kinsmen in Kabul. A list was sent with the goods. It is not known whether Gulbadan got hold of the list at some point in time or she reconstructed it all from her memories, which was very unlikely, but she tried to give an exact account of the precious gifts sent for the inmates of the palace. Apart from the *ashrafis* and *shahrukhis*[15] (coins), jewels and other things, Gulbadan writes that each Begam of Babur received a dancing girl from Hindustan. It is not known whether these dancing girls entertained the Begams, for she does not mention their presence in any of the royal occasions. The tradition of sending dancing girls as gifts to women certainly needs to be seen critically. Orthodox Islam would forbid dance, and Babur, as a Sunni Muslim, must have known this. Did he then send these nautches only for his female relatives for that very reason? Having thus deliberated on the problematic implications of gendered subject with regard to religion, we also need to take into account this act of human

---

[14] Battles at Panipat were fought thrice: first, by Babur against Ibrahim and the Lodis in 1526, second, was fought by Akbar against the Indian Afghans in 1556, and the third by Ahmad Shah Durrani against the Marathas in 1761. Panipat is now part of the Indian state Haryana.

[15] Ashrafis are gold coins and shahrukhis are silver coins.

trafficking that should unfailingly lead to a condemnation of the dark side of the empire. As a historian-commentator who perceived this early in her maiden life and came to write about it at quite a mature age, Gulbadan's glossing over the deep implications of Babur's gift of these nautches only reinforces the repressive potential of the harem as aviary.

Moreover, Gulbadan records Babur's gifts for his sons, but nothing is told about his gifts to his daughters. Beveridge praises Babur's choice of gifts. She mentions a jeweled inkstand, a stool inlaid with mother of pearl, a short robe of Babur's own and an alphabet that Babur sent to Hindal in 1528. She writes, "What could be better for the royal schoolboy of ten?" (Beveridge 2018, 16). It was most unlikely that Babur did not send gifts for his daughters, but lack of a mention must be taken into consideration too. That women were to be ignored was etched as a fact in the mind of women too, who internalized the teaching of patriarchy.

Gulbadan also tells the story of how Babur made fun of Asas, an old servant (possibly a night-guard, according to Beveridge), with a huge ashrafi that he sent for him. Asas initially fussed about the fact that Babur had sent him only one ashrafi. Babur ordered that Asas should be blindfolded and the ashrafi would be hung round his neck through a hole. Asas was helpless in the beginning but when he felt that the ashrafi was huge, he became very happy. He treasured it with care. The Begams also gave him ten or twelve ashrafis. This episode also tells much of Babur's sense of humor and affection for a minor inmate of his palace. The intimate side of an emperor's nature hardly surfaces in mainstream history in such minute detail, though such accounts definitely provide interesting trivia. Hence, Gulbadan's narration brings in that hitherto unknown alterity to otherwise known subjects and events, in ways that the entire narrative gets a new color. Ruby Lal's remark is important here,

> Gulbadan's record of her father's inventory is striking for several reasons. It brings to life questions of correct deportment in the preparations of gifts and the manner of presenting (and accepting) them – so central to the sensibilities of the Timurid-Mughal world. It is particularly notable for depicting Babur's domestic life. The Begam gives us glimpses of the range of Babur's domestic relationships and associations, with the old as well as the young. The list of gifts is a pointer to the centrality and the hierarchical character of these relationships. (Lal, 2004, 591)[16]

---

[16] Lal's comment is quoted from "Historicizing the Harem: The Challenge of a Princess's Memoir" published in *Feminist Studies*, 30(3), 2004, pp 590-616. Internet source: https://www.jstor.org/stable/20458986, accessed on 25 May 2021.

In Lal's perception, the sending of gifts was obviously a wise step as part of Babur's "building alliances" and reinforcing kinship solidarities", as her book inadvertently suggests, because right after this event, Babur sent an urgent call through letters in which he asked his people to join him in Hindustan. Gulbadan quotes the call,

> We shall take into full favor all who enter our service, and especially such as served our father and grandfather and ancestors. If such will come to us, they will receive fitting benefits. Whoever there may be of the families of Sahib-qiran and Chingiz[17] Khan, let them turn towards our court. The most High has given us sovereignty in Hindustan; let them come that we may see prosperity together. (2018, 97)

This letter of Babur constitutes the democratic spirit of the empire in Hindustan. He won his people's opinion by a kind of soft diplomacy. A bunch of women of Babur's extended family responded to this call. It was very important for the women to join him in Hindustan, as there was already some chaotic news regarding the problems of the royal ladies in Kabul under Mirza Kamran. Kamran was unable to settle the disputes of the elderly and powerful women. On the other hand, Babur needed to have his people around him. Gulbadan's writing obviously eludes these references, her translator Beveridge mentions these in her introduction,

> The migration was amply dictated to many of the party by Babur's wish to see his own people again; but it is clear that the enforced *levee en masse* of the ladies was a result of considerations of policy and peace. The city was full of women who, by birth or marriage, were attached to various branches of the Timurids, and there was conflict of aims and palpable friction. It may well be that Kamran's government provoked unrest, because he was the son of a mother of less birth than were very many of the resident Begams of Kabul. (2018, 17)

In this context, it is interesting to take cognizance of Beveridge's hint of the presence of women chiefs in Kabul. In her 'Introduction' to the translation of *Humayun-Nama,* Beveridge refers to Babur's reply to Khwaja Kilan's letter written in 1528. The crux of Babur's letter relates to the impossibility of settling or regularizing anything in a land where there were seven or eight female chiefs; his reference being to his own sisters who enjoyed enormous authority. In this context, Gulbadan takes note of Babur's urgent instructions to his friend Khwaja Kilan to arrange for these women of his family to be sent to Hindustan without delay. Here again, it is surprising that Gulbadan's memoir does not

---

[17] Genghis Khan

make much ado about this fact of this displacement of powerful women of the harem that Babur had to effect in order to keep peace at home.

Gulbadan herself traveled to Hindustan with Maham Begam in 1529, and gives an account of all other ladies who traveled with them, "In short, all the Begams and Khanams went, ninety-six persons in all, and all received houses and lands and gifts to their heart's desire" (2018, 97). Babur used to meet his paternal aunts every Friday, and cheer them with his presence. He even ordered the architect Khwaja Qasim to obey the aunts' orders whenever they desired any construction or renovation in their palaces.

Gulbadan described some of the constructions in Agra under Babur's instructions. One learns from this memoir that Babur ordered the construction of several buildings facing the Agra fort. The fort was in use since the Lodis or even before them; Babur captured it and used it as his residence. He built a stepwell inside it. The reminiscence of the buildings and tanks made at that time are still there in and around the new fort in Agra (built by Emperor Akbar) that was declared a world heritage site by UNESCO in 1983. Gulbadan's vivid description brings back the history of the construction of the city.

One of the best war episodes in the memoir is between Babur and his former enemies gathered under Rana Sanga.[18] Gulbadan describes the dramatic episode in an intimate way. A year after Ibrahim Lodi's defeat and death, the amirs and ranas and rajas[19] who paid taxes to Babur gathered under the Rana. This shows that the Hindustani races were born fighters and would not give up easily. Babur was alone and helpless compared to the huge number of leaders gathered on the opposite camp. The court astrologer Mohammad Sharif declared that Babur should not fight with these people as his reading of the constellation was not in favor. The soldiers were in drooping spirits after hearing this. To revive the morale of his men, Babur called for an assembly where he said that it was imperative to undertake the battle and win the field if they desired to return to their birthplace. Such a win would consecrate them in history as avengers for the cause of God (Gazi); and even if they perished, they would do so as martyrs (Shahid). In either case, they would have to depend on their fate. Hearing this, his men swore by the divorce of their wives and by the holy book that they would fight if they were alive. Babur renounced wine and all other forbidden things. Four hundred men followed Babur's example and swore the same. Babur was looking for reinforcements. Dramatically, the night

---

[18] Rana Sanga is the popular name of Maharana Sangram Singh Sisodia (1482-1528) was the ruler of Mewar. He headed the Rajput confederacy during the 16th century against Babur.

[19] Both Rana and Raja meaning 'king', were titles used by Hindu monarchs in the Indian subcontinent.

before the battle commenced, some fifty men arrived from a relative Qasim Sultan. Babur sent about a thousand from his troops to accompany Qasim Sultan to deceive the enemies who would be scared thinking that reinforcement had arrived in time. Gulbadan's details show that Babur was both adventurous and adept in the art of warfare, an able successor of his Timurid ancestor.

Gulbadan's mention of her own arrival in Hindustan is engaging, and here again she unlocks her father's loving family-man avatar. A child with wide-open eyes to see the world, she traveled all the way from Kabul with Maham Begam. While they were two or three miles away from the court, Babur set out on foot to welcome his wife and daughter. Finally, she met her royal father, and she writes in her memoir, "I fell at his feet; he asked me many questions, and took me for a time in his arms, and then this insignificant person felt such happiness that greater could not be imagined" (2018, 102). This is what most royal kids of this nomadic race felt, perhaps this is what they were fated to observe: meeting with a long-absent parent from time to time. This episode shows that the princesses were groomed to show reverence and proper greetings to the people of rank. There is a description of the meeting between Gulbadan and his father's Khalifa[20] and his wife that confirms this. The way the Mughal children learned through action is witnessed here.

Gulbadan brings in such nuanced information about the lives of children and women on many occasions. More royal women (Babur's sisters) arrived from Kabul, and Babur gave them honorable reception. Babur's eldest sister Khanzada was among the women, and all women gathered in her quarters and paid respect to Babur. All the Begams received houses from the emperor. Women, as is understood, enjoyed liberty under Babur's rule, but liberty with limits. None could do anything against the wishes of the sovereign. Within their limits, they could move and work freely, and this limited freedom brings back the aviary that has been used metaphorically in the title of this book.

Gulbadan highlights many shades of Babur's character, one of which is obviously his love for gardens. Usually, we are informed of this through the many gardens he established, but never has anyone described them in the intimate way as Gulbadan does. After a few days of the Begams' arrival, Babur made an excursion to *Bagh-i-zar-Afshan*[21] or the Gold-scattering Garden,

---

[20] Khalifa means successor, ruler, deputy. It usually refers to the Caliphate, or the leaders among the followers of the prophet of Islam, but is also used as a title among various Islamic religious groups and orders. Gulbadan refers to Babur's vizir Sayyid or Khwaja Nizam-d-din Balras, who was also a distant relative of Babur. (Beveridge's note in pg 101)
[21] Bagh-i-zar-Afshan was constructed by Babur in 1526. It was modelled after the gardens Babur had seen in Samarkand. This garden was also called Bagh-i-Gul-Afshan (the flower-

where he declared that he intended to give up the throne to Humayun and wished to retire to this garden. This emotional outburst is what makes the emperor a human, and Babur surely was a human with a philosophical nature. Gulbadan not only shows this philosophical side of her father; at times, she shows Babur in a mystic light, and the life exchange episode[22] is the strongest example of this. Upon receiving the news of Humayun's illness his mother Maham Begam immediately left for Delhi and came to Mathura where she met Humayun, who was in turn trying to reach Agra. From there, the mother and son came to Agra. Gulbadan did not accompany Maham Begam in this journey. She writes, "When they arrived, this insignificant one went with her own sisters to visit that royal angel of goodness (2018, 104). She always talks of herself as 'the insignificant one', and 'the angel of goodness' is undoubtedly Humayun. This proliferation of words of compliment in her memoir testifies to Gulbadan's fondness and loyalty for the Mughal pillars of society. What is important here is her account of Babur's self-surrender for the sake of Humayun's life. This description is interesting primarily because of the life exchange prayers. Beveridge finds it 'puzzling to translate' as she writes in a note. This episode remains a mystery to the historians and the mysticism of prayers has inspired different pieces of literature in the Subcontinent. In a Bangla poem called "Baburer Prarthana" (Babur's Prayers), for example, the poet Sankha Ghosh (1932-2021) writes,

> Here I kneel in supplication before the western sky-
> Which is barren like a spring without flowers.
> Destroy me if you wish Oh Lord,
> Let my offspring live on in dreams.
> Where has his radiant youth fled,
> Where does the secret decay eat away at mortal flesh?
> Shadows lurk beneath his defeated eyes
> Poison courses through lungs and veins.
> Let the melancholy call for prayer
> Echo from the city's center to the edge.
> Turn me into petrified mass, if you will.

---

scattering garden) and Bagh-i-Nur-Afshan (the light-scattering garden). Babur's body was initially lain in this garden before being transferred to Kabul for burial. It was renamed Ram Bagh by the Marathas in the eighteenth century and currently is called by that.

[22] The life exchange episode is a mysterious event. Humayun fell seriously ill towards the end of 1530, and when all doctors failed to treat him, Babur prayed for consecutive nights to save his son's life. It is strongly believed that Babur pledged his own life to Allah in exchange of Humayun's. As things transpired, Babur gradually began to fall ill while Humayun was recovering, and finally when Humayun recovered, Babur met his death.

Let my offspring live on in dreams.
Or is it that the germs of sin
That infest this body
Prohibit all chances of redemption?
Or have the exultant cries of my barbaric victories
Ushered in death into this house?
Or is it that the unbearable brilliance of the palace
Burns down bones and hearts?
As millions of heedless insects
Lodge inside his body?
You have bestowed much bounty
Upon me, Lord
Showered me with immense riches;
Where will you take him
Stripped and bare?
Destroy me my Lord
Let my offspring live on in dreams. (Tr. Sonia Nishat Amin, unpublished)

Evidently, this is quite an emotional interpretation of supplication of a father for a son's life. Gulbadan's description of the episode makes a smooth passage between one's departure and another's entry. Historians across ages have created an image of Babur whom they have valorized as a gutsy conqueror whose claim to fame rests solely on being the founder of the Mughal empire in Hindustan. While this is true in the realm of public history, had Gulbadan not written about this episode, the humane and emotional father underlying the empire builder would never have come to light.

Since the beginning of her deliberation of Humayun's coming of age, Babur's gradual dependence and trust on him became part of the history though she never explained how through each event of that history Humayun was maturing in his ascending journey to become the monarch. Humayun takes charge naturally and pays homage to the women in the harem as Babur used to do. Hindal Mirza comes to meet his brother, now the emperor, who is received in kindness. Gulbadan writes that Humayun took care of Babur's death rituals with proper care. Muhammad Ali (*Asas*, or night guard) was appointed as the guardian of his tomb and sixty good reciters of the *Quran* were appointed for recitation and prayers. Maham Begam made an allowance of food twice daily, and Gulbadan's memoir provides a detailed account of this. Humayun used to visit his harem in Maham Begam's dwelling and later, he would visit Gulbadan in her tent where other married women would gather to meet the new emperor. Gulbadan feels soothed by her brother's treatment of her, and out of extreme gratitude, writes,

In short, after the death of my royal father and my lady, his Majesty, in the fulness of his affection, showed this broken one such favor, and spoke with such boundless compassion to this helpless one, that she did not know she was orphaned and headless. (2018, 111)

This is certainly a proof of Gulbadan's love for her brother, and henceforth she vividly narrates how her brother confronts new enemies. In the same breath, she also narrates the private life of Humayun, and his weakness for younger women that caused trouble in the harem. It is important to note that Maham Begam used to encourage Humayun's dalliance with these young women explicitly because she was eager to have Humayun beget a male heir. The women of the harem would naturally become jealous of each other, and resort to unethical means to win the emperor's heart. She describes the episode of the false pregnancy of Maywa-jan, who was lately married to Humayun. This is the first hint of the fraudulence of some women of the harem, which eventually takes a full frame in Jahanara's description. The poisoning of Babur's food by the mother of his enemy Ibrahim Sultan[23] was another mention of such acts. This depravity on the part of a woman who, though outside the family, was given no less a position than that of an insider by the monarch, shows the hideous intrigues women of the palace could indulge in. This second instance of conspiracy in the harem was a serious issue, though Gulbadan does not explicitly proclaim it as conspiracy. Gulbadan's veiled language tries to keep the readers at bay from the harem politics, but one cannot deny the fact that the ladies in the harem understood politics of power connected with the birth of the legitimate heir to the throne. Falsehood, backbiting and killing thus existed in the apparently secure aviary. Though the covert sexual politics of the harem surfaces in her plain-faced narration, the modern reader is wont to find her version of history complicit in its acquiescence.

Gulbadan's memoir, thus, bears testimony to the cunning nature of women, and she instantly picks on a grand feast arranged by Maham Begam to divert the readers from this complicated issue. The memoir serves as a wonderful record of rituals and feasts. Gulbadan describes the monarch's pleasure trips in which women participate. Feasts arranged within the premises of the palace also show how women of royal descent exercised power. Gulbadan's memoir serves as a detailed record of the Persianate culture that the Mughals still

---

[23] After defeating and beheading Ibrahim Sultan, Babur invited Sultan's mother to stay in the palace out of generosity. He wanted to comfort the old woman. He also employed Sultan's cooks in the kitchen so that she could enjoy the food she was habituated with. Babur would also taste the food the new cook could offer him. Ibrahim Sultan's mother forced the cook to mix poison in Babur's food, which did not take his life but kept him severely ill for weeks.

carried as a legacy. The Mystic Feast that Khanzada Begam arranged is another of those events that vividly records the royal culture of the time. The feast took place in the Mystic House, a grand structure built after the nomadic tent culture of the Timurid clans. Gulbadan gives almost a photographic description of the event. The bazars were lit up as well as people's homes and the soldiers' quarters. This illumination was the first of its kind in India, as claimed by Beveridge. A jeweled throne was made with gold hangings on it, large audience tents were erected with European brocade inside and Portuguese sheets outside. The jeweled throne was set for the Padshah, and Humayun and Khanzada sat together on a divan in front of it. The festival took place for several days, while enemies continued to disturb the reign of Humayun simultaneously. There is random mention of names and a casual reader stands the mischance of losing track of Gulbadan's description. From this description, the readers also learn of the hierarchy that the empire maintained. Three specific houses with proper names were built for the occasion. The military men and politicians dominated the empire for which they belonged to the House of Dominion. The theologians and ascetics enjoyed power too, because the Mughals revered them and dedicated the House of Good Fortune. The name is significantly indicating at the Mughals' faith in fortune that comes with the blessings of religious leaders. The third House of Pleasure, belongs to the emperor and his harem who have a natural claim on pleasure and luxury. As history evidences, Babur and Humayun could not enjoy much luxury due to their constant moves from one place to another. They mostly lived in huge royal tents. The Mughal rulers after them gradually lost ties with their nomadic culture, built palaces and monuments and enjoyed luxurious life in India. After the Mystic Feast Mirza Hindal's wedding feast takes place in the same house. Gulbadan again leaves a mark of her photographic memory in the description.

Gulbadan's sharp daily observances bring out the fact that the life of the royal people was however not one of just peace and leisure. Humayun as a king, had to face the troubles that often rocked the zenana. During his stay in the garden, all ladies of Humayun's harem would stay with him. The royal ladies had their separate tents and had offices inside those. These royal tents were visited by Humayun. Upon such occasions, Humayun usually visited his mothers and sisters. Gulbadan gives an account of a day when Humayun was visiting her tent. Usually, all the women would gather in the same tent while the emperor was there. On that particular day, while all were reposing after the enjoyments during the early morning prayers, one of Humayun's wives named Bega Begam made a complaint that Humayun does not visit 'their' (wives') tents. She literally meant herself and perhaps Gulbarg Begam, according to Beveridge. In response, Humayun said nothing and went to prayers. In the first hour of the day, he called his mothers, sisters and begams, and responded to Bega Begam's complaints. Gulbadan quotes him,

"Bibi, what ill-treatment at my hands did you complain of this morning?" And "That was not the place to make a complaint. You all know that I have been to the quarters of the elder relations of you all. It is a necessity laid on me to make them happy. Nevertheless, I am ashamed before them because I see them so rarely. It has long been in my mind to ask from you all a signed declaration, and it is as well that you have brought me to the speaking-point. I am an opium-eater. If there should be delay in my comings and goings, do not be angry with me. Rather, write me a letter, and say: "Whether it please you to come or whether it please you not to come, we are content and are thankful to you." (2018, 131)

Gulbarg Begam wrote the letter at once, but Bega Begam hesitated a little before finally writing a note to the same effect. This strengthens the aviary imagery; the Mughal rulers were generous but they were determined to give their women limited freedom and whenever necessary, they could regiment them under strict rules. Gulbadan does not ponder on Humayun's addiction to opium that, in fact, became his strangest shortcoming. He was the unattractive son of the charismatic leader and strong statesman that Babur was. This episode shows that his wives were not very happy with his arbitrary nature. Later, when he married Hamida Banu Begam (Akbar's mother), he became too attached to her to pay attention to his other wives. The harem was evidently not an equally pleasant place for all its inhabitants.

Gulbadan describes Humayun's battles in many places of Hindustan and surroundings. Gujarat, Champanir (Champaner),[24] Ahmadabad (Ahmedabad), Bahruch (Bharuch), Palan—many names connected with these conflicts help mapping the Mughal empire[25] and how Humayun was expanding it. In such a map, one can visualize him literally moving from west to east (north-east) and annexing different parts of Gangetic Uttar Pradesh, and then moving towards Gaur in Bengal. This description is not just about the geography of Mughal expansion, it also foregrounds the history of betrayal by siblings. Humayun's was a miserable life, because brothers and close relations conspired against him. It is a historical fact that Babur made Humayun promise that he would not kill any of his brothers, but perhaps his brothers were not happy with Babur's selection of heir. The law of primogeniture was not the basis for selection of heirs; Babur's fondness for Humayun as Maham Begam's son was the reason.

---

[24] Ancient city in Gujarat. The city was the capital of the Sultanate of Gujarat for some years.
[25] *Ahmadabad, Bahruch and Palan (as spelled by Beveridge) are part of Gujarat.* Ahmedabad is the largest *city* and former capital of the Indian state of Gujarat. Bharuch, also known by its former name Broach, is situated at the mouth of the river Narmada. It is the administrative headquarters of Bharuch District. Palan is a large village located in Valsad district. All three were part of the Gujarat Sultanate in the sixteenth century.

Humayun was a weak ruler, and his weakness emboldened his brothers to aspire for the position of the monarch.

Gulbadan's memoir shows the last years of his sad reign that were spent in resisting Shir Khan in Hindustan and fighting his brother Kamran in Kabul. Around that time, his obedient brother Hindal also stood against him. Hindal was misguided by some courtiers who informed that in the absence of Padshah Humayun, some mirzas (whom Hindal had defeated on earlier occasions) were trying to raise their heads against him. Hindal killed Shaikh Bahlul, the servitor, for treason. Hearing this, Humayun started for Agra and on his way back, was defeated by Shir Khan. Gulbadan writes, "His Majesty's own blessed hand was wounded" (2018, 135). He came back to the bank of river Yamuna safely with the help of Raja Birbahan. But before he arrived at Agra, he had heard that Shir Khan was coming from the direction of Chausa. Humayun lost three women of his harem including his six-year-old daughter Aqiqa in that encounter. Whether they fell in the river or what happened to them nobody knew. This is the first time the Mughal women were hurt during a battle and Humayun promised that he would never again take his harem with him in battles. This sanctioned the aviary image of the harem; Mughal rulers were caring and responsible for the safety of their women. As history witnesses, women lived in apparent peace and security in Mughal zenana, but once any of them rebelled or opposed the Mughal sovereign, she was severely punished. Jahanara's imprisonment along with her father Shah Jahan by her brother Aurangzeb, and Zeb-un-Nissa's life imprisonment are ready examples.

Humayun is usually considered an ill-fated monarch as his brothers were the worst of his enemies. Gulbadan's memoir shows how he tried to keep them satisfied but to not much avail. Hindal was the only brother who constantly supported him, even though he also had bouts of unpleasant conflicts with Humayun, one of which is mentioned above. Gulbadan becomes emotional when she narrates one such quarrel between these two brothers, to appease which Humayun asked for help from her and Dildar Begam. Humayun said to them: "Hindal is my strength and my spear; the desirable light of my eyes, the might of my arm, the desired, the beloved. May what I do be right! [...]" (2018, 139). He took the Holy Book (the *Quran*) and vowed with it that he did not nurture any anger against him. It was settled that Dildar Begam would go to fetch Hindal from Alwar. The bonding between Humayun and Hindal stayed till Hindal's untimely death in the battle against Kamran. This memoir is a family saga in all senses.

Gulbadan's memoir also serves as a wonderful source of myth and fairytale. She describes a fantastic event: Humayun was saved by a *visti* or water-carrier in the river at Chausa when all his female companions were lost. When Humayun asked the visti what reward he wanted for saving his life, he playfully said he wanted to be the king for two days. To keep his promise Humayun made the servant sit on the throne and compelled all his amirs to make obeisance to him. This man enjoyed royal power for two days. Mirza Hindal was at Alwar for gathering arms. Mirza Kamran was annoyed at this and did not come to the court. While Shir Khan was as near as Lakhnau, it was unimaginable that Humayun was playing with his water-carrier just to keep his promise. But such was Humayun, and this story was later anthologized as a tale for children.

Gulbadan at times becomes prejudiced while describing fraternal conflicts, ostensibly because she was personally affected by those. One such example is of Mirza Kamran's taking her forcefully to Lahore. Kamran was sick for a few weeks and he suspected Humayun had given him poison. Humayun swore he did not do any such thing, but Kamran did not believe it. He left Kamran in Agra to act for him while he would be fighting with Shir Khan in Kanauj[26], but Kamran took a treacherous decision. He left for Lahore when he heard that Humayun had made a bridge of boats and crossed the Ganges. He made Gulbadan go with him against her will, "Then he took me by main force, with a hundred weepings and complaints and laments, away from my mothers, and my own mother and my sisters, and my father's people, and my brothers, and parted us who had all grown up together from infancy" (2018, 142). Gulbadan's narration clearly shows her dislike for Kamran though this journey with Kamran actually secured her life. Many amirs sent their wives with Mirza Kamran to Lahore for safety, and Kamran perhaps thought of Gulbadan's safety. Had she gone with Humayun, who was fighting with Shir Khan in Kanauj by the Ganges, which he eventually lost with his two wives and six-year-old daughter, Gulbadan could have died too. At this point, in Humayun's comment that it would be better if he killed his daughter, the readers get to have a clear idea of the Mughal understanding of gallantry that was a preferred mode to save the honor of their women. Hindal later escorts the Mughal women to safety in Lahore. Gulbadan's sisterly affection for Humayun and Hindal is illustrious, and she could equally give some credit to Kamran too. Beveridge writes in this regard,

> She (Gulbadan) bewailed herself as parting from those with whom she had grown up, and no uninitiated reader could guess that she was going with her father' son. She was a clever and attractive girl whose society was welcome to all her brothers, but in Kamran's wish to take her now there is something more. It is possible that he who liked her, thought of her safety; it is probable that, as he had attached two of her husband's

---

[26] Kanauj or Kannauj is administrative headquarters of Kannauj districtin Uttar Pradesh. It is an ancient city built up in the Maukhari dynasty around the sixth century.

> brothers, Yasin-Daulat and Mahdi, and perhaps the third, Masud, he desired to have Khizr (Gulbadan's husband) too. Gulbadan's departure from the home circle was perhaps her first adventure into the foreign world as a married woman. By going when she did and under the escort of Kamran's strong force, she was spared a terrible journey which her mother and the rest of the royal party made under care of Hindal, with foes in front and behind, and at great peril. (Beveridge, 2018, 32)

Kamran was clearly not her favorite, and she would not give him any credit. Was this part of state politics or simply a sisterly grudge? Given the old age[27] at which she was writing the memoir, whatever grudge she had had against Kamran should have been neutralized.

As a narrator, Gulbadan is not a simpleton, she has her own agenda, and that becomes clear in the second instance of her silence. She does not explicitly mention her marriage too. She records an evening of the day Humayun returned from Gaur when the ladies met him. Humayun notices something and says to her: "I did not know you at first, because when I led the army to Gaur Bangala, you wore a high cap (*taq*)[28], and now when I saw the Muslin coif I did not recognise you" (2018, 138). The coif was a sign of her marriage. Gulbadan, as a narrator, has taken the liberty to elide over a few facts she did not like to bring to limelight. Her biographer Rumer Godden claims that she did not have a very happy conjugal life with her second cousin, Khizr Khwaja Khan, and spent her old age at Akbar's court instead of accompanying Khizr Khan to Lahore. Perhaps that lack of conjugal satiety, if not the cultural grooming of the Mughal women to keep personal life behind the scenes prompted Gulbadan's reticence about her marriage.

This however does not stop Gulbadan from vividly narrating Humayun's romance with his would-be wife, Hamida Banu Begam. She gives a full account of how Humayun persuaded Hamida Banu to marry, even if he was not in a position to pay the alimony at that time. Godden comments that Hamida Banu might have been in love with Hindal. Gulbadan does not give any hint to that, rather she writes that Hindal made objections when Humayun proposed marriage, saying: 'I look on this girl as a sister and child of my own' (2018, 150). Humayun was determined to marry her, perhaps because she was of the lineage of the Terrible Elephant, which was connected to one of his dreams

---

[27] Gulbadan was commissioned by Akbar to write the memoir when she was more than sixty years of age.
[28] *Taq* is a cap and *lachak* is a wife's coiffure, clarifies Beveridge in the introduction to her translation. It would be very difficult to learn of Gulbadan's marriage from her narration had Beveridge not explained the significance of the objects.

about a male heir. Humayun was superstitious since childhood. One day during his distressful days in Sind and Multan he dreamt of a venerable man who foretold him of a son's birth who would be called Jalaluddin Muhammad Akbar. The man in the dream also informed that the child would be of the lineage of the Terrible Elephant, Ahmad of Jam (visibly referring to Hamida's father). After forty days of persuasion, Hamida Banu consented to this marriage. Humayun had to engage in battles again after this marriage. It is a sad episode while Humayun was traveling through the battlegrounds with a pregnant Hamida Banu as his companion. In regular history books that mainly focus on the broad narrative of battles fought between sovereigns, we never come across such domestic details of the battlefield, and such intimate details are possible only by a female historian and biographer.

It has already been mentioned that Gulbadan's memoir serves as a source for Abul Fazl's *Akbarnama*, and Akbar's birth is described in this to some detail, even though she remains mysteriously indifferent while informing of the birth. She mentions that Akbar was born in Umarkot when Humayun was thirty miles away, and was facing his enemies one after another. Humayun fails to negotiate with his brothers through messengers, and in sheer helplessness he exasperates: "What is to be done? Where am I to go?" (2018, 165). History books rarely familiarize readers with such frustrating moments in a sovereign's life. Humayun is seen as hopeful of getting reinforcement from the Afghans of Shal-mastan to confront his brother Askari. As soon as Askari reached Shal-mastan[29] Humayun fled with such haste that he managed to take only his wife Hamida Banu with him, leaving even his infant son Akbar in the abandoned camp. Askari arrived with his 2000 troops and took Akbar. Askari's wife Sultanam took great care of Akbar, as Gulbadan writes in her memoir. Askari sent Akbar to Mirza Kamran in Kabul where Khanzada Begam got his custody. Gulbadan writes that Khanzada used to kiss Akbar's hands and feet and would say that those were exactly like the hands and feet of her brother Babur. In retrospect, it seems difficult to adequately comprehend both the workings of Humayun's mind with regard to his near ones and Gulbadan's motivation behind what she chooses to dwell upon or exclude in her narrative. As for Humayun, his desertion at it were, of the very male child that he so desperately wanted, is strange to say the least. On the other hand, while describing this episode, Gulbadan's inexplicable matter-of-fact manner is equally bewildering, given that this is the same person who earlier narrated with much elan Humayun's gratuitous thinking that she was not with him during his ill-fated battle of Chausa.

Humayun's eventual sufferings are intimately described by Gulbadan though she was not present among the thirty people that were with him at that time.

---

[29] A place in the north of Kabul.

Humayun had his most trustworthy men with him. Gulbadan records these events from the stories told by Khwaza Ghazi and Hamida Banu Begam. It gives the reader a shudder to know that in sheer hunger and cold Humayun ordered to kill a horse which they would boil in a helmet, and the Emperor himself roasted some meat. In the same breath, Gulbadan shows how Humayun's charismatic personality could bring a magical effect on his enemies. She narrates Humayun's confrontation with the Baluchis[30] of the region. There is an order issued by Mirza Askari that the Baluchis must imprison Humayun and his followers. That does not happen because of the Baluchi leader's transformation after seeing Humayun's angelic appearance. She quotes the leader,

> As I had not seen your Majesty. I at first had this evil thought, but now I will sacrifice my life and the lives of my family, I have five or six sons, for your Majesty's head, or rather for one hair of it. Go where you wish. God protect you. Mirza Askari may do what he likes' (2018, 168).

Gulbadan gives a glimpse of international ties that existed at that time. Humayun managed to go to Khurasan in Iraq, and the Shah of Khurasan was happy to receive him. The two rulers spent time in friendly conversations. Gulbadan focuses on the women who were also engaged in partying. Hamida Banu Begam and the Shah's sister Shahzada Sultanam are seen having splendid enjoyments in her description. Sultanam arranged a big gathering in honor of Hamida Banu Begam four miles away from the city in which about a thousand women participated. The Shah accompanied Humayun during Hamida Banu's absence. This description of freedom and power enjoyed by women in those days counters the stilted Orientalist straitjacketing of the Mughal harem as a space for unmitigated male promiscuity and female bondage. The harem was in reality an ambivalent space suitably expressed with the metaphor of the aviary.

On several occasions, Gulbadan is explicit about women's intervention in state polity. Khanzada Begam was sent by Mirza Kamran to Qandahar to make peace between him and Humayun. On the way at Qabal-chak, Khanzada died of fever. Gulbadan does not ponder much over her death; she only makes passing mention of her first burial in Qabal-chak, and then of her remains being brought to Kabul to be laid by the grave of Babur. This detail leads one to feel that women whose lives were lived in conformity with patriarchy were allowed to exercise limited power in life and were also revered in death. As somebody who had willingly sacrificed her individuality in exchange of the life

---

[30] Baluchis or the Baloch people live mainly in the Balochistan, which is a Persian plateau thatencompasses, apart from the greater part of Iran, Afghanistan and Pakistan.They speak the Balochi language.

of Babur, Khanzada did receive her rewards in the form of privilege and power with Babur and Humayun. As a contrast, there is Zeb-un-Nissa (taken up in Chapter 4) whose dissenting nature earned her the wrath of Aurangzeb till she perished in captivity.

Humayun allocated pension, rations, water and land and servants to the widows and families of the soldiers wounded and killed at Chausa, Kanauj and Bhakkar, and all people were happy under his reign. On the other hand, in Humayun's absence, Mirza Kamran returned to Kabul and recaptured the fort in Kabul. Gulbadan narrates Mirza's ill manners with the women of Humayun's harem, which was rather unusual for the Mughals. He imprisoned the Begams in Mirza Askari's house, and shut them up in a room with bricks and plasters. The ladies were supplied food and water from over the walls. He plundered the houses of those men who had left him for Humayun, and behaved very badly with their families. Gulbadan also mentions Kamran's rough behavior towards her and her mother. He ordered Dildar Begam to reside in the armorer's house and asked Gulbadan to stay in his own house. The intentions of Kamran behind keeping Gulbadan with him, as she speculates, might have been to get the help of Gulbadan's husband, a fact mentioned earlier. Kamran asked Gulbadan to write a letter to her husband but she did not oblige. She reveals in the memoir that she had already told her husband not to leave Humayun's side even if his (Khan's) brothers supported Mirza Kamran, which her husband followed.

At this point, Gulbadan mentions the birth of Humayun's children by Mah Chuchak Begam. Amidst the din of warfare this sudden diversion might look somewhat awkward, but perhaps she means to reflect upon the eternal cycle of life where deaths do not stall the continuance of the human race. Amidst the quite long narration of warfare in different places involving different sets of soldiers, she describes an event when her brothers come to an agreement of peace and Humayun gives them provinces –Kulab to Kamran, Qila-i-zafar to Mirza Sulaiman, Qandahar (or Kunduz, Beveridge seems confused) to Mirza Hindal and Taliqan to Mirza Askari. Thus, while the unfortunate elder brother kept his promise to their dead father till the end, in return however he did not receive his brothers' fidelity. However, on the particular occasion of this distribution, the brothers ate together, which was instigated by Gulbadan's wish. It must have been a moment of happiness for her when she writes,

> At this gathering, his Majesty graciously remembered this lowly person, and said to his brothers: 'Gulbadan Begam used to say in Lahore(e): "I wish I could see all my brothers together!" As we have been seated together since early morning, her words have occurred to my mind. If it be the will of the most high God, may our assembly be kept in His own place! He knows without shadow that it lies not in my heart's depths to seek any Musalman's ill; how then should I seek the hurt of my brothers?

May God grant to you all the same divine and beneficent guidance, so that our agreement and concord may endure! (2018, 187-188)

This is self-fashioning; a 'lowly' person excels in goodness of character for which the royal brother illustrates her. The Mughals loved to listen to their women in serious times and shared leisure time with them in lighter mood. This gives an insight into the private life of the Mughals: the emperor participating in recitation, singing and story-telling with his wives and female relatives must be a different sort of orientation of the empire.

The memoir ends with Kamran's enmity that becomes unmitigable. He instigates different tribes to attack on Humayun when he travels out of Kabul. Such a one is the Quibchaq[31], when Humayun was deeply hurt. Gulbadan writes: "Since such was the Divine will, a barbarian, –inwardly blind, an ill-fated oppressor and ill-omened tyrant, – inflicted a wound on the Emperor" (2018, 195). This is Gulbadan's assessment of Mirza Kamran; comment of a sister, of a woman, above all, of a witness of the tragic history of the ill-fated brother. Gulbadan compares Humayun's head injury at Quibchaq with Babur's injury in the head in a previous Mughal war. Was she thinking of other similarities between the father and the son? Humayun became a surrogate father for her after Babur's death, as the treatise shows. However, finally Humayun was no more in the position to forgive Kamran, as he made a pact with his amirs long irritated by Kamran's continuous offenses. He sent a letter to Haram Begam in Badakhshan and asked for reinforcement. This is a very significant episode in Humayun's history, though Gulbadan does not throw much light on the issue of a woman overseeing a platoon. A woman's military reputation must be considered if one is to judge pre-modern Indian history. It is so unlike the miraculous transformation of Joan of Arc in fifteenth-century Europe; it is rather part of the tradition of the Afghan tribes to have women chiefs who were able to lead the soldiers. Gulbadan could have done more justice to this part of her Timurid ancestry. She, however, describes the face-to-face fight with Kamran either at Charikaran[32] or at Qara Bagh[33], and Kamran being defeated flees to Lamghanat[34].

In the last pages of her writing, Gulbadan becomes emotional and narrates the last days of Hindal and Kamran in minute details. Hindal's death happened in the war. Brave-hearted as he was, Hindal asked Humayun to take the high ground with child Akbar and took the lower ground himself, which was a

---

[31] A passage near Kabul.
[32] Charikaran is probably *Charikar*, the capital of the present-day Parwan province in northern Afghanistan.
[33] Qara Bagh or Qarabaghis a district in eastern Afghanistan.
[34] Lamghanat is Laghman, a province in eastern Afghanistan.

vulnerable position. He posted his men and took preparation. Here Gulbadan refers to an incident that shows the Mughals were superstitious. Hindal called for his own cuirass, surtout, high cap and helmet. His wardrobe-keeper went to bring his things and while he lifted his wallet someone sneezed. The wardrobe-keeper set Hindal's armor down and waited for a while. This delayed Hindal's preparation. Hearing this Hindal told the man: "You were wrong. (You should have) said rather: "May there be a blessed martyrdom" (2018, 198). That very day, Hindal's servant was attacked in the trench. No other person advanced to help him, and Hindal went down into the trench. Arrows came from the enemies and Hindal was martyred. Gulbadan expresses her anguish passionately,

> I do not know what pitiless oppressor slew that harmless youth with his tyrant sword! Would to heaven that merciless sword had touched my heart and eyes, or Sadat Yar, my son's, or Khizr Khwaja Khan's! Alas! A hundred regrets! Alas! A thousand times alas! (2018, 199)

The attachment she had with her brother was rather too deep; at one point, she writes that she would be less sad had her own son died instead of Hindal. Humayun was also deeply hurt by Hindal's death, but he had to keep majestic patience. Gulbadan's husband took Hindal's dead body to be buried in his jagir Jui-shahi (modern-day Jalalabad). Gulbadan's lament soon turns into accusation, "If that slayer of a brother, that stranger's friend, the monster, Mirza Kamran had not come that night, this calamity would not have descended from the heavens" (2018, 199-200). The women in Kabul were tremendously shocked and according to Gulbadan's description, "Doors and walls wept and bewailed the death of the happy, martyred mirza" (2018, 200).

Gulbadan then narrates Kamran's predicament. Kamran lost more of his luck through Hindal's death. Since then, all started to disbelieve him as he was a brother slayer. He went to Salim Shah, the son of Shir Khan, Humayun's lifelong foe, to ask for help. Salim Shah did not tell him anything directly, but in private, told his own people that it was impossible for him to help a man who had killed his own brother. He would rather destroy him and bring him to justice. Mirza Kamran overheard this and without even counseling his own people, fled from there. Consequently, Salim Shah imprisoned many of his followers. When Kamran went as far as Bhira[35] and Kush-ab[36], Adam Ghakkar captured him and brought him to Humayun.

---

[35] Bhira or Bhera is a city in present-day Sargodha District in Punjab province of Pakistan. In 1519 Babur took it, and in 1540 Sher Shah founded a new city in Bhira. Therefore, his son was the owner of Bhira when Kamran went to ask for his help.
[36] Kush-ab or Kushab is Khushab, a city situated between Sargodha and Mianwali in Punjab province of Pakistan.

Humayun could not show any mercy to Kamran this time because all his amirs and followers unanimously demanded Kamran's punishment. They said: "Brotherly custom has nothing to do with ruling and reigning. If you wish to act as a brother, abandon the throne. If you wish to be king, put aside brotherly sentiment... (Begam, 2018, 201). They expressed their wrath at Hindal's death. They also referred to Kamran's cruelty with their wives and children on previous occasions. Being so pressurized, Humayun asked them to write what they demanded, and they all wrote "It is well to lower the head of the breacher of the kingdom" (Begam, 2018, 201). Humayun then passed an order and Sayyid Muhammad executed it. He blinded both eyes of Mirza Kamran. Gulbadan's manuscript breaks off here with "After the blinding, his Majesty the Emperor... (Begam, 2018, 201).

Gulbadan's manuscript does not really announce her unbearable misery at Kamran's blinding for which she would have decided not to narrate Humayun's last years. Especially of those years when, being free of his tyrannous brothers Kamran and Askari, Humayun was able to reconquer Hindustan. Nonetheless, Godden suspects that the rest of the manuscript was simply lost or perhaps Gulbadan could not bear to describe what happened afterwards. However, being commissioned to write Humayun's history, Gulbadan would keep it incomplete in the way it is, looks improbable. There is no way to know what happened to the last pages of Gulbadan's manuscript. The only tattered copy of the manuscript is preserved in the British Library. It was found by Colonel Hamilton with other Indian manuscripts that he personally collected. Later, it was sold by Hamilton's widow to the British Library in 1868. Annette S. Beveridge's translation of it in 1901 made the extant text known to the world.

### How to appreciate *Humayun-Nama* today

*Humayun-Nama* is a 16$^{th}$ century manuscript that tells the history of a man, or of men to be more precise, by a woman. Emperor Akbar did not expect a full-fledged history of the Mughal dynasty from his paternal aunt Gulbadan; he wanted information from a close witness of the reign of Akbar's father and paternal grandfather so that his own biographer could use it for *Akbar-Nama*, that was meant as eulogy. So, basically Gulbadan's writing is the source for Abul Fazl's biography of Akbar. However, one may find some information about Akbar's birth and childhood in this book, but perhaps it serves Gulbadan's own persisting memory more. The sixty-year-old Timurid woman living in Agra and Delhi in the last years of her life with zero possibility of travelling back to her roots in Kabul was perhaps living in her memories, and the sudden 'order' of the Emperor created an opportunity for her to officially indulge in retracing a stream of consciousness, albeit from a vantage point. So, this history of Humayun is not only about Babur, Humayun or Akbar, it is also quite much about Gulbadan herself. Even though it was not meant to be self-reflexive as the modern-day autobiographies, it becomes so by virtue of what she chooses to narrate and what to refrain from. It depicts the wonderful world of a girl who travels from Kabul to Hindustan with women, dangers of the passage always lurking at the back of her mind. It gives a glimpse of a Timurid girl seeing India for the first time. When she writes about mangoes and Indian food, she talks about her own acculturation. When she narrates the construction of palaces, tanks, and gardens by her father, she relives the history of the empire. She is a biographer, autobiographer, and historian in one. The details found in her treatise are hardly found in books of mainstream history, not to speak of the approach she takes. She has given a close orientation with each episode she has narrated, though sometimes she loses trails and it becomes difficult to conceive of what she writes. Even then, her style of writing gives the readers of this century two very important messages. First, a woman writing in the sixteenth century had that intellectual capability to put down the turbulent history of a nomadic race that was crossing cultures every now and then. Second, she had the prerogative to comment on the power equations both in the male circle and in the harem. Her letter to her husband, instructing him to join Humayun's force instead of Kamran's, is ample testimony to Gulbadan's searing wisdom in reconnoitering between public and private worlds.

What are her weak points? Gulbadan serves as a brilliant pioneer for the succeeding generations of historians who have written about Islamic dynasties. Indeed, much of her book remains a puzzle until historians like Leslie P. Peirce have explained some events further to bridge the gap of five hundred years between Gulbadan's time and ours. Gulbadan just mentions Humayun's first journey to Badakhshan in which Babur and Maham Begam accompanied him. The readers would understand its significance properly when they read Peirce's description of an Ottoman prince's royal departure for his provincial capital. The basic difference between Gulbadan and Peirce is that of the treatment of the event from their different viewpoints; while Peirce concentrates on a logical causality of events, Gulbadan narrates without much reasoning. There lies the difference between an immediate observer and a trained historian. While Gulbadan writes for an informed royal historian namely Abul Fazl, and misses the point that her narration may puzzle readers after a few centuries, Peirce explains,

> A prince's departure for his provincial capital was the occasion of a ceremonialcelebration marking his political coming of age. He may have been theobject of previous public celebrations—his circumcision and, until the lapseof foreign marriages, his wedding—but these were occasions that demonstratedthe power, majesty, and beneficence of his father. (1993, 46)

Gulbadan mentions both parents accompanying the prince or following him, but she does not spell out that it was usually a custom for the mothers to accompany their sons to their deputed territories, a fact Peirce clarifies contextually in her book. Apart from these gaps, Gulbadan's memoir substantially contributes to women's history of pre-modern India. She opens the wonderful world of Mughal women in front of the readers of the subsequent generations. Women traveled on elephants or horseback from Kabul to Hindustan and from one region to another within Hindustan, sometimes without enough safeguards, is vividly visible in her writing. In this connection, I would give one personal anecdote. In 2015, I was visiting Hyderabad with a group of university teachers. Seeing two ladies in a burqa with only two chinks for the eyes, one riding a motorcycle and the other a pillion, a male professor in my group commented, "Look, that is what I call modernity." This anecdote becomes important if one wants to understand modernity in terms of women's emancipation. What modernity was the male professor referring to? Modernity in the sense of women's mobility and *purdah* not being a hindrance to it? There are numerous records of women being raped in public vehicles in the so-called cosmopolitan cities of the Indian Subcontinent in the present century, which makes it difficult to determine modernity by women's mobility. Compared to modernity or post-modernity, both women and men in pre-modern India seem to be more emancipated. It is true that women were used as pawns in the settlement of conflicts, as Khanzada was, or afterwards, many of Akbar's non-Muslim wives were. Conversely, it is equally true that women at that time were important decision-makers too, and on many occasions, women acted as royal messengers. Khanzada Begam was sent to Humayun by Kamran and Dildar Begam was sent to Hindal by Humayun as messengers, as we come to know from Gulbadan's writings. These women were knowledgeable and courageous, but above all, they were respected by males in their surroundings.

Gulbadan mentions two women while she describes the feast in the Mystic House. They are possibly Shad Begam, daughter of a paternal aunt of Humayun and Mihr Angez Begam, daughter of Muzaffar Husain Mirza, both grand-daughters of Sultan Husain Mirza. Gulbadan writes that they had a great friendship and used to wear men's clothes, played polo, shot with bows and arrows. They also played musical instruments. The existence of such women during that time must have been supported by royalty, and this can be one great example of liberty enjoyed by women.

Women also served as soldiers and commanders. Haram Begam is an important example in this case. Haram Begam was the daughter of Sultan Wais Kulabi Qibchaq Mughal and wife of Sulaiman Mirza Miran-shahi, son of Khan Mirza (Wais), who was the Governor of Qandahar. Annette S. Beveridge refers to her military prowess. Gulbadan mentions that while her husband was in Humayun's attendance in Kabul, Humayun sent a message to her, and in response, she spearheaded thousand-armed men to assist Humayun. On another occasion, Gulbadan mentions that Haram Begam got very angry with Kamran. She was the sister of Kamran's wife Mah Begam and his brother Mirza Sulaiman's wife. Kamran, being cheated by a woman, sent her a love letter and a handkerchief. Haram Begam made her husband behead the woman who brought the letter and kerchief. Sunita Sharma writes that historians usually saw Mughal India as "patrimonial bureaucratic structure" (Sharma 2012, 358) in which the women's role is shown as stereotypical, while Mughal women played an important role to raise and support the rulers. She mentions Babur's rise from the mirza of Faghana to the great founder of the Mughal dynasty in Hindustan, but from Gulbadan's writing, we come to know of the role of women in the sustenance of Humayun too, if not of Akbar. This history is a treatise of the Mughal domestic life within which the women's role becomes prominent, and also serves as a window to the state affairs in which women played vital roles.

Gulbadan's ability to combine the public and the private worlds of her time is borne out by instances beyond her famed letter to her husband as well. She takes the readers into the private quarters of the women, and at the same time, shares her experiences of how women were affected by war and conquest. An emperor's many wives, their desires, and frustrations, sometimes their shared maternal roles, are vividly presented by her. Her mother Dildar had to give her and her elder brother Hindal to Babur's favorite wife, Maham Begam; and even though Gulbadan is quite reticent about it, it is understandable how hierarchy within the harem was created. Maham's frustration for the death of her many children as well as Dildar's untold miseries for losing the custody of two living children are revealed. Women's ties are complicated, and the nature of the link between the Timurid and Chinghizid families is also a matter of important research for the historians. Gulbadan not only provides a "view of the Other" among the very male, very monopolized territory of mainstream history of the pre-modern period that neglected these; she also creates a 'narrative of the Other' in terms of European monopoly of early Mughal history too. Jyotsna G. Singh writes in this regard,

> Although a seemingly unfamiliar work among the many biographies and manuscripts of the Mughals, including her father's more famous *Baburnama* (ca. 1528-1530, translated into Persian in 1589), Gulbadan's narrative is unique in illuminating the world of early modern Islamic kingdoms and cultures from a Muslim woman's perspective. And, importantly, in offering a non-European perspective, Gulbadan's memoir pluralizes and interrogates subsequent European history of the early modern period by charting the formation of Hindustan through the

writing of the "culturally other" within intra-Islamic social, political, and cultural formations. (2012, 231-2)

She writes that the Europeans started to know the Mughal culture through their travels for business and commerce, explorations, and gradually they colonized Mughal Hindustan, but often they would fail to translate this culture. The traffic in goods and people brought this culture, especially the Ottoman empire close to Europe, but intra-Islamic interactions remained beyond the Europeans' purview and "Christian Europe remained the center of inquiry" (2012, 233). Gulbadan's memoir and narrative of early Mughal history offers a "detailed exposition of a highly localized profusion of characters to counter the broad thrust of European memory-making" (Singh, 2012, 233). Having spent her life under three Mughal rulers, Gulbadan acquired a unique vision of the nomadic culture of her Timurid people who were slowly transforming into a settled dynasty in Hindustan. The many travels of Babur and his clan described in the manuscript witness the nomadic life they lived. At the same time, this reports the porous borders in the territory. The Uzbegs and Afghans dominated in some parts of the land across Central Asia and parts of Hindustan; the Hindu Ranas and kings reigned in other parts of Hindustan; and the Mughals traveled through these territories without much hazard. Sometimes they would take prior reports how they would fare in these territories, but many a time they were pushed by their enemies to traveling without prior news or invites. Especially in Humayun's time, his followers moved here and there for months and life did not know any peaceful rest. Nationalism was unknown to these lands; there were communal feelings, but even within one community, there were fractions. For example, Babur and his sons were Sunni Muslims, whereas there were Shi'as and Sufis who would not submit to the demand of the Sunnis just because they were Muslims. There were tribal leaders as well whose territories were different, but the borders were never fixed.

Gulbadan's memoir also opens a world of cruelty, intrigues, and killings. She provides a history of the Subcontinent parallel to that of the European history which is also tarnished with treachery and bloodshed. Babur's helplessness when his cousins and close relatives fail him and fight against him, or intrigues of Kamran against Humayun, or the several lapses of Humayun and Hindal – all give an insight into the vices of royalty. At the same time, she gives an account of friendship between rulers. The friendship between the Shah Tahmas of Khurasan (Iraq) and Humayun can be an example. Humayun received unbelievably warm hospitality from the Shah that restored him to good health and mind after his defeat by Sher Shah, and prepared him for the treachery of his brothers that was to follow. The memoir is also a very early treatise giving a glimpse of the multiple communities living in Hindustan, and can be considered as a herald of the mingling of the Mughal and the locally diversified communities that was forthcoming.

The ultimate culmination of this cultural exchange happens during Emperor Akbar's reign. The Mughals built edifices and gardens (for which they must have transformed some old architectures), and tried their best to settle in Hindustan, but there was always a sense of alienation in the Hindu land. Babur's speech before his men during the battle against Rana Sanga reminds one of the battles fought by the prophet of Islam during his days: a Muslim dying in a battle against a non-Muslim is a martyr and winning against a Hindu in Hindustan would mark him as a soldier of God.

History indeed does repeat itself! In 1992 a mosque in Ayodhya (in the Indian state of Uttar Pradesh) known as the Babri Masjid was demolished by the Hindu sectarian groups who claimed that the mosque was built by Babur's general Mir Baqi in 1528-1529 at the site of the birthplace of the Hindu deity Rama. The demolition ignited fierce communal riots. After much politicking and a prolonged legal battle, the Supreme Court of India decreed the land to the Hindu claimants in 2019.

It will not be entirely out of place to connect the riots and subsequent violent killings of the Muslims in Delhi and across India to this aftermath of Hindu ascendancy and the granting of legitimacy to a piece of controversial history, basing upon details that are at best unsubstantiated. Very recently in an excavation of the place it has been revealed that the site was a Buddhist monastery. What Gulbadan narrated in the 16$^{th}$ century as an observer, though she was a quiet one, has developed into ferocious communal and political atrocities in the 21$^{st}$ century. Her memoir has currency in that respect. One of the shortcomings of her treatise is that she never talks about the class dynamics within the Mughal clan, nor does she write of the people of Indian origin. Her world evolved around her Timurid identity and culture that gives her writing somewhat of a limited outlook when viewed in hindsight.

## What happened to Gulbadan afterwards

Gulbadan's incomplete history *Humayun-Nama* ends with Kamran's punishment in 1552, but history did not stop there. She lived many more years to see Humayun reconquer Hindustan and her nephew the great king Akbar expanding the Mughal territory to impossible circumferences. Shir Khan's short dynasty was over when Humayun recaptured Hindustan in 1555. However, Humayun did not live long after that. Just after one year, he died of an accident. He was always inclined to astrology and in his later years, he grew more passionate about it and used to go to the roof of his palace-tower to watch the planets and stars. One evening, he went there but while coming down fell from the stairs.

Afterwards, his son Akbar, a young boy of thirteen, was crowned on 14 February 1556. Gulbadan came to Hindustan in the second year of Akbar's reign. Khizr Khwaja Khan was appointed the Governor of Lahore, but as is evidenced in different records, instead of staying with her husband, Gulbadan lived close to Akbar's court, but outside of his harem. She witnessed, perhaps with much dissatisfaction, Akbar's cruelty, and growth. Rumer Godden comments more than once that Gulbadan was saddened by Akbar's activities regarding religious practices in the palace and taking wives of different religions. Akbar's experiments of amalgamating religions were almost blasphemy to a Sunni Muslim like her. She was eager to go to Mecca for Hajj but Akbar turned down her petition several times before he finally let her go. Gulbadan stayed away from Akbar for almost seven years among which she was in Arabia for three and half years. When she was well over sixty, Akbar passed the 'order' to record what she knew of Babur and Humayun.

In 1589 Akbar conquered Kashmir, and Gulbadan traveled one last time in her life with Hamida Banu, this time to see the beautiful gardens and valleys of Kashmir. However, they set out to meet Akbar there, but on their way, they heard that the emperor had already left for Kabul and, instead of going to Kahsmir they went to Kabul to meet him. The rose-body princess got to see her hometown one last time. In 1603 she died of fever and Akbar himself is said to have helped carry her bier to some distance towards her graveyard.

Though Akbar was quite caring and respectful towards his aunt, Gulbadan seems to have been too formal about him in her writing. She never addresses him as 'Akbar', but as "Emperor Akbar" (often his full name is written) even when she informs of Akbar's birth in Humayun's history. This manuscript, even though focused on the women of the time, caters round the great rulers, the heroes of the Chingizid dynasty. She sets a tradition of self-writing for the next scholarly women in the family, and the biography of Khwaja Moinuddin Chishti and Mullah Shah written by Princess Jahanara are examples of how Gulbadan became a pioneering figure for the women of pre-modern India.

# 3
# Jahanara's Hagiographies:
# The Mind of a Matriarch

> What is civilization? I answer, the power of good women.
> – (Emerson quoted in Rowe, 1997, 38) [1]

Jahanara Begam is, perhaps, the most striking of all the Mughal princesses. This statement stands not on speculations; the plethora of fictional writings on this royal woman confirms the fact that her captivating persona became the subject of imagination for writers of later generations. There are at least half a dozen historical novels written on Jahanara's life in recent times, most of which focus on her participation in harem politics; some concentrate on her charismatic leadership with respect to the strong patriarchy of the Mughal empire; and the rest capitalize on her supposed romantic liaisons with men. The existence of these writings as well as rumors about Jahanara's incestuous relation with her father, the fifth of the mighty Mughals, emperor Shah Jahan[2], initiate a lot of questions. How do rumors function? In terms of reception, it is perhaps not interesting to be powerful without sharing the scandals that accompany power. Jahanara was, apart from her step-grandmother Nur Jahan, the single most powerful woman in Mughal India. She stepped into her mother's shoes when she became the *Padshah Begam*[3] after Shah Jahan's beloved wife, Mumtaz

---

[1] Ralph Waldo Emerson said this in a lecture read before the Woman's Rights Convention on September 20, 1855 in Boston. It later appeared in *The Complete Works of Ralph Waldo Emerson: Miscellanies* [Vol. 11], page 409. Accessed on https://quod.lib.umich.edu/e/emerson/4957107.0011.001/1:26?rgn=div1;view=fulltext.
John Carlos Rowe mentioned this in *At Emerson's Tomb: The Politics of Classic American Literature*, Columbia University Press, NY, 1997, page 38.
[2] William Dalrymple in his book *City of Djinns* relates to an anecdote by the French physician at the Mughal court named François Bernier, in which Bernier indicates at the incestuous relationship between Shah Jahan and his daughter Jahanara. This rumor is particularly an invention of the European travelers who were amazed to witness Jahanara's influence at the Mughal court.
[3] Padshah Begam or Lady Emperor was used to be bestowed upon the chief or principal wife, a sister, or a favored daughter of the Mughal Emperors. This title was enjoyed by several Mughal women: Babur's wife Maham Begam; Jahangir's wife Saliha Banu Begam

Mahal, died in 1631. She enjoyed her father's proximity and the power he bestowed upon her; and her major responsibility was of looking after her broken-hearted widower father and younger siblings. Jahanara also took interest in Sufism and became a devotee of the Qadiriya[4] order in India. It is not that a woman leading a mystic life in public, cannot have her secret romances in private, but the authentically obtained facts about Jahanara's life do not lead towards the conclusion that she was involved in illicit affairs.

### Mystification of Jahanara's life in recent fictional writings:

Two vital points have come out of Bernadette Andrea's analysis (2007) of early modern English literary reception of Muslim women: first, the fact that women writers of the West during pre-modern period were replacing Orientalism with Feminist Orientalism, as they were looking at the Ottoman women as their 'Others'; and second, a somewhat alarming fact that recent studies have taken more interest in the gendered representations of male-authored travel narratives neglecting the archive of early modern women's writings on the English-Ottoman relationships. Therefore, Andrea claims that there is a lot of misogyny in the recent turn of western historiography.

Nonetheless, the underlined fact that needs to be reaccentuated that no such archive was ever existent on English-Mughal women's relationships as these empires did not have strong links as such for which English women writers of the period could have frequently traveled to India as we see in the case of the Ottoman empire. Only in the beginning of the 18th century the British East India Company was surfacing as a strong foreign power though they had come to India in the early seventeenth century. Throughout the seventeenth century, the officers of the company, especially the doctors, built some connection with the royal families, and travel narratives and memoirs of several such officers were the only English records of the Mughal harem during that time. Women's studies in Europe developed methodologies to uncover and recover alternatives of

---

and after her death, Nur Jahan; Shah Jahan's chief wife Mumtaz Mahal; and after her death, Shah Jahan's eldest daughter Jahanara. When the title is used by a princess it means 'Empress of the princesses.' Roushanara enjoyed it for some time during Aurangzeb's reign, but Aurangzeb gave it back to Jahanara after Shah Jahan's death. Aurangzeb's own daughter Zinat-ul-Nisa also enjoyed this title.

[4] The Qadiriya tariqa is a Sufi order that was initiated by Abdul Qadir Gilani (1077-1166), a Hanbali scholar from Gilan in Iran. The order was later spread across the Indian subcontinent. It has many offshoots in the Arab speaking countries as well. Hanbali being one of the four major Sunni schools, the Qadiriya order relies strongly upon adherence to the fundamentals of Sunni Islam. On the other hand, the Chishtiyah order is known for its adherence to love, tolerance, and openness.

male-dominated historical sources since the 1980s, for which Andrea or her colleagues in the field could write their books on English literary trends of recording lives of Ottoman women; but the Mughal women were not as fortunate as their Ottoman sisters. The men from Europe who traveled to India always had the "pleasure principle" (Freud quoted in Lal, 2005, 3) in their assessment of the Mughal harem, and their records have been the only source and guiding principle for the recent fictional works on Jahanara and other Mughal women, some of which need to be countered.

As a mysterious woman with beauty and power, Jahanara has been a lucrative figure to readers and writers of recent historical fiction. Andrea Butenschon published *The Life of a Mogul Princess Jahanara Begum* in 1931. The title of this book is confusing because it pretends to be a biography of the princess, which it is not. Butenschon narrates the life of Jahanara in a make-believe fashion; and she manages to claim that she has written Jahanara's story based on a tattered diary found by accident while she was visiting the Jasmine Tower of the Agra Fort. The manuscript seems to have fallen into her hands from behind a marble slab, which she later translated and published. What was there in the book written after almost 300 years of Jahanara's existence? It expresses the sufferings of Jahanara who was house-arrested by her brother Aurangzeb along with her father. As a result, in the book, her expressed anger and hatred towards Aurangzeb, and at the same time, she does not spare her father. She utters "the white serpent" several times in the book to refer to Aurangzeb, and points out that it was a label given to Aurangzeb by her father. Her father is called the "tiger" and a "panther" because he was equally ferocious and selfish. The book also records Jahanara's aspirations of becoming a great builder like her father, and she wants to build a palace holding a thousand minarets. She describes the Mughal gardens like Anguri Bagh, Shalimar Bagh, Hayat Baksh Bagh, and Mahtab Bagh in different Indian cities and expresses deep fondness for them. When one reads such books, one is tempted to assume reading of actual history, which then becomes a deceptive process. Historical fiction thus twists history in various ways, most often to its political interest. Butenschon, a Swedish author, apparently has no political end to achieve through the pseudo history she creates. As the emperor's eldest child, Jahanara was the rightful heir to monarchy in Butenschon's European understanding of the law of primogeniture. To show the injustice of patriarchal regal system Butenschon may have written this. Jahanara's 'masculine' prowess that was historically undermined when she was being judged only by her gendered identity (read biological attributes) that the book may have intended to oppose. Butenschon's book was reprinted in 2004, which shows that there is continued interest for it among the readers of the new millennium. Had this been a one-off phenomenon, this fictional work could be put aside as a light reading, but somehow all subsequent historical fictional works on Jahanara have taken the shape of memoirs or diaries.

More recently, Kathryn Lasky in her *Royal Diaries* series published a fictional diary by Jahanara as *Princess of Princesses of India 1627* (2002). In this, she also uses the phrase "the Serpent", but this utterance by Jahanara is not about Aurangzeb; this time it is accorded to Nur Jahan, Jahanara's step-grandmother. In this fictional work, Lasky introduces a few things like enacting Shah Jahan's feigned death to put paid Nur Jahan's plotting against him, poisoning of Shah Jahan's Hindu wife Indira (fictional name) by Aurangzeb and Roushanara, Aurangzeb's close connection with Nur Jahan (which is not supported by historical evidences) and a "yellow-haired Englishman with sapphire eyes" called Peter Mundy (fictional name) who Jahanara meets in the Flirting Bazaar. 'Flirting Bazaar' is a derogatory term for *Meena Bazar*. *Meena* in Persian is drawn from its Arabic origin that means 'glass beads'; Omar Khayyam[5] has used the word as "decorated glass of precious stones" (used to serve wine) in his poetry. Lasky's colonial imagination used 'Flirting' to show the hypocrisy of the harem women whose public modesty was her target of criticism; who wore veils in public spaces but supposedly performed all kinds of arbitrary acts indoors. Jahanara's 'flirtation' with the 'blue-eyed' East India Company officer Peter Mundy also contributes to this colonial narrative. The problem of historical fiction is, in this the fictional elements are curated in a way that one may tend to believe that all of it actually happened. Apart from introducing Jahanara's emotional turmoil for the English officer, Lasky introduces her intimate feelings for Queen Elizabeth I. The book shows that Jahanara gets a pendant miniature of the queen as a present from her father and keeps it hanging around her neck as her inspirational icon. Lasky writes (in Jahanara's persona), "This woman gives me courage – for what, I am not sure, but she gives me courage" (2002, 44). There are several other references to the queen. When Jahanara claims that she studies hard being inspired by the image of the English queen, or her doubts whether it is better to marry than to rule the country are solved by the virgin queen's history, one cannot but take the fictional diary as a colonial come-back of the English imagination that uses the Mughal princess's life as a raw material.

At the same time, Aurangzeb's hatred for the Hindus highlighted in the book also serves the postcolonial Indian nationalism that looks back at the Mughal conquest of India as a way to perpetrate communal aggression and expansion

---

[5] Omar Khayyam (1048 – 1131) was a Persian polymath adept in poetry, philosophy, mathematics and astronomy. The most popular volume of ruba'is in the world is his *Rubaiyat of Omar Khayyam*, the English translation of which by Edward FitzGerald was published in 1859.

of religion. Since the partition of the Subcontinent in 1947, violent upsurge of communal feelings has been witnessed in the region. About two hundred years of British colonial regime and its "divide and rule" policy have injected in the colonized Indians a communal hatred and mistrust that has become a legacy for the successive generations. Indian politicians are also adept at capitalizing communal mistrust in the name of ethnic purity. The Mughal period is once again at the center of subversive discussion in India today because this nationalism tends to investigate the roots of civilization with a desire to go back to its ethnic roots, for which all colonial eras are being re-scrutinized.

In August 2015, a road stretching towards Mansingh Road, Shahjahan Road, Humayun Road, Prithviraj Road in the north-east, and towards Mustafa Kemal Atatürk Marg in the south-west end in New Delhi's Lutyen's Bungalow zone was renamed. Earlier called *Aurangzeb Road* it is now known as Dr A P J Abdul Kalam Road. This event is one of the examples of how colonial history has been under constant scrutiny and is creating controversy at present. Emperor Aurangzeb, who was infamous for his religious oppression, is now being judged as a tyrant ruler in whose reign lies the root of communal conflict, and thus, it is decided by the Indian Parliament that he should not be memorialized. However, the petition of the Delhi Sikh Gurdwara Management Committee to the Indian Prime Minister that initiated this change in 2014, was not honored. They had appealed to rename the road after Guru Tegh Bahadur, the ninth Sikh *Guru*, who was executed in Delhi on Aurangzeb's order. Conversely, Maheish Girri, a Bharatiya Janata Party (BJP) Member of the Indian Parliament for East Delhi, proposed the name of former Indian President Dr A P J Adbul Kalam, which was accepted by New Delhi Municipal Council. Replacing a name of a Muslim with that of another Muslim is a political correctness of the government; and this being the rehash of the Mughal history in the political arena, it is natural that the creative writers would also find new avenues of representation. Jahanara was instrumental in the construction of Shahjahanabad or Old Delhi. When old monuments, structures and historical artefacts are being perceived in new lights, the name of Jahanara must have been resurging in the new political-cultural scenario. The sudden appearance of Lasky's book and a bunch of other historical novels on Jahanara can be connected to this resurgence.

Nonetheless, the fact that the feminist voice of Lasky emerges through Jahanara's persona is another interesting aspect of this fictional writing. The author stresses the power of the Mughal harem through the character of Indira, Shah Jahan's Hindu wife, who tells Jahanara,

> What disturbs me, Begum Sahib, is this notion of yours that we women of the harem have no power. Have you learned nothing in your almost fifteen years of life? Yes, it is true that we must keep purdah and sit veiled and screened to the rest of the world. But have we not become the

keenest observers, the best listeners? And do you not think your father listens to us? Why, right now as we speak, your mother is in the Diwan-i-Khas, albeit behind a screen, but right next to the Emperor as the petitioners come, the widows, the orphans, the scholars, or nobles. She listens to their pleas. And later, the Emperor will discuss them with her. And do you not notice that every time the Emperor has a meeting with the gentlemen from the East India Company or if they are invited to sit at his table, he always asks me to be present behind the jalis? He knows that my father had many dealings with the factors, the commerce men of the East India Company, and was very clever. So he often asks me about his business dealings with the company. (Lasky, 2002, 101-102)

Being persuaded by Indira, she accompanies her to the Diwan-i-Khas when Shah Jahan meets the men of East India Company, and she realizes how the Mughal harem has the power of "the best kind – it is hidden" (Lasky, 2002, 102). This description reminds us of Ruby Lal's refutation of understanding the harem as a solely private place. Lal claims that the women of nobility were involved in the public-political affairs, much of which used to take place in the inner quarters of the palace, and thus the domestic life of these women was not only for raising children and caring for husbands (Lal, 2005, 3-4). Lasky looks at these royal women with awe and wonder as the travelers of the time were wont to, but perhaps her intention is to show that it was more for the intellect and understanding these women showed, rather than their sexual appeal which led the monarchs to trust their judgement. If so, Lasky's attempt at logically explaining their power over the monarchs is what was long needed to counter available narratives by Niccolao Manucci[6] *et al.*, whose writings are proliferated with erotic suggestions about these women. Lasky follows the line of Ruby Lal though her colonial superiority in portraying Elizabeth I disturbs her fairmindedness to some extent.

Subhadra Sengupta's *The Teenage Diary of Jahanara* is a children's book on Jahanara written in a diary-writing fashion. Here the author describes Jahanara's life up to the time of Shah Jahan's coronation. Emperor Jahangir as an affectionate grandfather of Shah Jahan's children takes much space in the book; and even though it is children's fiction, the bloody murder of Prince

---

[6] Niccolao Manucci (1638–1717) was a Venetian doctor and traveler, whose first-hand accounts of the Mughal Empire have become important source for the historians. Juliana Diaz da Costa (1658–1733), Gabriel Boughton (date of birth and death unknown), William Hamilton (1730-1803) are some other European doctors and high officials who also contributed to the history of the period. *The Mughal Harem* (Aditya Prakashan, 1988) by Kishori Saran Lal draws upon Manucci's work on the Mughal empire. Ayushi Dhawan wrote her PhD dissertation on all four at Leiden University in 2017.

Khusrau and his son by Shah Jahan is presented in it. Here we find Jahanara recalling these murders and saying, "I really don't like being a Mughal" (Sengupta, 2019, 194). Under the garb of a children's book, there exists a motivational attempt at initiating dislike in children for the Mughals; suspicion and distrust being the weapons in today's ideological wars. One may even align such books with the agenda of spreading anger and hatred for a particular religious community and their ancestral roots, exemplified in the act of erasing all proofs of Aurangzeb's social welfare activities and underscoring his hatred for the Hindus, which is what would find majoritarian acceptance in India today.

Each of these fictional diaries touches upon the private life of the Mughal princess. It is a fact that diary writing as a phenomenon is contemporaneous with Jahanara's era; the first known diary writer Samuel Pepys having belonged to the 17th century, but then, women as renowned diary writers were discovered much later in the 19th century. Why then do these writers take the genre of memoir writing as their fictional form? Is it because diary writing, as a form of intimate expressions of one's private life, makes it easy for these authors to ensure the readers' "willing suspension of disbelief"[7] that is essential to the success of their method?

Two historical novels by Ruchir Gupta and Indu Sundaresan in their takes of Jahanara's life bring new twists. Gupta has written *The Mughal Intrigues: Mistress of the Throne* in the first-person narrative, in which Jahanara's lifelong battle with her destiny is retold. This book takes Jahanara's romance with Gabriel Boughton (an English doctor working under the East India Company) to its extreme, and it even marks the celebrated Chandni Chowk in Old Delhi as an epitome of her love for Gabriel. Several history books, including Charles Stewart's *The History of Bengal from the First Mohammedan Invasion until the Virtual Conquest of that Country by the English A.D. 1757* mention Gabriel Boughton's name as the doctor who healed Jahanara's burns. However, none of these give any hint of her private relationship with the doctor. Gupta depicts Jahanara's romance with the English doctor in an intimate way through their secret meetings and physical union. Jahanara's connection with Sufism and Mullah Shah Badakhshi gets much attention by Gupta, but unfortunately, there is not a single hint at the treatises Jahanara wrote in his book. Gupta favors Jahanara by challenging the rumor of her incest with Shah Jahan. He shows Shah Jahan as an old man with desires for young girls. The character of a street

---

[7] British romantic poet Samuel Taylor Coleridge introduced the term in 1817 in his *Biographia Literaria* that suggested that a writer needs to mix "human interest and a semblance of truth" with fantasy, so that the reader would suspend judgement concerning the implausibility of the narrative.

girl called Chamani Begam is invented by him. He shows that Chamani is of the same age and physical structure as Jahanara; and Roushanara sees her with Shah Jahan in an awkward situation and spreads the rumor of incest between her father and sister. Therefore, one sister is saved at the expense of the other. Indeed, the conflict between Jahanara and Roushanara is legendary and one cannot blame the author for thinking of such a plot. One can always connect this with Jahanara's utterance in her second hagiography *Risala-i-Ṣahibiya* (henceforth, *Sahibiya*) that she has a "wasted life", and try to understand how hard she tried to get away from these palace intrigues and intended to lead a blissful life under Sufism.

In *Shadow Princess: A Novel* Indu Sundaresan portrays Jahanara's romantic life with Mirza Najabat Khan, a nobleman at the Mughal court of Persian royal descent. According to her book, Jahanara's mother Mumtaz Mahal wanted to arrange her marriage with this man, but as she died in childbirth, the marriage between Jahanara and Najabat Khan never took place. Shah Jahan selfishly craved for the company and support of his elder daughter, for which he never thought of her marriage. Sundaresan shows how Jahanara fulfilled her sexual desires in secret through her amorous relationship with Najabat Khan. And when Najabat refuses to meet her, being misguided by the rumor of Jahanara's incestuous relationship with her father, Jahanara finds solace in sexual intercourse with a hired youth, some "musician's son". However, Najabat Khan responds to Jahanara's love when he realizes that the rumor is baseless and it was spread by princess Roushanara, who cunningly wanted to win him as her husband. Sundaresan thus rescues her from the rumor of incest, but she questions Jahanara's lifelong passion for Sufism by showing her Sufi mission as a camouflage. Her book portrays Jahanara's pregnancy and motherhood; she and Najabat Khan have a son who is later patronized by Aurangzeb. The episode of Jahanara's pilgrimage to Ajmer (which is a major event in *Sahibiya*) is put into question, because Sundaresan claims that Jahanara did not go to Ajmer; instead, she went to Kashmir to Najabat Khan's house to give birth to their son. Jahanara's mysticism and involvement with the *Qadiriya*[8] order do not get attention by the writer although there are minute details of some other historical events in the book. The realistic tone of the book thus misguides a contemporary reader.

It remains a question why all of Jahanara's fictional biographies voyeuristically dote on a speculated life of romance instead of dwelling upon the specifics of a life that she actually led. Is it so because our subversive taste in reading is not

---

[8] Qadiriya order is a major branch of Sufism that was established by Abd al-Qadir al-Jilani (b. 470/1077, d. 561/1166), originally a native of the Persian-speaking region of Gilan, spent most of his life in Baghdad. The order became popular in India during Shah Jahan's reign.

satiated with a purely mystic and ordinary life of a woman? Sometimes it becomes difficult to discover the 'real' Jahanara from the palimpsest that her persona has become in these writings. She is a victim of fictional romance without which historical fiction or fictional biography can hardly thrive in today's publication industry where the search for novelty gets obsessive to the point of inaccuracy. Such writings about Jahanara mostly emerge in the twenty-first century though some such books about her were already available in the twentieth century. It is not possible to discover the person behind the many layers of imagined entities by triangulating the fictional claims against facts of history. It is rather easy to comment on her level of emancipation from the imprints of history and through analyzing her writings, and at best, we can comment on how her writings performed as coming from the pen of a woman in pre-modern Indian setting. First of her hagiographies, *Munis-ul-Arwah* is a biography of Hadrat Sheikh Nizamuddin Auliya[9] and some of his close associates, and the second *Sahibiya* is a biography of Mullah Shah Badakhshi, and Jahanara's own connection to the Sufi order. Both hagiographies trace a history of Islam in the Subcontinent as well as a parallel history of the Mughal expansion. These are important sources for a contrapuntal reading of the Mughal empire, and thereby locate some of the humanitarian sides of it that have been subverted in the recent times.

### A brief history of Jahanara

Jahanara Begam was born on 23 March 1614 as the eldest daughter of the Mughal Emperor Shah Jahan by his beloved wife Arjumand Banu Begam, famously known as Mumtaz Mahal. Mumtaz gave birth to fourteen children, and Jahanara was the eldest among her seven surviving children. Muhammad Dara Shikoh was the second, and after him were sequentially Shah Shuja, Roushanara Begam, Muhi-ud-Din Muhammad (known as Aurangzeb), Muhammad Murad Baksh and the youngest Gouharara Begam with whose birth their mother expired. Jahanara was honored with the title *Begam Sahiba* or "The Princess of Princesses" when her father ascended the Mughal throne in 1628 because she was Shah Jahan's eldest child, and became the unrivaled ruler of a huge territory that spanned from Kabul to the Deccan. Later, when Jahanara's mother died in 1631, she became Padshah Begam, the head of the imperial harem who was also given the power of using the great imperial seal *Muhr Uzak*. Shah Jahan depended much on Jahanara's counselling, as history

---

[9] Nizamuddin Auliya (ca. 1238 –1325), was an Indian Sufi saint who established the Chishti order in the Subcontinent. The Mughal rulers were followers of this order, though during Shah Jahan's time the Qadiriya order also gained popularity. Nizamuddin's mausoleum is located in old Delhi, where Jahanara is also buried.

witnesses, and he favored her and her brother Dara Shikoh over his other children. Jahanara was honored with the title *Sahibat al-Zamani* (Lady of the Age) posthumously by Aurangzeb, because she played a pivotal role in Mughal politics throughout her life as the most trusted counsellor to two great emperors, Shah Jahan and Aurangzeb. Jahanara and her sisters spent their lives in celibacy. During the first two Mughal rulers' reign, the princesses were married and had their own families, but since the time of Jahanara's great-grandfather, Emperor Akbar, the Mughal princesses remained unmarried until the rule of Aurangzeb. It was so decided perhaps to avoid contestation over the crown. However, there are uncountable rumors about love affair of these women with men of rank or below rank that affected their public image; the numerous speculations surrounding Jahanara's life having been the staple of much literature mentioned in the earlier section.

Jahanara's education was covered by the tuition mostly of Sati-al-Nisa Khanam, who taught her Persian, the *Quran*, and most probably, she also taught her the manners of a princess. Sati was the sister to Jahangir's poet laureate, Talib Amuli. A woman accomplished in etiquette, housekeeping and medicine, Sati served as principal lady-in-waiting for Mumtaz Mahal, and was much revered by her pupil Jahanara and the harem of Shah Jahan. Jahanara's talent in playing chess, polo, and hunting, writing poetry and painting is not much known though many of the high-class Mughal women were accomplished in these. Apart from her two Sufi treatises *Munis-ul-Arwah* and *Risala-i-Sahibiya*, she wrote a few Persian verses, and some of her letters to Aurangzeb have survived that tell of her literary talents. Jahanara got acquainted with her great-grandfather Akbar's library in early childhood and she must have enjoyed books on world religions and literature that the library had among its large collection. It is strongly believed that Jahanara's initial writings were sparked by the influence of Sati-al-Nisa and that great library.

Jahanara's generosity as a daughter and sister as well as her diplomatic skills are highly appreciated by the authors of both fiction and non-fiction. She exists in several historical treatises though most historians and biographers of Mughal emperors mention her rather passingly. Jadunath Sarkar, who dedicated much of his scholarly life to Aurangzeb's history, mentions Jahanara as a dear child of Shah Jahan in both volumes of Aurangzeb's biography. He writes,

> She was the best loved child of Shah Jahan, and well did he deserve his affection. Ever since her mother's death, her care and forethought had saved him from domestic worries. Her sweetness of temper and greatness of heart, even more than her mental accomplishments, soothed his mind in fatigue and anxiety, while her loving kindness healed all discords in the imperial family, and spreading beyond the narrow circle of her kinsfolk made her the channel of the royal bounty

to orphans, widows, and the poor. In the full blaze of prosperity and power her name was known in the land only for her bounty and graciousness. In adversity she rose to a nobler eminence and became an Antigone to her captive father. Happier than the daughter of much-enduring Oedipus, she finally won her father's forgiveness for the son who had wronged him so cruelly. (Sarkar, 1989, 73-74)

The Antigone image is worthwhile because Jahanara looked after her aged and imprisoned father till his death and managed to make a final conciliation between Shah Jahan and his rebel son Aurangzeb. However, this was not the only evidence of Jahanara's efforts to bring peace between these two. There are other significant examples. Jahanara was heavily burnt in the evening of Nowroz[10] in 1644 as her muslin dress caught fire from a candle, and she was almost dead. Two of her maids died in their efforts to save her. Shah Jahan tried all sorts of treatment for her, and she was finally cured after several months of suffering. Sarkar mentions the episode of Jahanara's burning in 1644 and her eventual treatment; and he mentions how Jahanara, post- recovery, convinced Shah Jahan to reconcile with Aurangzeb and return him his rank and respect that the emperor father had snatched for his son's previous offenses. This shows her motherly attitude towards her younger siblings. Dara Shikoh's wedding is another event that witnesses Jahanara's care and dedication. That wedding is considered to be the most expensive wedding in Mughal history. In 1657-1658, when Shah Jahan fell ill and his sons were engaged in a war of succession, Jahanara supported Dara Shikoh. Aurangzeb's victory and ascension to the throne left Jahanara with the choices between freedom and captivity; and as her response to the love and care she had received from her father, she chose to accompany him during his house-arrest in the Red Fort of Agra. She took care of her old father until his death in 1666. It is a fact that she finally managed to have Shah Jahan say that he had forgiven Aurangzeb, which gave Aurangzeb some consolation while he was repenting for his cruelty towards his old father. Hence, Sarkar ascribes Jahanara the Antigone image. Afterwards, Aurangzeb granted her a handsome allowance and returned her the position of the Empress of Princesses that she enjoyed until her death in 1681.

Historians did not do justice to Jahanara or other Mughal princesses, as they more than often connected these women with immoral sexual behavior. For example, Chob Singh Verma calls Jahanara 'lascivious princess' (1996, 129), and he writes that since Shah Jahan remembered Akbar's verdict that daughters must not be given in marriage, Jahanara's confirmed fiancé Najabat Khan could not marry her. So Jahanara, in Verma's understanding, contended herself with

---

[10] Nowroz is the Persian new year.

lovers. Verma mentions Dulara, the son of a dancer, another young man named Shakil, and a Persian steward who were Jahanara's favorite sex partners. The accident during Nowroz or the fire episode is also darkened by Verma; he mentions Jahanara's drunkenness and pastimes with dancers and lovers, during one of which a dancing girl caught fire and Jahanara burnt herself while trying to rescue her. The English doctor Gabriel Boughton who treated her after the accident also became part of the gossip.

In popular literature, Jahanara is portrayed as a co-planner of the famous Taj Mahal with her father, and she is seen assisting and instructing the architects who were invited from India and Persia to build the great structure. Such fictional writings are based on historical facts as the writers claim to have researched in Mughal court chronicles and documents. Even if one is not prepared to accept the credibility of these writings and acknowledge Jahanara's contribution for the Taj, one must admit that Jahanara was the architect of the Chandni Chowk, the famous business street in Shahjahanabad, present-day old Delhi, which was a thriving beautiful space for the city dwellers of her time. She planned the canals and houses around it. Chandni Chowk is bisected by the canal called Paradise Canal, and Jahanara's projects in the area included a royal Muslim architectural complex with a mosque, a public bath, and a caravanserai. She commissioned a Timurid-Mughal garden called Caharbag that was a place of entertainment for imperial women and children. All these indicate that she had a progressive mind with love and care for her community and environment.

In her thirties, Jahanara was influenced by her elder brother Dara Shikoh's Sufi thoughts and became a disciple of Mullah Shah Badakhshi, who initiated her into the Qadiriya order. It was a Sufi order surviving the Chishtiyah order in India that was established by Moinuddin Chishti. Jahanara wrote the biography of Moinuddin Chishti and a few other Sufi masters titled *Munis ul-Arwah*[11], a text that still survives. Another biography, that of Mullah Shah Badakhshi, titled *Risala-i-Ṣaḥibiya*, in which Jahanara described her initiation into the Qadiriya order by him. Sunil Sharma writes in his *Mughal Arcadia: Persian Literature in an Indian Court*, "Both works reveal the facets of her personality that enable us to view her as a sensitive but strong person" (Sharma, 2017, 162). To exemplify Jahanara's qualities, Sharma refers to an extract in *Ṣaḥibiya* in which Jahanara describes the perseverance that won her the attention of Mulla Shah. She mentions that Shah Jahan went to Kashmir as he used to do in the summer every year. She reached there on 31 March 1640, and since she had no

---

[11] *Munis ul-Arwah* or *Munis al-Arvah* is translated as *The Master of Pure Souls* by its translators Valiur Rahman and Mohammed Adil. Sunil Sharma translated the title as "Confidant of spirits" (Sharma, 2017, 162)

knowledge of several saints arriving from the Persian region and living there, she was surprised when she heard of the existence of Mullah Shah. High-flown language in Persian about Mulla Shah's qualities that has been translated into the language of equal merit in English shows her enthusiasm,

> From the auspiciousness of his blessed feet this place has become heaven's partner, but rather it makes a higher claim than that. In the feat and exalted Qadiri order from the magnificence of companions and most virtuous disciples, Hazrat[12] Mia Mir is the possessor of saintly virtues, first in the list of great *shaikhs*, leader of renowned saints, informed of the esoteric and exoteric, leader of the small and big." (Tr. Sharma, unpublished)

She also praises Dara Shikoh in the same inflated manner – "My successful brother, of lofty nature and exalted rank" (Tr. Sharma, unpublished), and even calls him "knower of God" that could be assessed as blasphemy had it been the time of Joan of Arc in northern Europe.[13] Dara was already a follower of Mulla Shah, and she heard of the virtues of the Sufi saint from him and accepted Mullah Shah as her guide. The amount of satisfaction for getting accepted in the order can be understood from her exalted expression: "Whoever seeks something will find", and her letter written to Mulla Shah: "If that sun-like visage becomes accessible to me / I will make a claim of lordship, not just of kingship." In *Sahibiya* she also mentions her cooking of naan and saag for the saint, and eating the rest of his food that gives the reader a sense of physical reunion between her and the master. It is evident that Mullah Shah knew that the Mughals needed him for legitimizing their empire, and would avoid them because he did not want religion or his order to be used for political purposes. Nonetheless, he had to give in to Jahanara's repeated pleas, as she writes,

> "My exalted brother who was in his service continuously spoke about my sincerity and belief. Later by his discovery and inner light he found me to be sincere in my search and need and knew that my true intention was nothing but searching for the path of God. Out of kindness he answered my notes bit by bit and the scent of perfect hope that he would

---

[12] Hadhrat is the other variant of the same title.
[13] Joan of Arc is the national heroine of France. She came from a peasant family in Domrémy, and during the Hundred Years' War, led the French army that earned the portentous victory at Orléans. The English thus failing to conquer France, was determined to avenge on her; and even though she was canonized in 1620 as a saint, she was captured after a year, and burned her to death by the English and their French collaborators. The premises on which she was burned was that she claimed to be acting under God's direct guidance and so she was a heretic.

guide me reached the olfactory part of my soul" (Sharma's own unpublished translation of *Sahibiya* quoted in Sharma, 2017, 162-163).

Jahanara wrote *Sahibiya* soon after her encounter with Mullah Shah. In the treatise, she mentions an Islamic saint, a woman called Rabi'a, who Mullah Shah held in his reverence for her spiritual power and considered as "not one woman but a hundred men from head to toe" (Sunil Sharma's translation quoted in Mukhoty, 2017, 107). To show that men and women are equal in matters of faith, Jahanara quotes the Sufi hagiographer Attar; Attar once uttered about Rabi'a, "When a woman becomes a man in the path to God, she is a man and one cannot anymore call her a woman" (quoted in Mukhoty, 2017, 107). In Jahanara's case, unfortunately, her devotion and faith remained the prerogative of her gender, and she was not given any extra credit for it. Mullah Shah was very impressed with Jahanara's progress in the Sufi line and would have nominated her his successor in the Qadiriya, but the rules of the order did not allow a woman to be a leader in the path. Mukhoty's comments regarding this can be justified,

> Sufism, which arose as reaction to the increasingly formalized structure of orthodox Islam, was generally more tolerant of female involvement. In Sufism, a woman could be seen as a symbol for the yearning soul, seeking union with God. The main traits of Sufism, such as weeping, fasting, poverty, suffering and ardent love for the Beloved or God, made it easy to accept women as personifications of the soul. The attitude towards gender in general was more nuanced, with the emphasis clearly on the soul and its potential rather than its physical attributes of the seeker. But Sufism was still within the framework of Islam, and there were reminders of the way women were seen as essentially 'defective' and of a 'week' nature. (Mukhoty, 2017, 107)

In this chapter *Munis-ul-Arwaḥ* and *Risala-i-Sahibiya* are read discursively to see how Jahanara through a subjective style used these as ways of expressing some of her inner thoughts that will provide a fresh understanding about her and the Mughal empire. Some misgivings about her and misrepresentation of her persona may also get resolved. The manuscript of the first text was written around 1639, and exists in the manuscript section of the Bodleian Libraries at Oxford; the manuscript of the second probably completed at the end of 1641, is unavailable. Maulavi Muhammad Abdul Samad Sahib Kalim Qadri Uwaisi translated *Munis-ul-Arwaḥ* into Urdu (year unknown) as *Moin-ul-Arwah*. Its first English translation came out in 2015. The translation was a collaboration between Valiur Rahman and Mohammed Adil, who took Uwaisi's Urdu translation as the root text. The transcribed Persian text of *Risala-i-Sahibiya* was edited by Muhammad Aslam in Pakistan, and an Urdu translation of it is available in volume 17, No 1 of *Journal of the Research Society of Pakistan* published in 1980. An English translation from the Persian was attempted by Professor Sunil Sharma in 2007 which was used by Afshan Bokhari for her PhD dissertation. Bokhari herself attempted a translation of Tanvir Alvi's Urdu transcription of the book in collaboration with Dr Yunus Jaffrey in Delhi in January 2007. All quotes from *Risala-i-Sahibiya* are either borrowed from Professor Sharma's unpublished translation (hence, no page number of the text is given) or parts of his translation published in secondary sources. The unavailability of a published English translation is rather unfortunate and indicates the fact that in today's publication industry, which is captured by corporate market politics, Jahanara is doubly marginalized as a Sufi and a woman.

### *Munis-ul-Arwah* or The Master of Pure Souls

Jahanara's biography of Moinuddin Chishti (popularly called Khwaja Gharib Nawaz in India)[14] is the first biography of the Sufi preacher of Islam in the Subcontinent by any woman. This is a fine example of hagiography regarded for its literary quality. Jahanara calls Moinuddin 'the master of pure souls' and regards him as having initiated her spiritually four centuries after his death. She also describes her pilgrimage to Ajmer[15]. The translators Valiur Rahman and Mohammed Adil have divided the treatise into eight short chapters and have given subtitles to different sections in the chapters which were not there in the original. There is also Jahanara's preface. Jahanara begins the preface with reference to Allah ('Almighty' is used in the translation) who is "Merciful" and is the "Appointing Authority of the worlds and universes". She dedicates a long passage in describing the creator's aspects that touch both physical and metaphysical worlds. She writes that God has created the worlds, incarnated great spirits and pure souls to lead human beings to glory and devotion. She repeatedly addresses God and thanks him for protecting the world from all evils and unacceptable forces, and asks for blessing.

After this, she mentions the last prophet of Islam and the 'Holy chain of God' with which the Prophet binds all men and women for their redemption on Judgement Day. There is a description of the Judgment Day: a day comprising fifty thousand years and horrifying to most except for the men and women who would stand under the flags of their spiritual teachers. She is following here the *Quran* and the fundamentals of Islam. Allah, the Prophet, and the Judgment

---

[14] Moinuddin Chishti was a Muslim preacher and Sufi master from Sistan, Iran, who was the promulgator of the Chishtiya order in the Indian Subcontinent. He was famous for his asceticism, scholarship, philosophy, and mysticism.

[15] oinuddin Chishti's grave is turned into a beautiful shrine in Ajmer in Rajasthan, India. It is the most important Sufi mausoleum in the Subcontinent.

Day are part of the basics in which one has to keep faith as a Muslim. In connection with the Judgment Day she refers to the Chishtiyah order, which, according to her, is a "blessed thing of the world made of a direct link to the Almighty God". Thousands of verses in praise of the order fail to express its height as sublime. She writes that this order is the only spiritual chain in Hindustan and influences many other lands beyond Hindustan. Then she addresses herself,

> O You! Keep a desire to speak and write about the greatest leaders of Islam and a spiritual leading man of Hindustan, the master of Chisht of Hindustan in the mind of this poor, aged, and a weak daughter of Emperor Shahjahan Namazi. O! I wish I had tongues to all parts and organs of my body to speak about these great leaders and masters. And this sinner is a disciple of the master of pure souls and leader of friends to God, the secret knower about the chosen people of God and the master of sublime spiritual height, Hadhrat Khwaja Moinuddin Hasan Sazsi Chishti (ra)… (Jahanara, 2015, n pag.)

She then names fifteen great Muslim leaders who were of direct descent (spiritually) of the Prophet of Islam. Here one gets to know about the temperament of the author. As a devout Muslim, Jahanara was well versed in the tradition of hagiographies, which had been part of the training in religious studies since a very old time. It was believed that through writing the biography of saints, religious knowledge could be shared and spread, and as was the custom, Muslim authors used to start their texts in the name of Allah. On the other hand, Jahanara was also to serve the Mughal dynasty through her writing. In the beginning, she calls herself "poor, aged and weak" and her father "Namazi". While the first attributes show her modesty, the last obviously calls for an appraisal for Shah Jahan. "Namazi" means one who offers his namaz or prayers regularly, and by calling the emperor Namazi, she certainly wants to underscore the religiosity of her father. Apart from military prowess, the Mughal Empire stood firmly in Hindustan also on religious grounds, as is witnessed in Gulbadan's description of Babur's governance. Jahanara's ancestors strengthened and perpetuated their authority in Hindustan through hard and soft powers equally, though the spread of Islam through bloodshed and destruction of other religions in their time gets highlighted by historians. It needs to be noted that many saints and Sufis came to Hindustan following the trail of the Mughals guiding the emperors and endorsing their spiritual supremacy before the common people. In fact, if the Mughal emperors could project themselves as the chosen of God, it was because of the influence of these saints. Jahanara here connects her father with the long line of Khwaja Moinuddin Chishti, and Chishti's reference, on the other hand, connects the Emperor with the Prophet of Islam. Thus the "spiritual chain" mentioned by Jahanara is extended from the prophet of Islam to the Mughal ruler.

Jahanara mentions Dara Shikoh's book *Safinat-ul-Aulia*, which is another example of her service to her own clan. She writes that the title of her book *Munis-ul-Arwah* is guided by Dara's book that will continue to guide people on the true path of God. It becomes evident that she has a deep faith in the rightful heir of the Mughal kingdom because he possesses that spiritual quality. Here she is hinting at a parallel "chain" that has come to exist from the days of Babur, and will continue with Dara. Given the fact that Mughal women's contribution to the empire has never been acknowledged, the obfuscating of Jahanara's work and the politics of foregrounding her fictionalized personal life is indeed a good example of the systematic obliteration of women's contribution from history. Only recently, Afshan Bokhari has resurrected her true importance in her PhD dissertation. Bokhari comments that the Sufi treatises of Jahanara are her contributions to male agenda of the Mughal empire in India. Islamic law and religious teaching formed the foundation for the Timurid-Mughal imperial ideology and Sufism helped them legitimize their conquest of India. As a mystical belief system, the essence of Sufism could some of the most "deeply felt social and spiritual needs of the Mughal elite and commoners" that orthodox Islam could not have addressed. Contemporary history witnesses to the fact that Sufi saints served as "political and social advisors" to the Mughal emperors. The emperors' intervention in India would often be informed by religious texts and Sufi ideology. Sufism configured frames of spirituality for the conquerors, according to Bokhari.[16]

Jahanara describes Chishti's life from his birth, and names of places and people are cited in the writing as well as a list of miraculous events, all of which add to the exotic and mystic nature of the Orient. Sajastan[17] in Khurasan and several other places are mentioned in a manner as if these places are already always holy, being the birth places of saints. The miracles add to their charm. Jahanara narrates a miraculous episode of Chishti meeting a *faqir* Hadhrat Ibrahim. Hadhrat Ibrahim is a prophet of Islam who is considered the first prophet of the present form of Islam that prohibits idolatry. He is the founder of the *Qaba*[18], and of the tradition of animal sacrifice during Eid ul Adha. In the

---

[16] References to this can be found in Afshan Bokhari's PhD dissertation (2009, 22).
[17] Sajastan is Sijistan or Sistan, a desert city in the eastern border of Iran touching south Afghanistan.
[18] Qaba or Kaaba is the most sacred site in Islam. It is at the center of the *Masjid al-Haram* in Mecca, Saudi Arabia.It is considered by Muslims to be the *Bait Allah or* House of God, and is the direction of prayer for Muslims around the world.

dream Hadhrat Ibrahim appears in Chishti's garden and Chishti invites him and offers him grapes. Hadhrat Ibrahim offers Chishti a piece of bread and after taking a bite from it, Chishti feels enlightenment of his heart. Eventually, he sells all his properties and distributes the money among the poor. He then goes to Samarqand in Bukhara and acquires his knowledge of the *Quran*. Finally, he reaches Harun at Nisapur[19] and presents himself in the service of Khwaja Uthman-i-Haruni. Jahanara ends her preface here and commences the new section of the treatise with Uthman-i-Haruni. Apparently, this preface is written simply to eulogize the Mughals and put Islam in support of their subjugation of India, while at the same time, she must have been offering some signs of defining her subjectivity with regard to the empire. Why else would the sacrifice of Chishti be of such importance to her? *Munis-ul-Arwah* has adequate hints to suggest that in foregrounding the sacrifice of Chishti, Jahanara reflects upon her own life as well, destined as it is to be sacrificed for dynasty and power. Whenever a glimpse of her personal life gets exposed in her hagiographies, a strong sense of self-effacement also surfaces; which is perhaps in a way her self-proclamation, because she equates herself with her Sufi masters. A critical understanding of her text is necessary to comment on this. Bokhari observes in her study, "Her [Jahanara's] writings denote how an imperial female attempted to subjectively narrate and weave her persona through the religious, imperial, and political values of the court using creative and cultural processes of autobiographical/history writing and architectural commissions" (Bokhari, 2013, 166). Jahanara's self-assertion is more direct in *Sahibiya*, but in this one too, we can trace her act of underscoring the Mughal agenda in which she also participated as an active agent.

The translators of the book divided the second section of the book titled "A Talk about Hadhrat Khwaja Gharib Nawaz (ra)" into subsections that give structure to the biographical sketches of several Sufi masters put together. The first section is about Harun at Nisapur and Uthman Haruni. Jahanara aptly presents miracles after miracles in the episodic journey of the Sufi masters in which her primary intention seems to have been a kind of legitimizing the conversion of idol worshippers to Islam. It happens with her description of Uthman Haruni's visit to *Magun*;[20] she describes the fire temple at Nisapur and

---

[19] Nisapur or Nishapur is a city located in the eastern province of Khorasan. It was established during the Sasanian dynasty and through the medieval ages served as the seat of the governor and commander in chief of the province.

[20] *Magun*, as the translators of *Munis-ul-Arwah* explains, refers to a fire temple in Harun at Nisapur in the medieval age when fire worshippers or Zoroastrians used to live there. The translators write in their note that these people were called Magun. Perhaps *Magi*,

Uthman Haruni's miraculous entry into the fire kindled for worship by the fire worshippers of the temple. Haruni was fasting that day and while one of his disciples was preparing the *iftar* (food for breaking the fast), he challenged a fire worshipper and wanted him to see how fire could not harm him because he was a pure devotee of God. He took the man's child in his arms and entered the fire, and after some time came out without a hair on his body burnt. The fire worshipper asked the child what he saw inside the fire, and was amazed to hear what the child claimed to have witnessed: a divine garden with many varieties of flowers. Instantly the fire worshipper recited the *kalima*[21] and converted to Islam. Jahanara mentions the new Muslim names of the man and his child: Abdullah and Ibrahim. They became *Wali-Allah* (friend to God). Eventually, the man demolishes the temple and builds a mosque there. Here Jahanara introduces the world of holy saints of Islam who travelled far and wide to spread its messages. Moinuddin Chishti was a disciple of Uthman Haruni and perhaps the conversion of the Zoroastrian was witnessed by him as one traveling in his group. Her record of how one place of worship for one religious group is turned into the same for a different faith becomes a universal picture of world history and change of civilization. Jahanara allegedly sets the process of Islamization as a major agenda in her book, which conversely legitimizes the Mughal sovereignty as a major agency behind the spread of Islam across Hindustan.

One interesting element in Jahanara's narrative is her description of the journeys undertaken by Chishti and other Sufis. There is a scenic description of Chishti's journey from Sajastan to Ajmer, where he served Uthman Haruni for long twenty years and six months. His services included carrying water pot and utensils, blankets and prayer mats while traveling with his master, and in exchange, the master blessed him and included him in the holy chain. Then he went to Sanjar in Iran and stayed for two months and fifteen days. Afterwards he moved to Jilan and served Hadhrat Abdul Qadir Jilani. He stayed there for five months and seven days. Such mention of days clearly shows how meticulous and accurate she was in her narration. Her aptness and knowledge in the field as a writer is evident, and she possesses full authority. She upholds the dignity of faith through the sacrificial mode that was a constant

---

the term used for Zoroastrian priests, came from this word. However, Sufi hagiographer Attar in his book *Tadkiratu'l-awliya* mentions them as *gabr.*

[21] Kalima refers to texts to memorize to learn the fundamentals of Islam. There are six kalimas. Kalima at *Tayyibah* is the first that reads "There is no deity but Allah, and Muhammad is the messenger of God". When one converts to Islam, one usually recites this to allege faith.

complement of these great Sufis' character. Sometimes their physical ordeals to abide by the Islamic *sharia* or law, sometimes their meagre food habit, or sometimes their tattered attires are highlighted. Her mention of the *Fawaidul Fawaid*[22] is obviously a recalling of Sufism that flourished in India with the advent of the Turkish and Mughals that form the backdrop of this work.

Jahanara posits the physical travel of the Sufis as their allegorical or spiritual journey. Chishti's fondness for graveyards as his abode of isolation, his avoidance of human intrusion, and his surreptitiousness about his miraculous power, all lead to the idea that the true beauty of faith lies in modesty, not in boastfulness. Places like Baghdad, Tabrez, Istrabad, and Herat[23] that find mention in her writing remind of the Islamic golden age when conversion of opposers of Islam through the power of piety was a goal of Islamic saints. Jahanara mentions how Chishti converted a notorious man called Yadgar into his disciple when he went to Herat. Later, the man gave away everything in charity. This kind of narrative of conversion can significantly contribute to construct an alternative narrative against the history of more coercive and destructive processes of conversion to Islam during the Mughal period claimed by the present Indian ethno-political nationalist forces. Jahanara was surely defending Islam in Hindustan and simultaneously legitimizing the sovereignty of the Mughals who acted as a strong agency for the spread of Islam in the region.

In addition to chanting miraculous episodes, Jahanara's graphic description of the Sufi masters' life can be treated as a cultural treatise. She writes how a *haqim* or doctor called Ziyauddin who hated Sufism came to meet Chishti at Balkh, and returned entirely transformed. After each transformation, we find the Peer or the Sufi master dining with his followers; and the practice of sharing food, at times even from the same plate, as part of Persian culture contributes in a major way to this social interaction that strengthens the bond between the master and his disciples. Apart from the obvious context of spiritual delight that arises with such sharing of food, this account also attests to Jahanara's claim that her treatise can be read as an important cultural text of traditional Persian culinary delights. We ought to remember that Arabian and Persian cultures of

---

[22] *Fawaidul Fawaid* is a compilation of spiritual and literary discourses on *Shari'ah* (Islamic religious law) and *Tariqah* (school of Sufism) by Shaikh Nizamuddin Auliya written in the form of recorded conversations. It is compiled by Hazrat Khawaja Ameer Hasan Ala Sijzi. It provides useful information about a large number of Sufi saints and knowledgeable persons in Islam. Nizamuddin Auliya spoke on the necessity of love, tolerance, forgiveness, patience, forbearance, etc. in practical life.

[23] Herat is a city of Afghanistan situated in the valley of the Hari River in the western part of the country.

food have largely influenced the Indian Subcontinent since the advent of the Mughals.

The presentation of dreams is a popular trope in Jahanara's narrative, and she uses it to highlight the spiritual connections of Chishti, which is again a way of upholding the missionary spirit of Islam. Chishti moved from Lahore to Delhi, and then went to Medina and stayed there for a long time before he finally moved to Ajmer. He was unable to stay at one place as he was continuously persecuted by curious people and followers. To maintain that his decision of going to Ajmer is ordained by the divine will, Jahanara describes Chishti's dream of prophet Mohammad who asked him to go to Ajmer to enlighten the disbelievers. This is quite tricky to comment on, as most of the hagiographies on Islamic saints use this dream trope, and the only source for these is hearsay that has come down to the present time in our oral tradition. Jahanara is a biographer whose forte is actual events in Chishti's life, but she uses a great portion of imagination where dreams play an important part. The Prophet's arrival in dreams is highly appreciated in religious exegeses as this is explained as the supreme form of divine assurance in Islam. Jahanara refers to her own dream in *Sahibiya* in which she saw the Prophet of Islam addressing her and Dara Shikoh as 'Timurid lights'. That dream became an assurance to Mullah Shah Badakhshi that her entry into the Qadiriya order has been blessed. The dream of Chishti in *Munis-ul-Arwah* is evidently sharing a positive conviction that the expedition by the exponents of Sufism to the Subcontinent is established as a peaceful missionary arrangement guided by the Prophet. This gives Jahanara the opportunity to reiterate that as the Mughals complemented the Prophet's mission with their military prowess, their sovereignty must be sanctioned as holy.

The final settlement of Chishti at Ajmer was a decisive moment of history; and Jahanara's hagiography includes the defeat of the Hindu king of Ajmer called Prithwiraj Chauhan[24], who used to be guided by his mother's astrological speculations. When the Sufi master arrived at Ajmer, he had to face antagonism from Chauhan's men. Chishti cast a spell on all camels of the area so that they could not get up from the grazing grounds. Later, when his disciples were forbidden by Chauhan's forces to use water of Ana Sagar Lake, he caused the lake to dry up. Chauhan appointed a magician called Ajay Pal to have a face-off with Chishti. After many efforts, Ajay Pal failed and submitted to the master.

---

[24] Prithwiraj Chauhan/ Prithviraj Chauhan/ Prithviraja III (ca. 1178–1192), was a king from the Chauhan dynasty. He ruled the Chahamana territory, in present-day northwestern India that included Rajasthan, Haryana, Delhi, parts of Punjab, Madhya Pradesh and Uttar Pradesh. His capital was located at Ajayameru (modern Ajmer).

Then the master forgave him and returned the lake and the camels their previous states. A djinn[25] called Shadi is also present in this description. This adds another supernatural element in the literary features of the hagiography. Jahanara's writing could have been influenced by the traditional *Arabian Nights* stories, as the book must have been part of the imperial library. However, Jahanara's story offers a different approach to retribution; it is not punishment and reconciliation but light of knowledge that settles the confrontation between Ajay Pal and Chishti. Ajay Pal's curiosity about the master's spiritual power was high and to satiate his thirst Chishti took Pal to a voyage through the superlunary universe that is explained in Sufi cosmology. Jahanara uses terms like *Arsh e Muallah*[26], *Mujar e Manjil*[27], etc. that are key terms explaining the cosmic layers that man's soul crosses to meet the divine. Ajay Pal completely transforms after this journey with the saint and converts to Islam. Jahanara writes that people believe that Ajay Pal still traverses the Mausoleum of the Sufi master as he substituted Shadi djinn as the master's servant, and this comment comes from her own faith in the existence of the everlasting soul. After this Jahanara writes. "Islam was initiated and finished the unbelievers" (n. pag.). This statement can be a reference to the tumultuous history of the Subcontinent that was repeatedly attacked by Turkish and Afghan clans, and finally, the Mughals established the rule of Islam, that was undoubtedly a matter of pride for Jahanara.

The hagiography has a philosophical undertone; and towards the end of it Jahanara mentions some Sufi principles. She states that the heart of the seeker is like a rivulet, which finds peace only in the unity with the Holy one. There are three kinds of men who are accepted in the Divine realm: those having the quality of rivers, of moonlight and of earth. She further writes that a spiritual follower needs to avoid all kinds of evil deeds, and is always in fear of losing the Beloved (God). It is very difficult to know whether she includes 'women' in her conceptualization of divine 'men' because terms like *Arif* and *salik*[28] that are

---

[25] Jinn or djinn or genies are spirits or demons, supernatural creatures in early pre-Islamic Arabian and later Islamic mythology and theology.
[26] *Arsh e Muallah* is a time and space where Allah exists alone as all creations are annihilated. The translators refer to the superlunary universe here.
[27] *Mujar e Manjil* is referred to as the universe of divine dialogue.
[28] The translators explain *Arif* as a Sufi identifier or a gnostic. Arif is actually the one who knows. Arif is the one who resides in ma'rifat or the mystical knowledge of spiritual truth attained through ecstatic experiences, rather than acquired rationally. Jahanara writes that Arif is he who sees anything he wants to see, knows anything he wants to know, and gets reply from anyone or anything he wants. Arif cleans his heart with the help of extreme devotion and passionate spiritual love to God. In loving God, he becomes alone

explained as part of the Sufi philosophy by Jahanara are all 'male' oriented words.

The book carries in-depth teaching of Sufism. Moinuddin Chishti's teaching of four jewels of senses: *Durvesi, Sakhawat, Andogahni*[29] and Blessings can enrich anyone's knowledge about the *nafs*(the self), the richness of heart, sympathy, friendliness towards enemies – the teaching of which is absolutely needed to understand Islam. Jahanara also mentions Uthman Haruni's teaching of maintaining three things: care of friend and carelessness of hunger (*fikr o faka*), homesickness and isolation (*bimari*) and Death (*mautiikhtiyari*). She also explains who a *dervish* (who knows the ultimate truth is with him) is, *Mutwakil* (far from the reactions of praise and condemnation) and *Arifkarimkhalk* (knower of God). It shows that Jahanara had a thorough learning of the Chishtiyah order and also kept much command on the terms like *nadamat* (feeling of shame), *qitama'malat* (manners) and *tark e masiyat* (to leave sinful act) that are connected with *Marifat* (the knowledge of Truth). She is also knowledgeable about the qualities a friend to God has: one has the power of maintaining fast, is involved in powerful prayers and is the embodiment of constant remembrance of God and His sincere friends. *Arif* or friend to God who has all the knowledge, humility, patience, and power to see *Uqba* (Day of Judgment, *akhirat*). These terms can be of interest to one having knack in Sufi philosophy, but the ultimate use of this knowledge could be to defend the learning of Islam against the status of a religion that encourages militancy. The essence of Islam is love for humanity, and Jahanara comments that the true lovers are those that suffer the pain given in love without complaints. Her writing has a fabular quality. She exemplifies this through a story of Ra'bia al Basra[30], that involves a *faqir* (a pure man) who was meditating beside a grave and heard of the suffering of the man inside the grave as he had the power to hear the dead. The translation is a little incoherent in this part, and yet the comments on *baqaa* (permanency) and *tagrid* (isolation) match with this because death is related with isolation in the grave and permanence of soul. It is a pity that just because of her womanhood

---

and isolated, and removes everything related to hindrances to loving His sincere and trusted friends. Through these he reaches the state of *Marifat* or truth. Conversely, *Salik* is also a man who knows but connects with his creator directly. A salik must go through the state of *ma'rifat*.

[29] *Durveshi, Sakhawat* and *Andogahni* are explained as sainthood, friendliness, and sympathy by the translators.

[30] Ra'bia of Basra/ Hazrat Bibi Rabia Basri (living in the eighth century in Basra,Iraq)was a Muslim saint and Sufi mystic. Her life has been recounted by Farid ud-Din Attar, a later Sufi saint,poet and hagiographer.

Jahanara was not proclaimed a learned Sufi master, and the spiritual side of her character is erased in most of the recent books.

The treatise tries to show how Sufism is different from the more rigid aspects of Islam; perhaps because she wanted to establish a more generous and open Islam against Aurangzeb's unbending attitude. Her anecdote regarding a man's punishment for deceiving one of Chishti's disciples teaches how sinfulness is prohibited in Islam, but Islam is also for forgiveness and humanity. Chishti was basically a soft-hearted person, who loved songs and Hindustani musical notations; he would always be in an ecstatic state. A western reader of 21 century would certainly feel surprised because the current orientation of tenets of Islam has happened either through the Kingdom of Saudi Arabia or the IS, both of which present a strong unforgiving and militant version of the religion.

An important aspect of the book is Jahanara's subjective appearance though it is more visible in the second book. Here acceptance by the Lord and acceptance by the master repeatedly surfaces in Jahanara's vocabulary. She refers to Chishti's recitation of the *Quran* two times a day and after each completion, he would hear "I accept". Jahanara gives a prelude to this 'acceptance' in another anecdote. Moinuddin Chishti's master, Uthman Haruni, once took the disciple's hands in his, and prayed to God: Accept him and accept his prayers" (n. pag), and his prayers were responded with: "I accept him as one of Friends to Me. I include him among leaders and guides of the world" (n. pag). This happened when Haruni found his disciple perfect as a dervish through his acts of piety, and so his love for the follower increased. Such acceptance or assurance is important in any Sufi apprentice's life; and when Jahanara's repeatedly mentions her "low/abject/wasted" existence vis-à-vis her own spiritual transformation through learning Chishti's life, it becomes obvious that she has become a person beyond the mundanity of life. In this way, she used "Sufi ideology and mystical semantics to cultivate an aura and also perceptions of her spiritual subjectivity that cast her in a leading role on the male-dominated Sufi-Mughal stage" (Bokhari, 2015, 167).

Jahanara ends the treatise in a rather cumbersome manner. In a short space, she tries to familiarize five followers and saints of the Chishti order: Hadhrat Qutubuddin Uwaisi[31], Hadhrat Sheikh Hamiduddin Sufi Nagori[32], Sheikh

---

[31] Qutubuddin Uwaisior Qutb ul Aqtab Khwaja Sayyid Muhammad Bakhtiyar Al Hussaini Qutbuddin Bakhtiar Kaki (ca.1173-1235) was the disciple and the spiritual successor of Moinuddin Chishti. The Qutb Minar in Delhi is dedicated to him.

[32] Hadhrat Sheikh Hamiduddin Sufi Nagori was a Sufi saint, a follower of Moinuddin Chishti. He came from Bukhara province in Uzbekistan. He was the Qazi of Nagor.

Fariduddin Masud Ajodhni Sakarganj (Ganjesakar)[33], Sheikh Nizamuddin Auliya[34] and Sheikh Nasiruddin Mahmud Awadhi.[35]There is ample element of knowledge as well as humor in this, for instance, she refers to Ganjesakar's naming that has an interesting history. Sakar means sugar in English, and once when Fariduddin was sitting at his master's feet he tasted dust and it turned into sugar in his mouth. Since then, he was called Ganjesakar.

Jahanara ends the short description of each of these five saints with their last wish for several objects to be buried with their bodies: a blanket, long stick, counting beads, wooden stoop, and footwear. One may connect this part of the book with Jahanara's own last wish of covering her grave with only grass. She was buried at the mausoleum of Nizamuddin Auliya in Delhi with the favorite inscription "There cannot be any other curtain of my tomb except the humble covering of grass; Grass alone is sufficient to cover the grave of a poor person, as I am" (Nath and Nath, 2018, 122)[36]. It clearly shows that even though she physically lived a court life full of intrigues and corruption, her spiritual life of Sufi ideology was equally strong, and such individuality and personal choice mark her progressive stride in a pre-modern India. Remaining steady in her faith and ideology as a Sufi woman while upholding Mughal patriarchy, she juxtaposed her individual self on a self-proclaimed matriarch.

### *Risala-i-Sahibiya* or **Begam Sahiba's Treatise**

Jahanara Begam begins her second treatise in a traditional way invoking Allah and the last Prophet, the practice of Muslim authors for opening only religious writings nowadays, but it was a custom for all kinds of writings in the Islamic kingdoms. Such invocation is evidenced in Christian or pre-Christian authors

---

[33] Farid al-Din Masud Ganj-i-Shakar (ca.1179–1266) was a 12th-century Muslim preacher and mystic from Punjab. He was one of Khawaja Qutbuddin Baktiyar's prominent disciples, whose mausoleum is at Pakpattan in Pakistan. He is known reverentially as Baba Farid or Shaikh Farid or Fariduddin Ganjshakar.

[34] Fariduddin Ganj-i-Shakar's most famous disciple was Nizamuddin Auliya, as history supports. He used to be called Mahboob-i-Ilahi (God's beloved). His mausoleum is located in old Delhi. Jahanara is buried there.

[35] Was also known as Nasiruddin Mahmud Chirag-Dehlavi. He was the last important Sufi of the Chishtiyah Oder from Delhi.

[36] Sir Sayyid Ahmad Khan (1817-98), the founder of Aligarh Muslim University, was a historian interested in the monuments of Delhi. He wrote a book titled Athar'al-Sanadid in Urdu, which was translated into English by Prof. Ram Nath and was first published under the title *Monuments of Delhi: A Historical Study* in 1978. Ram Nath and Ajay Nath later edited that translation and this is published as *Monuments of Delhi: Architectural and Historical* by The Heritage press in 2018. This book has consulted the 2018 edition of Sir Sayyid Ahmad Khan's book.

too, and gradually more secular writing styles have been adopted by authors of the later generations. What is interesting is that Jahanara refers to the "nobles and companions of his munificence (the Prophet) and writes, "peace be upon them, each one of whom is a unitarian in the court of monism, steadfast, and propagator of the religion of Muhammad, and they have no other duty but to follow that leader." For Jahanara, it must have been both style and fashion; it was a custom, true, but she must have been aware that she was writing a Sufi treatise where invocation to God was necessarily evinced beyond the level of practice. She must have been also aware of Hindustan as a land where millions of people from diverse religious backgrounds lived under the Mughal empire. This invocation serves as a reminder of her own position both as a Sufi and an empress who had to uphold the Mughal ideology. Bokhari writes that Jahanara's texts, especially *Sahibiya*, function as rhetorical devices for articulating and perpetuating Mughal ideology as well as objectifying her representation of the female self within the Sufi tradition (Bokhari, 2015, 166). Bokhari's claim is congealed in the next long comment by Jahanara in which she calls herself "the abject *faqira*, weak, lowly person and servant of the saints of God, believer in the faqirs of the gate of God" even though she is Jahanara, the daughter of Badshah Shah Jahan; the way she continues is interesting for various reasons,

> May God pardon her (herself) sins and conceal her faults, has written as a compendium of the felicitous circumstances of the protector of saintliness Hazrat—apparatus of direction and guidance, leader of the wise men of the age, pride of the researchers of the ages, knower of the secrets, the renowned lofty sheikh, pride of the monotheists, chosen of glorious God, model of the high-ranking saints, perfect master Hazrat Maulana Shah, may God protect him and grant him permanence, who is the master and guide of this abject one—and a bit of the disordered circumstances of myself—about becoming a disciple and acquiring the zeal for seeking awareness and taking the protector of saintliness Hazrat as master and clutching the auspicious skirt of that Hazrat with the hand of hope—and the circumstances around the writing of this treatise and called it the *Risala-i-Sahibiya*. (Tr. Sharma, unpublished)

Starting with a modest preamble, what disordered circumstances of herself she may have wanted to point at, becomes a reader's object of query – was it a daughter's concern for the children of her mother? Or a sister's worry for the younger siblings who showed hostility towards each other over inheritance and power? Or was it a devotee's struggle to reach her divine destination while all mundane circumstances were hindering her ways? Was it a matriarch's fight with the odds around her whose only solace was in divinity? Whatever it was, Jahanara never leaves the formal tone of the treatise to rip off the mask through which one can see her innermost self. Even though *Sahibiya* is a piece of self-writing, it focuses only on her relation with Mullah Shah Badakhshi, and there is no slip of words that can betray a Jahanara other than the Sufi devotee.

As history witnesses, the mystical belief system that Sufism propounds, had influenced the Mughals much. A Sufi-Mughal relationship can be traced back to the time of the Timurid patriarch, Amir Timur aka Tamerlane, which continued to exist till the reign of Shah Jahan. Amir Timur's connection with the Naqshabandi[37] order is well known; Shaikh Sa'di functioned as a moral guide to the great Mughal ancestor in the fourteenth century. Sufism and Sufi saints facilitated the kingship; and the guide-disciple relationship that existed between Sufi leaders and monarchs, never remained only a spiritual connection. The saint or the spiritual master became a political advisor to the murid or disciple. The pir himself was a major promoter of the political agenda of a Timurid leader. The relation between the Indian Mughal ruler and the Sufi master was sustained through the Chishtiyah Order. Babur retained a close connection with the Naqshbandi order, but its influence among the later Mughal emperors was minimal. Conversely, the Chishtiyah was already an established order in pre-Mughal India, especially in the northern territories. For that reason, the support from the Chishtiyah networks worked for legitimizing and expanding Mughal rule in India. She writes,

> The long-standing popular tradition of Sufi orders and saints in pre-Mughal India provided the strategic sociopolitical support for the Timurid-Mughal rulers in the nascent empire and allowed them to establish rightful rulership similar to Timur's status in the ancestral lands of Herat and Balkh, Afghanistan. The sovereign's inextricable connection to Sufi institutions was political and spiritual, solidified through the sponsorship of Sufi saints and their shrine complexes and through the magnanimous and visible support by the royal family. (Bokhari, 2015, 174)

The formal connections of the Mughal empire with the Chishtiyah order were established by Emperor Akbar who devoted himself to Shaikh Salim Chishti after the birth of his son Jahangir. He kept his wife Jodha Bai in the shrine of Salim Chishti for the whole period of her pregnancy to have the master's blessing for the birth of a son. Jahangir's auspicious birth is believed to have been anointed by Shaikh Salim, and after the son's birth, Akbar appointed the

---

[37] The Naqshbandi or Naqshbandiyah is a Sunni order of Sufism that originated and developed in Turkestan. The order takes its name from Khwaja Baha'uddin Naqshband Bukhari (1318–1389).

Sufi master as his son's protector. The connection with the *pir*[38] strengthened Akbar's sovereignty, as his rule was perceived as legitimized by God; and so it also validated the Mughal empire in India. Thus, the spiritual became the political and vice versa. The Mughal-sponsored shrines and mosques in India are living evidences of that; they disseminated and legitimized both their political and religious agenda through such public endowments. Bokhari compares the Mughal architectural expansion with textual representations, as both fall under the category of 'history writing' according to her. She calls such works "composite objectification of the patron", and their architectural designs as "coded" narratives of stock Mughal-Timurid iconography" that interconnected the *male* (emphasis added) sovereign and his subjectivities through the object of the structure.

What was a woman's function in this male agenda? The answer is obvious: to serve it. In their daily routine, the Mughal women practiced acts of piety, distributed alms, patronized and visited shrines and tombs. Those who had the means to commission building some structures, built mosques, squares, and gardens. Jahanara was the architect of several Mughal structures. She commissioned the famous Chandni Chowk in Old Delhi and the Jam-e-Masjid (Friday-prayer Mosque) in Agra. She used her imagination and power to build structures that would bear the glory of the empire. Her writings too were instrumental in recording the imperial history with its grandeur and ideology and at the same time legitimizing the sovereign's absolute governance. From *Babur Nama* to Shah Jahan*'s* biographies, all Mughal auto/biographies are about imperial authority. Apart from building, Mughal women also wrote biographies; Gulbadan Begam's *Humayun-Nama* is a pioneering work among those. Interestingly, none of these women wrote about themselves, nor did they write about other women of their time. It can be understood that self-portrayal was not allowed in such memoirs or biographies by women; and that it was only the prerogative of their male counterparts. *Humayun-Nama* is remarkably well written and in that Gulbadan exposes a lot of inside stories of the Mughal harem, but this does not happen in Jahanara's case as a writer, even though she was more powerful as a matriarch. Perhaps, because she lived too close to power all her life, she maintained that if a Mughal woman was to write it must be with the sole objective of contributing to the imperial ideology. She carried out her roles as the confidante of her father and an accomplice of her brother Dara Shikoh so religiously that it is not improper to believe that she had profound faith in those roles. She dedicated her energy to decorating her father's empire, and strove to keep up the sanctity of the sacred dimension of

---

[38] Pir or peer in Persian is a title for a Sufi spiritual master. It can be translated into English as 'saint'. In Sufism the Pir's role is to guide his disciples on the Sufi path.

the Mughal reign. *Sahibiya*, as we know, is autobiographical in nature. It is certainly different from the earlier hagiographies, but it neither goes beyond the codes of Mughal self-writing, nor does it ever become a mirror to Jahanara's own self. Bokhari claims the treatises written and the structures commissioned by Jahanara to be expressions of her masculine modes that are prevalent in her self-representation, but ultimately her political and spiritual agenda served "to illuminate Shah Jahan's divinely ordained flame, or *farr-iizadi*, and kingship" (Bokhari, 2015, 173).

Therefore, when in *Sahibiya* Jahanara mentions that she has "disordered circumstances" in which she has written the treatise, she is evidently referring to the disordered state of her father's kingdom, in which she sees signs of conflict over inheritance. This is a remarkable advance from the time when she wrote *Munis-ul-Arwah*, whereon she could either not visualize the gravity of the sibling conflict, or was not sure whether to refer to that in her writing. But around the time she wrote *Sahibiya*, she was much more apprehensive of the palace intrigues. She further utters that whatever this *faqira* (she) who "has wasted her life" writes with her 'broken pen', will be inadequate to describe the virtues of Mullah Shah. The 'broken pen' and 'faqira' images are understood as her writerly modesty, but 'wasted her life' may have a reference to the rhetorical journey of a Sufi woman through court politics. As a woman who is prohibited to get married, have children, and lead a life of her own, and at the same time who must mediate between brothers and sisters engaged in eternal personality conflicts, she must have found her philosophical bonding with Mullah Shah as her only breathing space.

Jahanara repeatedly mentions her writing abilities; and adds that she has read similar treatises written by Shaikhs on their own circumstances, and she has followed the tradition. Bokhari explains the 'tradition' as a patrilineal one and comments that Jahanara's Sufi treatises and commissioned architectural constructions aligned with those of her male ancestors. So, her writings served as "a form of objectified counsel" (Bokhari, 2015, 165). Babur's autobiography and Shah Jahan's biographies are examples that establish Bokhari's claim, and she rightly puts that "The habit of chronicling the deeds of each Mughal a consistency in governance, public confidence, and sociopolitical praxis" (2015, 165).

The act of self-effacement carried forward with the word "faqira" is well balanced with the patrilineal "tradition", but certainly, it was not patrilineal only. Her predecessor Gulbadan Begam's *Humayun-Nama* must have worked as an inspirational model for Jahanara's writings, giving her confidence to go beyond her "indigent weakling" self,

Otherwise, what am I but an indigent weakling and what can I do but be able to bring forth a drop from the sea of pleasing perfections and qualities of that Hazrat, or be able to pluck a rose from the garden of his pleasing virtues and excellences of that true master, and in what queue and multitude am I that I would want to write about my own disordered life. (Tr. Sunil Sharma, unpublished translation)

The use of metaphors is an obvious example of her training in the tradition. Persian poetry delighted in artifice, and was proliferated with the use of metaphors since very old times. Some common metaphors in Persian poetry relate to handicrafts that are woven, such as brocade, or piece of jewelry like pearl necklaces. These metaphors usually emphasize the aesthetic nature of writing. "The sea of pleasing perfections" and "the garden of pleasing virtues" actually come as a legacy of Persian literature. Attributes of this kind that Jahanara bestows on the master in the treatise emphasize upon the extraordinariness of the man, manifest in his ornamental qualities that he possessed. A careful perusal of *Sahibiya* leaves no doubt that as a royal disciple who has imbibed these qualities of her master Mullah Shah, Jahanara is the rightful claimant to the prerogative of writing the life of her Persian Sufi master. Self-writing or biography for Jahanara thus becomes a proof of her innermost feelings in that sense, even though she is consciously trying to evade it.

While reading about Mullah Shah's ancestry, when a reference to Rabi'a returns, a reader naturally understands that a saint of Islam who is famous for her sacrifices for religion is Jahanara's role model. Additionally, the first wife of the Prophet of Islam, Khadiza is also mentioned while describing Mullah Shah's mother. Jahanara's statement that she "was among the ascetic and perfect women" for her "spiritual exercises, strivings, lofty circumstances and stations", is rather intriguing. It is further problematized when she states that despite being of Qazi (justicer) descent, Mullah Shah did not consider a profession in the field of judiciary. Jahanara's language exalts in spiritual fervor while she writes of Mullah Shah's sole purpose of life being the attainment of God's favor. One asks if perfection in human nature in her understanding constituted unworldliness, how then was she endorsing the expansion of empire by the Mughals? She then mentions two brothers and a sister of Mullah Shah who went to different (of worldly interest) directions in life under the guidance of the Sufi leader. Here she refers to herself again; like Mullah Shah's sister she is "occupied in the inner world" as she has achieved spiritual perfection in his presence. Her master has illuminated his followers, including Jahanara herself through many odes, ghazals and quatrains, and she has obtained "endless bounty and limitless benefit from reading those luminous verses." Interestingly, she is connecting the mundane with the spiritual that are bridged by one's constant search for truth in verses.

Mullah Shah was capable of various miracles, Jahanara writes, but she does not exemplify any. Is it because she did not see him perform any? *Munis-ul-Arwah* was full of miracles, because Jahanara wrote that biography on the basis of information obtained from reading others, and she also depended much on hearsay. She mentions that telling people about miracles was forbidden by Shah, but it was perhaps impossible for her to narrate any incredible incident about the saint who she physically met, as she had a habit of being honest to herself. Ruchir Gupta's depiction of Mullah Shah's miraculous cure of Dara or opening the future-vision to Jahanara standing in a pond, is completely imaginary and exoticization of Jahanara's spirituality. Jahanara maintains this adherence to credibility throughout her book, because she was simultaneously legitimizing her own spiritual self too. She refers to Shah's abilities to perform miracles, but does not write explicitly nor exemplifies. She mentions that he could bring out the inside out, perhaps she means that he could tell the inner thoughts of men. She further writes that like Jesus Christ, her master could give life back to the dead "in the heart." Here Jahanara equates the two major Abrahamic religions, Islam and Christianity, by placing the prophet of Christianity on the same scale with a Muslim saint Mullah Shah. This can have a double meaning: first, bringing a physically dead man into life is a miracle to the commoners that could be performed by masters of both religions. Second, Islam as a religion receives prevalence, for even a saint is shown as being capable of performing the same miracle that Christ alone could deliver. It can also suggest the return of hard-hearted atheists to the life of a believer, which is a change of heart. Whatever it means, Jahanara emphasizes that Shah could perform miracles, although she could not describe any as Shah preferred to conceal his powers.

The settlement of Mullah Shah in Kashmir becomes important for Jahanara for legitimizing the presence of the Mughals in Hindustan. She mentions that after spending some years in Balkh, Shah set off for "paradisal India and he first illumined Kashmir with his emanating light" because that would give him God's proximity. He stayed in Kashmir for three years as a student, and afterwards moved from "charming Kashmir to luminous Lahore." Jahanara considered India her fatherland, as she did not have any tussle between her memories of Kabul and living in Hindustan, as was the case with Gulbadan. She unhesitatingly glorifies the Hindustani cities, and her various architectural projects also prove her love and concern for the land her forefathers conquered. Her fondness for Kashmir and Lahore is absolutely a Mughal legacy. Kashmir was annexed to the Mughal empire during 1585-86 under Akbar's reign, and Jahangir made Srinagar the empire's summer capital. On the other hand, Lahore was decorated by them in a luxurious way as Lahore was the hub between Kabul, the ancestral land of the Mughals and Hindustan, their new home. Jahanara writes that before Mullah Shah went to Lahore, it had been honored and illumined by the presence of Miyan Mir, Shah's spiritual master. Jahanara's skill in using eulogies in this panegyric is manifest in the lines –"the sheikh of mystics, the chief of uniters in one sea within truth, the heavenly soul of the shariat and tariqat[39], the mountain of dignity, renowned mystic, chief of the seekers of truth and cream of the mystics, of the great saints, of lofty shaikhs, followed by the people of the world, imam of the monotheists, knower of the secrets, opener of the veils and coverings, leader of the great and small, the second Junaid" (Tr. Sharma, unpublished translation) – Miyan Mir's qualities are thus perceived by the female Sufi devotee. Shah went to Lahore to serve Miyan Mir, but the master did not accept the disciple easily. Shah had to wait a whole year, persevering to attract the master's attention even to the point of not eating or drinking anything could he prove his zeal for "understanding of absolute existence" of his master. The master's attention opened the world of existence and spirits and semblances and the esoteric sciences to Shah, and that attention grew by days as the pupil increasingly proved his sincerity and integrity. After spending nineteen years in Miyan Mir's service, Shah returned to Kashmir. Jahanara comments that Shah never "put his sides on the ground" in those long nineteen years, some years before that and since the last five years after Miyan Mir had deceased. Essentially, it means that Shah, even when he sleeps, is ever vigilant regarding issues of spirituality. She refers to his mystic comments on his own wakefulness,

> "How long should I roar so that you wake up
> Wake up for sleep is the enemy of the heart."
>
> (Tr. Sharma, unpublished)

The sacrifice of mundane pleasures is thus, in Jahanara's Sufi ideology, an entry-level requirement for the world of *Jabarut*, *Malakut* and *Lahoot* – stages of cosmic connection and creation taking place, the knowledge of which Shah had acquired. Jahanara declares her devotion for him who does not "command too much of austerities, exercises, abandonment and abstinence for his friends and disciples," a special attribute of a Sufi mentor that is not generally found in ordinary Islamic tutors. The difference between Dara and Aurangzeb in religious issues are known to the world; Dara was trained in the Sufi tradition while Aurangzeb's Sunni Islam was full of strict rituals. But perhaps Jahanara also indicated at their different orientation of politics and monarchy. These brothers clashed for the throne, and Jahanara supported Dara Shikoh against Aurangzeb; as Dara's contention as the next Emperor must get the maximum support from the nobility who were mostly Muslim aristocrats, she mentioned Dara in both her treatises which witness her admiration for him. Though the

---

[39] *Shariat* is Islamic canonical law based on the teachings of the *Quran* and the *Hadith* (sayings and instructions of the Prophet). A *tariqa* is a school or order of Sufism, usually a concept for the mystical teaching and spiritual practices of such an order with the aim of seeking *haqiqa* or the "ulltimate truth".

struggle for Mughal throne formally started much later, it can be understood that she always had the agenda of Mughal succession in her subconscious and wanted to reveal that she had her approval for Dara's coronation.

Jahanara certainly explains why she chose the sacrificial self, while an equation of the feminine sacrifices within the Mughal harem and Sufi austerities is finally projected: "Perhaps God a bit into the wakefulness of night and at times by way of a hint commands us that for the other friends too we must sit, strive and endure austerities" (Tr. Sharma, unpublished). In Gulbadan's memoir and other Mughal writings there are references to women's fasting and prayers for the victory and safety of their spouses, Gulbadan's mention of Khanzada's sacrifice to ensure Babur's safety being an instance in point. Within the limited freedom of the aviary, a woman's life has its burden of self-effacement, and in this the Sufi and the woman have their meeting point. However, Jahanara is never to betray her feminine self, so she writes,

> The purpose of these words is the warning and censure of the lazy people. In the knowledge of unity and perception of the level of 'Wahdat al-Wujud' today he is the leader of monists on earth and chief of the investigators into the institutes of vahdat and the first of the exalted nation and head of this shining group. (Tr. Sharma, unpublished)

*Wahdat al-Wujud* is considered to be the unity of being or oneness of existence. The term is often ascribed to the Arab-Andalusian scholar Ibn Arabi who actually did not use it in his writings. It is explained as God and the creation as one, which goes against the notion upheld by Wahhabis who never associate anything with God. Jahanara indicates that Mullah Shah was able to be united with God and in her sheer ecstasy quotes the Sufi master's quatrains,

> "If the essence and nature is open in a person's face
> The house of the heart's knowledge becomes inhabited from them.
> He is a sultan and his beggar is Bayazid
> May his 'ma a'zam al-sha'n' be auspicious."
> And
> When a human is fettered by his body he is an animal
> He who falls into the heart's world is a human.
> He who falls into the body from the world of the heart bashed?
> 'Ma a'zam al-sha'ni' his words are merciful.
> (Tr. Sharma, unpublished)

Ma a'zam a-sha'ni refers to the proximity with God and Bayazid refers to another Sufi master Bayazid Bastami of Iran who is believed to be in mystical unity with God in death. Jahanara claims that similar union with God has been attained by Shah who is given miraculous power to turn people's mind with his sweet words. She refers to Shiahs' transformation into pure Sunnis, and nonbelievers becoming Muslims under his influence. She believes that her master converses with God, His prophet, saints, and whoever comes across the pious man must be transformed. Unlike weak believers, Shah's spirituality is long-lasting and he confidently claims to transport anyone to God. Here Jahanara gives a non-Muslim the idea about different sects of Islam, which becomes necessary for understanding sibling rivalry between Jahanara's brothers Dara and Aurangzeb. One has to remember that their differences in religious practice culminated in the goriest of fratricides in human history.

Among many of Shah's influences with men of rank is his ability to unite them for common causes, and this statement about Shah is again one on democratic spirit and egalitarian zeal that inhered the Sufi tent. Shah offers prayers with others; and only when a better leader is not present among them (Mulla Muhammad Sa'id, one of Mullah Shah's beloved friends, is an example of a better leader in the treatise), he leads the prayers. As a diligent follower of shariah, Shah adorned his exterior and interior with the truth of shariah (the day-to-day aspects of Islamic practice) but the staunch ulama (the Muslim scholars) who did not have spiritual knowledge criticized him even though they could not show a single feature contrary to shariah in Shah's lifestyle. Jahanara's treatise forebodes narrow bigotry and sectarian conflicts among Muslims in India that ensued in Shah Jahan's regime, and culminated in the conflict between his sons. For Jahanara the personal is thus becomes political.

Jahanara's understanding of the political world can be further witnessed when she portrays anti-populism in Shah's character: his refusal to accept gifts from followers being one major instance in point. She mentions that people are ready to sacrifice their lives and riches for him, but he would not accept anything from the worldly people, never more than one or two rupees even from the rulers or nobles. Whatever he receives anything he would instantly distribute that among his followers. He has only one or two men in his service. She describes his sitting postures in which there are expressions of surrender to God: "Sometimes he stretches his legs, sometimes he sits in the moonlight and sometimes in a dark house." If anyone from the worldly people comes to offer service, Mullah Shah asks his name and where he has come from, and dismisses the man with a recitation of *fatiha* and a polite goodbye. Jahanara dedicates lines at length to describe how Shah is always in union with the creator, how he is always smiling, how in his jests too there is always something to learn. Such objective appraisals sometimes turn into subjective amorous expressions that one needs to take into cognizance Bokhari's comments on "the sacral-secular modes of courtship/initiation, affirmation, and finally consummation/ mystical union" (2015, 183) are significant in this context. There were on the one hand these "delicate and sublime formal elements" that portray the pir as a "benevolent, sensitive, and charismatic master who lovingly inspires devotion" (Bokhari, 2015, 185); and on the other, there was a possibility of channelizing unrequited physical love towards him. Bokhari is quite candid when she comments that when Jahanara had written the *Sahibiya*, she was only twenty. She must have had youthful passions and it would not be irrational to infer that she may have "redirected/diffused her intense and unrequited amorous desires and carnal longings" from the mundane to the divine through the intervention of Mullah Shah. Bokhari associates Jahanara's expressions like "My beloved came easily into my arms on the nights of parting. . . . I was a crazed lover. . . . My yearning has finally rewarded me with you in embrace" with Jahanara's ecstasies, both physical and spiritual. Indeed, when Jahanara writes, "Oh Shah! You have finished me with one glance" (Bokhari, 2015, 185), and longs for physical union, one may certainly suspect so. Such a union is witnessed in *Sahibiya* in the episode of a physical meeting between her and Mullah Shah. She saw him when he came to Shah Jahan's summer palace (Jahanara calls it 'house') responding to the Emperor's invitation. She describes Mullah Shah's appearance in a rather abstract way,

> From the shining light that emanated from his clear forehead, the discerning eye and eye of belief were dazzled. From the auspiciousness of seeing him my belief and sincerity increased thousand-fold and the conditions I had made with myself that until I would see such a great man with my own eyes and learn his true story from my wise brother I would not take a master, were all met. (Tr. Sharma, unpublished)

Before this meeting, Dara Shikoh showed her a portrait of Mullah Shah painted by a renowned painter, and Jahanara writes that she used to imagine him through her mind's eye. This expression is undoubtedly for praising Mullah Shah, but it can also be interpreted as an expression of a woman's world proliferated with her emotions and power of imagination. She was in the making of an artist herself. It also reveals how eagerly the Mughal women waited for a glimpse from the outside world. Gulbadan described several journeys on elephants and horses, and it is understood that she saw much of the outside world though the world did not see much of her. Mughal women travelled but their lives were not for openness and exposure. Jahanara presents the other side of that secluded life. They were not allowed to meet outsiders and seeing a male outside of the family circle was a privilege for the women sitting in the *Diwan-i-Khaas* between which and the Emperor's court (*Diwan-i-Aam*)[40] there would always be a screened wall. Women used to remain eager when they would be asked to see through the screen when some special event

---

[40] The court of the commons. It was usually a place where the Emperor would listen to the complaints of the common subjects and declare his verdicts.

occurred in the court. Mughal miniature paintings with portraits of humans and objects, and other kinds of artefacts like Persian carpets and tapestries were used to be brought to them inside the zenana, and they would curiously observe them and purchase them if they liked. Her description of the divine also becomes a window to the mundane world of women in that sense.

Jahanara records three meetings with Mullah Shah; the first being in Kashmir, the second happened when Dara went with her to see Mullah Shah, and the third happened when Mullah Shah himself came forward to fulfill Jahanara's wish to meet her when she was returning from Lahore. Each time, they were surrounded by their servants. She compared the meetings with contemplating beauty personified in Mullah Shah "who was like the full moon in heaven and brilliant and bounteous sun." However, the meeting in Kashmir summer house brings a completely different mode of interaction. In the spiritual-sexual dialectic that continually binds Jahanara with Mullah Shah in Bokhari's understanding, the physical meeting with all elements connected to it became important. The dupatta or the scarf of Mullah Shah, for example, visibly substituted for his hands in a symbolic act of physical union, "He took off his dupatta (headscarf) . . . and gave it to me. . . I rubbed it over my eyes, lips, and chest, and then placed it on my head. I experienced immense joy. . . (Bokhari, 2015, 185). Whatever the emotion was, Jahanara never let the sexual side overpower the spiritual in this exchange, and her deliberation was more of a symbolic nature. Bokhari refers to a quatrain sent by Mullah Shah in praise of Jahanara's devotion, in which he wrote something like "The light of God that shines on your face, from it opens a path to the faces of everyone" (Bokhari, 2015, 184), in response to which Jahanara wrote him the letter mentioned earlier in the chapter. The last line of Jahanara's letter went like this: "Oh Shah, come on to me like the light of the sun" (2015, 184). This becomes a guiding principle in all her writings. She responds to this light of the master with her own mission of spreading the Timurid light across the empire. She uses an interesting strategy in *Sahibiya*: after a brief description of several enlightened and powerful followers of Mullah Shah in a modest style, she starts narrating how her own entry into the spiritual order happened. It would look incongruous to connect herself with the master had she not included his other followers among whom she could contain herself. And at this point, her self-fashioning or self-portrayal begins.

She gives a brief background of her Sufi inclination and particular interest for the yah order. By the time Jahanara turned twenty, she became quite familiar and fond of the Sufi order and had already visited the holy shrine of Ajmer several times. She then mentions her visit to Lahore to meet her royal father in 1049 Hijri year. She refers to Shah Jahan, "may God preserve his kingdom and power—on whom God almighty bestowed extreme grace of devotion, worship, and immense gratitude, the greatest happiness that his (Shah Jahan's) father and grandfather had been deprived of" is a very intriguing statement. It confirms that Mughal women contributed in legitimizing the emperor's position; Shah Jahan ascended the throne through fratricide, and yet Jahanara, a matriarch in the Mughal making, was upholding the monarch's dignity. Afterwards, her comments are directed towards Dara, "the powerful and successful brother, the sage of secrets, the master of zeal and presence, the light of the eye and source of light, full of meanings and illustrious actions, heir to the internal and external kingdom, felicitous in his search for God, of lofty rank" (Tr. Sharma, unpublished) for whom she has immense love. She elaborately mentions her spiritual bonding with her brother, the heir apparent to the empire. She even mentions the Kabul expedition in which Dara Shikoh led a huge army and the defeat brought him disrepute. This episode is portrayed by historians as a shameful military loss in Shah Jahan's reign brought about by Dara's lack of skills. In Jahanara's writing, however, it is not the adverse criticism of Dara Shikoh for having subjected the empire to huge material losses that is scrutinized; rather, she stands steadfast in defending him and persists in her overt preference of Dara. In her preferential treatment of Dara over Aurangzeb, a fact repeatedly brought out in history, Jahanara lets go of no occasion for voicing her political inclinations. She therefore emerges as a classic instance where an inmate of the Mughal harem is continuously placing herself as a matriarch who not only heads the domestic sphere but also declares her stand in the war of succession. The narration of history therefore offers interesting twists of political acts, depending on what point of view one is adopting to place even an oft discussed episode in perspective. As we see here, Jahanara deftly alters the narrative from insinuations at her brother's lack of military stratagem and presents the otherwise shameful defeat as a blessing in disguise, for it allowed Dara to be with her. From historical estimates of how deeply the failed military enterprise had drained the royal coffers to the expression of Jahanara's gratitude to God for keeping Dara close to her so that she might be able to spend days in religious enlightenment is an interesting turn that she gives to contemporary history, "Often I would sit with my wise brother who possessed virtues and talked about seeking God and the truth. From obtaining this desire, my zeal increased a thousand-fold and the fire of zeal for divine gnosis was thrown in me" (Tr. Sharma, unpublished).

This very zeal inspires Jahanara's search for a Sufi master, "My honorable life—every breath of which is dear and enriched, and since whatever passes cannot be obtained again—was wasted in nothingness and uselessness" (Tr. Sharma, unpublished). A woman of twenty-seven contemplating life as "wasted" and "useless" is not to be wondered at, as one knows her life and time. She was not allowed to get married, and the heavy burden of assisting a royal father bereft of his most beloved wife and playing role of a matriarch for her deceased mother's children must have embittered her life to some extent. And after a series of efforts, she finally reached Mullah Shah in Kashmir.

Jahanara's travel to Kashmir needs to be commented upon. 31 March 1640 was the exact date mentioned in her treatise when she reached the beautiful valley. As usual, she is all praise for the natural beauty of Kashmir, but unlike the available travel narratives based on the valley, she presents a completely different perspective. Her thrust is on the divine nature of Kashmir because of the saint who lived there, "From the auspiciousness of his blessed feet this land has become heaven's partner, but rather it makes a higher claim than that." As has been discussed earlier, here she cooked naan and sag for Mullah Shah and wrote that letter: "If that sun-like visage becomes accessible to me / I will make a claim of lordship, not just of kingship." It was quite in fashion for Mughal women to visit shrines and saints, but perhaps a note like that was a very bold step, and could only have come from someone whose words truly carried the weight of her convictions. It becomes clear from Jahanara's writing that Mullah Shah was not fond of royal people though they were frequenters at his shrine. Their intentions were also not always clean, and when she was accepted as a follower, it was obvious that she was certifying her intentions through Mullah Shah's acceptance.

To add to her intelligent mix of emotional and the political, one must admit that she always upheld Mughal women's act of piety and sacrifice. In *Sahibiya*, Jahanara mentions her first fasting according to Mullah Shah's instructions, and how she broke her fast with the food sent from him. Later that night she said her prayers in the mosque of the harem and then retiring in her chamber she sat in meditation with Mullah Shah's portrait in front. Such idolatry, needless to say, is not sanctioned by Islam; Jahanara's indulgence in it ostensibly reveals her internal conflict regarding the transition from Chishtiyah to Qadiriya order. The Qadiriya order was more open in nature and allowed space for personalized interactions between master and disciples in its practice. We can attribute Jahanara's conflict to the fact that while her forefathers followed the more strictly Sunni Chishtiyah order, she and her brother Dara dared to follow this new Qadiriya line that was less stringent in nature. She meditated, and in her dreams, she saw the vision of the Prophet of Islam and his disciples, among which group Mullah Shah also figured. There is reason to believe that Jahanara's dream sequence is an inadvertent result of her inherent conflict, and that she aspires to draw coefficients with real life to rationalize her decision regarding the change of order. So, she writes in *Sahibiya* that in her dream, she hears the Prophet telling Mullah Shah, "O Mulla Shah! You have lighted the lamp of the Timurids." To Jahanara, this is a revelation, and she continues to describe how in sheer ecstasy she had uttered,

O King, you are the one who saves through purity.
By God, your glance is a grace for the seekers.
Whoever you look at reaches his goal.
The light of your glance is perhaps the light of God.

(Tr. Sharma, unpublished)

Once her internal conflicts are resolved, one sees a confident Jahanara writing that she and Dara are the ones from the Timurid nobility, and that by choosing the path of Mullah Shah, the siblings have virtually emerged as the lights of this clan,

> My belief was strengthened a thousand-fold because I had I had tied the girdle of sincerity in ten places around my waist, put the ring of servitude to Hazrat in the ear of my soul, made him my master from the bottom of my heart, chosen to follow him as leader in this world and the next. (Tr. Sharma, unpublished)

Here she does not talk of herself only; her intention is also to legitimize the spiritual superiority of Dara and thereby to strengthen his claim on the Mughal empire. She writes, "My wise brother had experienced this felicity one day and by the auspicious attention of that brother, it reached me too and not anyone else from the lineage of Timur" (Tr. Sharma, unpublished). As proximity between the political and the spiritual has always remained a pattern in the Mughal empire, Jahanara's upholding of Dara's spirituality, albeit after he had led the forces to a humiliating defeat, might have been her application of soft power to try and legitimize his ascendence to the throne.

Jahanara stay in Kashmir for six months at a stretch allowed her to meet Mullah Shah and exchange gifts, but she hardly narrates any miracle. *Sahibiya* has only a single reference to some event that could be called nothing more than a coincidence. Before leaving Kashmir, she had a dream of Mullah Shah one Thursday evening in her meditation after evening prayer in which she saw Mullah Shah gifting her his with own scarf. Being agitated, she thought of sending a scarf of her own to her master for taking his blessing in it. However, before she could send someone, her chamberlain Puran came to her with Mullah Shah's scarf and said he had taken off the scarf and sent it for her. Jahanara records it as a miracle of the 'lowest' kind. Nonetheless, it is never to be the source of what the fictional writings have written about her. For example, Ruchir Gupta narrates Jahanara's meditations in the river nearby while she sees distant visions of the future reflected on the surface of the river. Gupta does not refer to *Sahibiya* at all; such meditative power commanded by Jahanara is therefore not based on historical sources.

Towards the end of her writing Jahanara praises God for sending the master as her spiritual guide. Along with this, she adds,

> Every person who does not possess this truth is not a person, and his existence is nothing and in vain. Each person who is blessed with that greatest felicity becomes the perfect human and the superior to all creatures. His existence is lost in the absolute existence and becomes a drop in the ocean, a ray of the sun, and a part of the whole.
>
> (Tr. Sharma, unpublished)

This comment offers a twofold meaning. The mention of "who does not possess this truth is not a person, and his existence is nothing and in vain" may carry political connotations. As history witnesses, Aurangzeb was contemptuous of the Sufi order, and Jahanara might have referred to his antagonism towards the spiritual order in her remarks. "Perfect human" or "superior to all creatures" are complements for Dara in that sense. However, the political is camouflaged by the religious fervor of the next sentence. Jahanara makes a reference to herself here, "Each person who has love for the absolute essence is a perfect human, even if she is a woman." Her intention to lift public appreciation of Dara as a future heir becomes almost explicit in the next few lines when she writes, "I obtained this great fortune and benefit through the means of my brother of lofty nature, master of perfection, perfect uniter, knower of God, Muhammad Dara Shikoh, the shadow of almighty God" (Tr. Sharma, unpublished).

A formal ending to *Sahibiya* proves Jahanara's craft in hagiography; she ends it with a concrete date (27 Ramadan 1051 Hijri year that the translator calculates as 30 December 1641) when she accomplishes the writing of the text, and adds with it a note of felicitation for the master. She writes about the writing itself; while she calls herself "abject" and "lowly one" as usual, terms every word of the treatise as "a precious gem" and every phrase as "a string of pearls" that composed "an ornament for the ears and necks of those travelling on the path of guidance." She expects the readers to be guided by her writing, and also desires her wasted life to remain under the shadow of the Sufi master,

> May his shadow be over our heads like a parasol,
> May his state be a veil for our lives.

It is a traditional text in the sense it brings out formal compliments for the Sufi master. One needs to delve deep into her expressions and match her comments with information retrieved from historical sources. Perhaps, one may find many layers other than the spiritual in this.

### Jahanara at the crossroads of modernity:

From the discussion of Jahanara's treatises, it is clear that these two texts can be of interest to scholars in New Historicism who maintain that literary documents respond to the conditions of their own production. Through joining the Qadiriya order, Jahanara primarily responded to the necessities of her own life. Her grievances in private life were subsided by acts of charity and divinity dictated by her Sufi masters, and at the same time, she could collect her dispersed thoughts through writing. She found solace and peace in Sufi thoughts and her responses to those ventilated her personal life to some extent. At the same time, she served as a voice of the Mughal sovereignty for which she dedicated her life and sacrificed her feminine desires. It is unfortunate that her writings did not get much attention of translators and did not reach readers of the subsequent generations. The unavailability of English translations is obviously a specific reason for this scanty readership of such texts. Sunil Sharma's translation of *Sahibiya* will be a good addition in this regard. *Munis ul-Arwah* needs a more qualified and coherent English translation. When translations of these writings and her verses become available, perhaps there will be a time to reassess her as a mystic and a writer proper.

Apart from being hagiographies, these two treatises are important attempts at alterity with historical documents because they give a glimpse of history of Muslim conquest of India from a different vantage point. Especially, *Munis-ul-Arwah* gives an alternative version of mainstream history. When the Turkish and Afghan races were invading parts of India, the Sufi saints came to India as their missionary counterpart for the sake of spreading Islam. This side of history is important because it records how Sufi philosophers applied soft diplomacy through their teaching of tolerance, sacrifice and sympathy and spread Islam across the continent. This is perhaps a gateway to go back to history and see the change of culture with a more holistic approach. Jahanara's books open new territories of understanding cultural change.

As a woman, Jahanara thus remains an unfathomable enigma. The power she wielded in the time of two of the greatest Mughal Emperors is unimaginable, and her private life is a lucrative raw material for any creative writer. As someone whose afterlife has been spent in darkness for over four centuries, she stands the possibility of resurrection from obscurity/ mindless fictionalizing when all kinds of front-line conceptualization along the lines of gender are in currency. To that effect, this chapter aims at getting beyond passing interest in adding layers of imagination on her already enigmatic and palimpsestic life, and foregrounding Jahanara as the subject of critical understanding at the crossroads of gender and modernity. It is amply evident that her originality of thoughts can, if analyzed seriously, serve as rich materials for understanding the dynamics of contemporary gender constructs within the harem. For example, Jahanara spoke of herself as a *faqira* to signify her vocation as a Sufi woman. Her repeated utterance about herself as "the lowly one" is a curious expression that differs in tone and meaning from its resonance in a 21$^{st}$ century female writer's expression, a living American poet called Hanna Gamble, who writes, "I wanted to make myself like the ravine." One can comment that Gamble maintains her womanly pride when she adds to her first line, "so that all good things/ would flow into me. / Because the ravine is lowly, / it receives an abundance". The abundance of the ravine ranges from a half-eaten apple to a semi-cooked mouse; danger lurks within the flow of the ravine; and one needs to shut the door on time to live untroubled days. Jahanara also mentions the *Herat* of the pious which is like the rivulet. On a second thought, one may not find much difference between what Jahanara meant by her lowly existence and what Gamble wants to mean by the abundance the ravine receives. A life of an empress with heavy responsibility of the royal seal and suffering the rumors of incest; a life that needed to be balanced between feuds and favors, could it but stay away from the consolation and the light that Sufism brought to it? God's abundance was there in the offerings of Sufism for Jahanara. It became her self-fashioning as well as self-consolation; it was her gateway to freedom and peace. The charisma and miraculous power of the Sufi saints gave Jahanara a certain faith that this life, if not the power of royalty, will give her eternal peace and security. She lived a life of strong convictions. Ruchir Gupta's Jahanara meets that life of convictions when Jahanara has visions of future in her meditation, or decides not to elope with the British doctor Gabriel Boughton to have a family in England. She finds herself in the Mughal empire, and wishes to keep her marks in the construction of the new city. She represents the Mother India trope in Gupta's fictional work.

In real life, Jahanara's individualism and free will reveal her modernist mind in the pre-modern era. History remembers her as powerful because she used to instruct her father and brother on maintaining political integrity and keeping communal peace within the kingdom; and her powerful personality was influential on Zeb-un-Nissa, her niece, to a great extent. Sufism gave her the tolerance necessary in an empire enriched with its cultural diversity; and added with it, her intelligence and self-awareness that get revealed in her treatises can be of interest for the scholars today and tomorrow.

# 4

# Dissenting Songbird in the Aviary: The Poetry of Zeb-un-Nissa

Women are never so strong as after their defeat.

– (Dumas, 1994)[1]

In refusing to attest much importance to the work of Zeb-un-Nissa, contemporary writers of romance have been the losers, for hers is a history that could have been ready material for fictioneers. She was an extremely beautiful princess born of the tyrant monarch Aurangzeb. One of the finest poets of the Indian School of Poetry in Persian, Zeb-un-Nissa's poems are at the core, reflections on love and melancholy. Her poetry flowed from the pores of her skin that tolerated the burning of a forever unfulfilled mundane love; and simultaneously, she indulged in metaphysical spasms of divine union with God. Her beauty and irrepressible poetic emotion attracted many admirers who could not however save her from the wrath of her father; and she had to spend the last twenty years of her life in captivity before her tragic end in the prison. Finally, the aviary at this stage stretched out of the limited confines of the Mughal zenana to the real incarceration within the walls of Salimgarh Fort in Delhi, where Zeb-un-Nissa awaited divine providence for days on end apparently to no good effect.

The first generation of Mughal women literati can be said to have ended with Gulbadan. In the second generation, Jahanara alternated between upholding the tradition of writing in favor of the Mughal patriarchy, and writing for her own self-fashioning that was inherent in the individual that she was. In the third generation, Zeb-un-Nissa appeared as a representative of those Mughal women born and brought up in Hindustan, the land whose ties with Central Asia were gradually fading; and they were in search of a strong footing in the new empire.

Influenced as she was by the Sufi spirit of her paternal uncle Dara Shikoh who was a poet of repute himself, Zeb-un-Nissa's forte too was poetry. As a

---

[1] From *La Reine Margot*, which is a historical novel written in 1845 by the French novelist Alexandre Dumas (1802-1870). There and several English translations of the novel; the source of the quote is *Queen Margot, or Marguerite de Valois* (Miramax Books, 1994).

contemporary of great Sufi poets like Bedil[2] (Mawlana Abdul Qader), Kalim Kashani[3], Saa'eb Tabrizi[4] and Ghani Kashmiri,[5] Zeb-un-Nissa is best known as a writer of ghazals[6] and ruba'is.[7] There is also a noticeable influence of Hafiz[8] on her poetic style. However, an Indianized poetic cult was visible in her ghazals and ruba'is in which she blended Persian forms with Indian imagery. Thematically her poetry surpassed the feminine mode that usually adhered to visible reticence in expression; and she boldly declared her state of mind, her passionate love and, occasionally, her complaints too.

Sufi poetry as a form was introduced and practiced by men, in which concepts of divinity and worldliness have very thin dividing lines. Love is a major theme, and the masculine mode has been dominant in this kind of poetry. In that sense, Zeb-un-Nissa as a Sufi poet stands unparalleled among her contemporaries. She wrote in secret under the pen name of 'Makhfi' or 'The hidden one' because though her father had initially appreciated her poetic bent of mind, he did not favor her vocation towards the mature phase of her career. As a fiercely independent woman, she could not agree with all of Aurangzeb's tyrannical and parochial activities. Her meddling in state politics, especially her connection with her brother Akbar who was in alliance with several Hindu and

---

[2] Abul-Maani Mirza Abdul-Qadir Bedil (1642–1720), was also known as Bidel Dehlavi. He was and Indian Sufi poet, who wrote during the reign of Aurangzeb. He was a representative of the later phase of the "Indian style" of Persian poetry. He is often considered to be the most challenging poet of the Safavid-Mughal poetry, who was difficult to understand.

[3] Abu Taleb aka Kalim Kasani (1581-1651) was a Persian poet and one of the leading exponents of the Indian style of Persian poetry. He was born in Hamadan, but as his student life was spent in Kasan where he started writing poetry, his pen name has Hamadani or Kasani. He went to the Deccan to seek his fortune at the court of Mughal Emperor Jahangir.

[4] Mirza Moḥammad Ali (pen name Saeb Tabrizi, 1592-1676) was a Persian poet of the later Safavid period. He came to Hindustan around Shah Jahan's time.

[5] Gani Kashmiri (1630 – c. 1669) was regarded the greatest writer of Persian in the Mughal Kashmir.

[6] The ghazal is a form of amorous poetry originating in the 7th century Arabic poetry tradition. This form spread to South Asia in the 12th century due to the influence of the Sufi mystics and the new Islamic Sultanate. It is one of the oldest poetic forms that still prominently existent in the poetry of many languages of the Indian subcontinent and Turkey.

[7] Ruba'I is a specific form of Persian poetry consisting of a quatrain or four lines. It is usually intensely lyrical and subjective.

[8] Hafiz/ Hafez was the pen name of Khwaja Shams-ud-Din Muḥammad Hafez-e Shirazi was a famous fourteenth century Persian poet. The theme of his ghazals is usually a lover's benedictions for love, and alsofaith and hypocrisy playing on two sides of love. He deals with love, wine, freedom from all kinds of physical and spiritual restrains and sometimes they are against religious and ruling establishments of the time. Aurangzeb banned reading his poetry in educational institutions, and also forbidden reading it in his harem.

Marathi chieftains against Aurangzeb, enraged her father to the point that he decided to imprison her. She continued writing in her imprisonment and proved that a songbird's 'caged voice' could not be strangled. Her writings have survived through centuries on account of their sheer merit, and today they bespeak the existence of a resolute woman whose discursive voice against injustice had the potential to interrogate Mughal patriarchy, albeit within her limited agency. Zeb-un-Nissa's poetry is best understood in relation to the remark by Ania Loomba and Ritty A. Lukose in their introduction to *South Asian Feminisms* (2012),

> But history has continued to be disproportionately central to feminist scholarship in South Asia, in part because of the nature of postcolonial politics in the entire region. The spectacular rise of communalism, sectarian violence, and militarism has necessitated a continued feminist engagement with histories of religious identity, community, and social memory. (2012, 5)

Zeb-un-Nissa's writings sprang from her unusual mental strength, of which she showed traces since childhood. She could celebrate poetry against Aurangzeb's prohibition at an early age; and such resilience enabled her to stand firm against the Mughal militarism and oppression at a later period. On a first view, her engagement with poetry might not appear overtly critical of the empire, but the underlying suggestion that she was striving towards a syncretic understanding of the empire, as was necessary for its sustenance in Hindustan, would have come across as an inherently problematic proposition. Be that as it may, it is this syncretic temperament in Zeb-un-Nissa's poetry that makes for its increasing relevance today, in order to challenge and dismantle an overtly prejudiced neo-nationalist agenda that the Mughal empire was the root of sectarianism in India. Religion has been one of the yardsticks to measure the Mughal empire, especially Aurangzeb's period, and that is proper to an extent indeed, for the spread of Islam was his primary agenda in the empire. Against this, Zeb-un-Nissa's resolute stand on the secular ground of poetry needs to be revisited in order to highlight the presence of a school of thought among the royal descendants that could speak of this 'other' history. Seen thus, the Mughal empire may not appear as cruel, parochial and sectarian as an establishment, that it is made out to be through the lens of nonchalant cultural nationalism in post-colonial India at present.

Attaching due importance to the body of her work in this reinterpretative light, this chapter peruses a few ghazals and ruba'is by Zeb-un-Nissa. The author is of the conviction that their analyses will comment on her poetic temperament, technique, and the innumerable ways in which she exerted her progressive and mature mind that traveled beyond her time to embrace modernity; and most importantly, reveal her secular and independent voice. As a point of comparison, one feels that while Jahanara was powerful as a great matriarch, she was neither determined to challenge patriarchy, nor could she develop the secular voice that was necessary for the acculturation of the Mughals in Hindustan. In that sense, Zeb-un-Nissa was beyond doubt a path breaker, a dissenter, who did not learn to submit to patriarchy.

### Life and education

The scant attention accorded to Zeb-un-Nissa is brought out by the fact that not much is known of her life other than passing mentions that historians have made of her in writing biographies of Mughal emperors. Zeb-un-Nissa was the eldest child of the last great Mughal Emperor Aurangzeb (also known by his regnal title *Alamgir*[9]). Her mother Dilras Banu Begam was a princess, daughter of Mirza Badi-uz-Zaman Safavi of the ruling Safavid dynasty of Persia (Iran). Zeb-un-Nissa was born at Daulatabad[10] on 15 February 1738. She had four other siblings by her own mother: Zinat-un-Nissa, Zubdat-un-Nissa, Muhammad Azam Shah and Sultan Muhammad Akabr. For the mention, Zinat-un-Nissa and Zubdat-un-Nissa also possessed poetic faculties that have equally remained unheeded. Aurangzeb had children from his other wives and concubines too. Muhammad Sultan, Bahadur Shah I and Badr-un-Nissa Begam were born of Nawab Bai, and Mehr-un-Nissa Begam was born of Aurangabadi Mahal, Muhammad Kam Bakhsh was born of a concubine named Udaipuri Mahal. It is recorded in history that among all these children, Zeb-un-Nissa was her father's favorite child to begin with, and when she had memorized the *Quran* in three years and became a *Hafiz*[11] at the age of seven, Aurangzeb even arranged for a huge celebration. There was a great feast and a public holiday. In the first volume of Aurangzeb's biography, Jadunath Sarkar writes,

> She seems to have inherited her father's keenness of intellect and literary tastes. Educated by a lady named Hafiza Mariam she committed the Quran to memory, for which she received a reward of 30,000 gold-pieces from her delighted father. A mistress of Persian and Arabic, she wrote different kinds of hand with neatness and grace. Her library surpassed all other private collections, and she employed many scholars

---

[9] Alamgir means "conqueror of the world". Aurangzeb was the sixth Mughal Emperor, who expanded the Mughal empire to its largest extent in terms of territories annexed to it. He ruled over almost the entire Indian subcontinent from 1666 to 1707. He ruled over a population estimated to be over 158 million subjects, with an annual revenue of $450 million. He was the richest man of the world during his reign.

[10] Daulatabad is a city in the Indian state of Maharashtra. It is situated in the outskirts of Aurangabad, which was the seat for Aurangzeb in the Deccan when Zeb-un-Nissa was born.

[11] Hafiz literally means "guardian" or "memorizer". It is a term used by Muslims for someone who has completely memorized the *Quran*.

on liberal salaries to produce literary works at her bidding or to copy manuscripts for her. As Aurangzib disliked poetry, her liberality compensated for the lack of Court patronage, and most of the poets of the age sought refuge with her. (Sarkar, 1912, 69)

It is to be noted that Mughal Emperors used to sanction money for the important women in their harems. Aurangzeb was one of the richest emperors (perhaps, the richest in his time) of the world. However, that amount of land and wealth came to him long after his ascension to the throne, and the event Sarkar describes had taken place when Aurangzeb was the Governor of Lahore. Therefore, Zeb-un-Nissa being rewarded 30,000 ashrafis or gold coins by her devout Muslim father for memorizing the entire *Quran*, though not surprising, is quite a serious matter. As far as is known, Zeb-un-Nissa had Miyabai as her tutor for Arabic. A second lady tutor named Hafiza Mariam is also mentioned as her mentor. As this name suggests, Mariam was a hafiz of *Quran*, and her appointment as Zeb-un-Nissa's tutor is understandable and more credible. Zeb-un-Nissa learned philosophy, mathematics, astronomy and literature, and other sciences of the time from a teacher named Mohammad Saeed Ashraf Mazandarani. She was fluent in Persian, Arabic and Urdu, and had expertise in calligraphy.

In available documents, it is claimed that Zeb-un-Nissa initiated her poetic vocation in Persian from the age of 14. Aurangzeb's rigid Islamist credentials and disliking for poetry evidently compelled Zeb-un-Nissa to keep her poetic pursuits under wraps; however, her teacher Ustad Bayaz discovered her secret and encouraged her to continue writing. Another source mentions that Shah Rustum Gazi, who was one of Zeb-un-Nissa's tutors, found copies of her verses among her exercise books. He is the one who prophesied her future greatness and persuaded Aurangzeb to invite poets and scholars from Persia and Kashmir and from all over the empire to form a fitting circle for the talented princess. At the cost of repetition, it must be mentioned that Aurangzeb did not like a poet's calling, and he had forbidden the works of Hafiz[12] to be taught in schools by boys or in the palace by Begams. But surprisingly, for his daughter's sake, he did heed the advice Rustum Gazi. The circle was formed and many renowned poets of the time were invited to participate in that circle. Nasir Ali Sayab, Shams Wali Ullah, Brahmin and Behraaz were among them. Some sources also claim that a literary circle that included great poets like Ghani Kashmiri, Naimatullah Khan and Aqil Khan Razi was formed secretly at Aurangzeb's court. This circle used

---

[12] Hafiz or Shams-od-Din Moḥammad Ḥafeẓ-e Shirazi (1315-1390) is best known for his *Divan of Hafiz*. He was a Persian Sufi poet primarily writing ghazals or lyric poetry. His style for expressing the ecstasy of divine inspiration in the mystical form of love poems was followed by Zeb-un-Nissa.

to hold literary and poetic conclaves in which princess Zeb-un-Nissa actively participated.

It was, therefore, no surprise that the news of her intellect and literary taste spread quickly. She had a huge collection of books, and her library surpassed all other private collections of the time. After ascending the Mughal throne when her father allocated her about 400,000 ashrafis per annum, she spent most of it for purposes of literary enrichment as a form of self-fashioning. Apart from being a poet herself, she spent generously for producing literary works or to have manuscripts copied for her, and also donated to literary circles. She employed calligraphers to copy rare books and employed translators to render Arabic and Sanskrit books into Persian. She even instituted a scriptorium in Kashmir because quality paper and scribes were available there. She became a patron of literary authors who would send her their works to her for approval, and she rewarded them according to the merit of their writings.

Zeb-un-Nissa was a proportionate blend of brains and beauty. Her beauty was widely renowned, and that she was smart and intelligent is evidenced in numerous documents. Paul Smith astutely writes,

> She was tall and slim, her face round and fair in colour, with two moles or beauty spots on her left cheek. Her eyes and abundant hair were very black, and she had thin lips and small teeth…She did not use missia for blackening between the teeth, nor antimony for darkening her eyelashes, even though this was the fashion of her time. Her voice was so beautiful that when she read the *Koran*[13] she moved those listening to tears. In dress she was simple and austere; in later life, she always wore white and her only ornament was a string of pearls around her neck. She is said to have invented a woman's garment, the angyakurti, a modification to suit Indian conditions of the dress of the women of Turkestan. It is known all over India. (Smith, 2012, 20)[14]

However, the Indian adage that a woman who is competent and pretty at that gets neither a husband nor a family, proved unfalteringly correct in the case of Zeb-un-Nissa! Though her unparalleled beauty and talent attracted many

---

[13] *The Quran.*

[14] *Diwan I Makhfi* is a collection of ruba'is and ghazals translated by Paul Smith that are published in a volume titled *Makhfi the Princess Sufi Poet Zeb-un-Nissa: A selection of Poems from her Divan* by New Humanity Books in 2012. In this book the translations of the first fifty ghazals by Jessie Duncan Westbrook, but most of the quotes are from Smith's translation. Westbrook's book contains only the first fifty ghazals and she has sequenced these with numbers. In Smith's translation the numbers are not maintained, and hence page number is mentioned.

suitors, she had to remain contented as a single woman in life. Emperor Shah Jahan, her grandfather, had betrothed her to Prince Sulaiman Shikoh, the eldest son of the Crown Prince Dara Shikoh. Shah Jahan perhaps thought that one day she would become the future Mughal Empress, because Sulaiman would be heir to the empire after Dara Shikoh. However, the war of succession made Dara Shikoh the worst enemy of Aurangzeb, leading finally to the assassinations of both Dara Shikoh and eventually Sulaiman. Here then was a future of a woman of substance besieged at the altar of Mughal royal polity and intrigue.

Zeb-un-Nissa allegedly enjoyed much freedom in her early years when her father became the powerful ruler of the empire. While she did have many suitors, Zeb-un-Nissa demanded to meet and test them when marriage was proposed. It was a *swayamvara*[15] kind of arrangement and many princes and noble young men came to ask for her hand. Among them one was Mirza Farukh, son of Shah Abbas II of Iran. Zeb-un-Nissa invited him to Delhi in writing and, as is known, he came with quite large a group of followers. The princess entertained his men in a pleasure-house in her garden and attended to him physically with a veil on her face. He allegedly asked for some kind of sweet using some words that also meant 'a kiss', something that deeply offended the lady who then refused to marry him. The incident clearly shows how independent and strong willed she was as a woman. However, the trivia that emerged out of this occasion is worth mentioning, for in that she left a mark of her poetic talent too. Mirza Farukh, also man of a poetic temperament, was determined to have her consent in marriage, and he sent her a verse: "I am determined never to leave this temple: here will I bow my head, here will I serve and here alone is happiness" (Smith, 2012, 16). To this, Zeb-un-Nissa wrote in reply: "How light you make of this game of love, O child. You know nothing of the fever of longing and the fire of separation and the burning flame of love" (Smith, 2012, 16-17). Mirza Farukh was thus left with no option but to abandon all hopes of marrying her. That a woman born as a princess, and endowed with a destiny was either to marry for the benefit of the kingdom or not marry at all, could dare such exercise of will, is certainly an episode that demands the right

---

[15] *Swayamvara* was a practice in ancient India that was arranged when a princess or an aristocratic girl would reach her marriageable age. A girl wishing to marry would select a husband from a group of suitors. Kings would sent messengers to outside lands. It was a custom among commoners too, in which case the girl's intention to marry would be spread within the local community. On the appointed day, the girl would offer a garland to the man of her choice and a ceremony would be held immediately to declare the marriage. In Mughal history this kind of arrangement was perhaps made only for Zeb-un-Nissa, though the arrangement was a little different. The suitors did not appear in the scene together.

kind of attention while formulating an estimate of Zeb-un-Nissa the person. Being the daughter of Aurangzeb who was a strictly principled orthodox practitioner of Islam, Zeb-un-Nissa's willful act of meeting and eventually refusing to marry the prince of Persia does leave a mark on how she perceived herself even while being a member of the Mughal harem that we here look upon as an aviary.

Conversely, there were rumors of Zeb-un-Nissa's secret love affair with Aqil Khan Razi[16], the governor of Lahore who was also a poet. In 1662 Aurangzeb was ill and as his physicians prescribed a change of air, he came to Lahore with his family and court. At that time, Akil Khan, the son of Aurangzeb's prime minister, was Governor of that city. Around this time, Zeb-un-Nissa allegedly had a brief affair with him that ended rather tragically.

It is difficult to say anything precisely about Zeb-un-Nissa because there is always a dialectical pattern about the historicity of the episodes in her life; what one historian describes is almost always nullified by another. Her supposed involvement with Akil Khan is not an aberration to this trend. As Paul Smith records in his introduction to a selection of her poetry, Akil Khan was so eager to meet her that he would ride around the walls of Aurangzeb's palace in Lahore with a wish to get a glimpse of Zeb-un-Nissa. One of those days, he saw her on a balcony and cried, "A vision in red on the balcony of the palace does appear." She heard it and replied, "Supplications nor force nor gold can ever win her" (Smith, 2012, 21). Akil Khan's desperate misadventures to woo the lady in the disguise of a mason inside the palace also finds mention in Smith. In his avatar as a mason, Khan sees the princess playing *chausar*[17] with her female companions, and utters, "In my longing for you, I've become like the dust, around the earth wandering" (Smith, 2012, 21-22). Zeb-un-Nissa immediately replied, "Even if you had become like the wind, you should not a lock of my hair be touching" (Smith, 2012, 22). This shows her quick wit that gives a razor-sharp edge to her poetic talent. The end of this affair with Akil Khan was tragic, or dare I say pathetic; according to contemporary rumors. The news reached Aurangzeb, and to stop their clandestine encores he wanted to have her married off. Zeb-

---

[16] Aqil Khan Razi was born as Muḥammad Taqi Khwafi to a family of Iranian *Sayyid*s. He received the title Aqil from Aurangzeb. His attribute "Razi" comes from the name of his spiritual instructor—the Ṣufi Shattari Burhan al-Din Burhanpuri. He is known for writing *The Waqiat-i-Alamgiri*, which is an account of the war of succession between the sons of Shah Jahan.

[17] Chausar of Chaupar is a kind of a board game that could be played indoors. However, Zeb-un-Nissa was perhaps playing it in the palace courtyard in the Mughal style. The first description of this was written in the 16th century, when it became a gambling sport that emperor Akbar popularized in Agra and Fatehpur Sikri. Hehad laid out in flagstones a huge "board" where he and his courtiers enjoyed the game, using slaves as the playing pieces.

un-Nissa asked her father to allow her to choose her groom. The portraits of the possible suitors were sent to her and she naturally chose Akil Khan. Aurangzeb wanted to fulfill her wish and sent for Akil Khan. Akil Khan was supposedly 'misled' by a rival suitor who wrote, "It is no child's play to be the lover of a daughter of a king. Aurangzeb knows your doings; as soon as you come to Delhi, you will reap the fruit of your love" (Smith, 2012, 22). The hitherto boisterous lover proved a coward and he turned turtle, never as much as daring to meet Aurangzeb and asking for his daughter's hand.

The subsequent turn of events was even more gruesome. As Akil Khan could not get past Zeb-un-Nissa in his mind, he continued to visit her in Delhi, and they used to meet in her garden. Aurangzeb was informed of this, and appeared during one such meeting. Zeb-un-Nissa, being out of wit, hid her lover in a large cooking vessel (*deg*), and when the emperor asked her what was there in the vessel, she replied it was only water to be heated. Aurangzeb was not convinced, and he ordered the servants to heat the vessel, but the princess could not say anything as she was apprehensive about her reputation. She came near the vessel and whispered to Akil Khan, "Keep silence if you are my true lover, for the sake of my honor" (Smith, 2012, 23). Smith connects this event with one of Zeb-un-Nissa's couplets that goes like this: "What is the fate of a lover? /It is to be sacrificed for the world's pleasure" (Smith, 2012, 23) and writes, "One wonders if when composing this she thought of Akil Khan's life" (Smith, 2012, 23). Different sources claimed that Akil Khan lived longer and had a natural death. Assumptions of this kind could proliferate about this lady, because her father destroyed every record of her out of rage when she united with her brother against him. The *Dictionary of Indo-Persian Literature* has an entry on Zeb-un-Nissa that writes,

> The India of Mughals irresistibly attracted the attention of post-renaissance Europeans, and its bazars thronged with men of every description from beyond the Mediterranean: traders, travelers, and free-lance adventurers, who roamed with eyes and ears wide open to inform themselves about everything odious. For, the East was "mysterious" and its institutions "barbarous". With frankly dehumanized attitude, it was not surprising if scandals concerning lives of Mughal ladies found free entry into their writings. Nor could Zeb un-Nissa be an exception. A sordid episode of her carnal romance with Aqil Khan Razi and his death inside a hot cauldron with burning fire under it, gained wider currency and was eagerly picked up by the vulgar populace. Nothing could be more absurd. 'Aqil Khan lived long as imperial servant and died a natural death. It was too late when a modern historian took stock of facts and data and wrote his vehement denunciation (Jadunath Sarkar: History of

Aurangzeb, vol III, p. 61) for, the damage to Zeb un-Nissa's personality had been already done. (Hadi, 1995, 639)

Hadi's comment reminisces the age-old tradition of travel writing that was captured by male imagination for quite a long time. Women travelers wrote, but their writings did not flourish until late. In "Women's Travel Writing 1750-1830", Catherine Turner writes that by 1800 there were only about twenty women who had published travel books while there had been several hundred travelogues published by men (Turner 2010, 48). She was giving only the statistics of the British literary geography; and in the rest of the world, the condition was even poorer. Therefore, it is normal that a woman's love life would become the gossip of the market, and would find a place in the travelogues written by males who lamented their misfortune of not having seen her. The loss was ultimately hers, because it was her history and her reputation that were put to stake. Moreover, the offense done to all records of her existence by her enraged father was not critically discussed by Nabi or any other writer of the subsequent times.

Zeb-un-Nissa's talent in state politics was widely known. She was only twenty-one when her father Aurangzeb became the emperor. Aurangzeb used to discuss political affairs with her, and would often take her opinions in court matters. It is believed that Aurangzeb would even pardon his offenders if Zeb-un-Nissa interceded on their behalf. Various sources also record that Aurangzeb used to send all the royal princes (her brothers) for the reception of Zeb-un-Nissa each time she entered the court; such was the father's fondness for the wise daughter. However, this trust and affection dramatically changed with time, and Aurangzeb became embittered with his daughter, and again there is no proper evidence to say for what good reasons. There are several speculations about it. That Aurangzeb could never forgive his daughter for her sympathies towards her uncle Dara Shikoh and his son is one of these. Being influenced by Dara's Sufi thoughts, she started interpreting Islam from the Sufi perspective, and this stood in opposition to her father's orthodoxy. Aurangzeb even went to the extent of stalling her *Quran* translation project, something that Zeb-un-Nissa began at the young age of fourteen. Another opinion was that for such free thinking of his daughter about religion, Aurangzeb did not allow Akil Khan to marry her. A group of historians believe that he did not want a subsequent rival to the Mughal throne from this talented daughter's progeny. In her introduction to the first fifty ghazals of Zeb-un-Nissa, Jessie Duncan Westbrook writes that after the affair with Akil Khan, Aurangzeb began to distrust his daughter, and eventually imprisoned her in the fortress of Salimgarh (Lal and Westbrook 17). She also mentions that the imprisonment might have happened because she supported her younger brother Muhammad Akbar who was involved in a conflict of succession. She was discovered to be having a steady correspondence with him during the rebellion in 1681,[18] and in one of those correspondences the prince publicly accused Aurangzeb of transgressions against Islamic law, for which both brother and sister might have been imprisoned. Yet another reason behind Aurangzeb's wrath as surmised by Westbrook was Zeb-un-Nissa's sympathy with the Maratha[19] chieftain Shivaji who lead the rebellion against Aurangzeb. Annie Krieger Krynicki, referring to the memoir of Italian traveler Niccolao Manucci (1638-1717), confirms all these in her biography of Zeb-un-Nissa. She gives a detailed background to the rebellion of Akbar and Zeb-un-Nissa. She writes that her brother Akbar was under Zeb-un-Nissa's tutelage for many years, and she tried to give him a thorough knowledge of religions, including Hinduism. Jahanara, their powerful aunt, also tried to do the same but with no effect. Zeb-un-Nissa was closer to Akbar and could succeed; and though strict about religion, Aurangzeb did not stop her. Krynicki writes,

> Aurangzeb had never forbidden his learned daughter in any way from teaching the doctrines of other religions to her ward; despite his reputation for being bigoted, he always respected Zebunissa's intellectual aspirations. But even under her tutelage, though Akbar developed an appreciation for poetry, he did not appear to pick up any interest in comparative religions and merely followed the accepted orthodox beliefs of his creed. (2005, 159)

But suddenly, in 1681, Akbar declared himself Emperor and planned the assassination of his father Aurangzeb. During this time, he developed some sympathy for Hinduism and became the champion of the Hindus. He wrote several letters to his sister about the tyranny and cruelty of their father, and received her replies. Krynicki informs that he espoused the cause of the Hindus

---

[18] The first half of 1681 was for the Mughals a busy time when contingents were dispatched to lay siege to different Maratha forts in present-day Gujarat, Maharashtra, Karnataka, and Madhya Pradesh. Sambhaji Bhosale, the eldest son of Shivaji, the founder of the Marathas, provided shelter to Aurangzeb's rebel son Sultan Muhammad Akbar. This angered the emperor, and led to a series of battles between the Mughals and Marathas that ended with Sambhaji's execution in 1869.

[19] The Marathas were a warrior clan that rose to prominence during the rule of the sultans of Bijapur and Ahmadnagar in the western Deccan. Shahji Bhonsle, was the first prominent member of the clan. One of his children, Shivaji Bhonsle, emerged as the most powerful figure in the clan to the west, while his other son Vyamkoji, half-brother of Shivaji, was able to gain control over the Kaveri River delta and the kingdom of Thanjavur in the 1670s. These chieftains became the possible threats in Aurangzeb's time with whom his own son Mohammad Akbar aligned.

because it seemed to benefit his political ambitions. Akbar raised the rebellion with the support of the Rathors[20] but could not sustain because of Aurangzeb's cunningness and political maturity. Akbar fled from his camp in haste after realizing that he had no means to fight with the emperor, but he left there the letters exchanged with Zeb-un-Nissa. All those eventually fell in Aurangzeb's hands. He was furious on both children for plotting against him. However, Akbar was subsequently acquitted of his offenses, but Zeb-un-Nissa was not. Krynicki explains the reason,

> The full fury of his wrath fell on the princess. He dealt with her most severely. Even Jahanara, who had supported Dara in the War of Succession and had often plotted against Aurangzeb, did not receive such harsh punishment, but then, he never loved his sister as much as he did his eldest daughter, and that made him feel doubly betrayed. He immediately stopped her annual pension of four lakh rupees, all her property was confiscated, and he ordered her to be imprisoned in the Fort of Salimgarh. Perhaps he even thought she had had a hand in the attempted assassination. (2005, 161-162)

Zeb-un-Nissa did not ask for mercy from her father. She was certainly shocked when she heard of Aurangzeb's decision, but according to Krynicki, she was in no condition to defend herself, "She was certainly not innocent, and her pride and highminded sensibility would not allow her to submit apologies or try to invent lies to cover up. A prince could escape or seek allies to help him, but she, sitting in the harem, could only accept her fate quietly." (2005, 162).

Some sources even suggest that for being a poetess and a musician Aurangzeb punished Zeb-un-Nissa, which is less credible because he was the one who initially allowed her involvement with the poetic circle formed at his court and invited many renowned poets of the time to interact with her. Whatever the reasons were, her life imprisonment and confiscation of her annual pension of 4 lakhs, and above all, the destruction of all records on her, mount up to a crime of a tyrannical father that history would never forgive. After 20 years of imprisonment Zeb-un-Nissa died in 1702, and at that time her father was on a trip to the Deccan. She was buried in the garden of "Thirty thousand trees" outside of the Kabuli Gate or the west gate of Delhi. Later, her remains were shifted to her great grandfather Akbar's mausoleum at Sikandra in Agra because a railway track was laid out by the British government in 1885 at Delhi which went straight over her tomb. Nonetheless, rumors about the existence of her

---

[20] Referring to Rathor Maharajas of Jodhpur, India. They were a military race and tried to remain free though they failed due to the lack of unity and harsh ecological conditions that prevailed in the region.

grave are also interesting. As she spent many years in Lahore and commissioned the construction of several gardens, and ran her charity there, some even believe that she was actually buried in the mausoleum of Nawa Kot on Multan Road in Lahore, Pakistan, which was also her favorite spot for meeting her lover Akil Khan. The story goes like this: Akil Khan, though refused to marry the princess in fear and doubt, was consumed by her love; and abandoning his wealth and property, started living like a mendicant. In her turn, Zeb-un-Nissa gave up living in the palace and came to stay in the garden of Nawa Kot. There she used to feed the needy, and one day Khan reached her, and here the lovers started to spend time together. The burning of Khan in a cauldron by Aurangzeb, according to this view, happened in this garden. This story is nullified by Manucci's records. Krynicki, who writes that Zeb-un-Nissa was forty-five when she was taken to Salimgarh, and around that time, Akil Khan (Aqil Khan Reza, as Krynicki puts it) took Aurangzeb's service once again. He was a long-time married man by then, and when the princess was taken a prisoner, a celebration of the birth of Akil Khan's grandson was going on. Zeb-un-Nissa's lines "Thou shalt attain success, / O happy lover, walking on the heights" from ghazal 44 (in Westbrook's translation) are connected to Akil Khan's rise in the court. However, the Archeological Department of Pakistan has preserved Nawa Kot as the tomb of Zeb-un-Nissa.

Memorialization becomes immaterial when an artist outlives all physical decay through works that have attained immortality. Zeb-un-Nissa is one such woman of her time whose long imprisonment, destruction of all her records, and an inconspicuous death could not erase her from public attention. Ruchir Gupta published a fiction on her secret poetic society titled *The Hidden One* in which he claims that Makhfi or 'the Hidden' was the name of the secret poetic society which was formed to overthrow Aurangzeb's tyrannical reign, which Gupta himself claims to be an imaginary idea. Jadunath Sarkar mentions that the same pen name was used by one of Akbar's wives too. In the imagination of current authors, her name Makhfi thus stands not as an individual's name only; it has gained the status of an institution. She is widely read all over India and Pakistan and her poetry is quite current for the intensity of passion and the artistry of language. A collection of her scattered writings that were compiled in 1724 under the name of the *Diwan-i-Makhfi*, literally meaning 'The Court of the Hidden One', is highly popular. It contained four hundred and twenty-one ghazals and several ruba'is. Subsequently, in 1730 other ghazals were added to the manuscript. Similar collections of poetry by her were printed in Delhi in 1929 and in Tehran in 2001. Its manuscripts are preserved in the National Library of Paris, the Library of the British Museum, the Library of Tübingen University in Germany and in the Mota Library in India. Apart from these poems, it is claimed that she also wrote *Monis-ul-Roh*, *Zeb-ul Monsha'at* and *Zeb-ul-Tafasir*, but there are controversies about the authenticity of her writings. Some even claim that she did not write all those verses of the *Diwan*.

In this chapter, several features and images used by her in the *Diwan-i-Makhfi* have been discussed to give a glimpse of her poetic temperament. These will show that she was individualistic, secular, and free that marked her as a dissenter in the empire.

## *Diwan-i-Makhfi* or the Diwan (Court) of the Hidden

*Diwan-i-Makhfi* is a collection of ghazals mostly and there are a few ruba'is too. The ruba'i originated in Persian literature and was imported into Arabic, Turkish, Urdu, English and other languages. The most popular volume of ruba'is in the world is *Rubaiyat of Omar Khayyam*[21], the English translation of a selection of Omar Khayyam's quatrains by Edward FitzGerald published in 1859. Conversely, a Ghazal is generally a short lyric poem that developed in the Islamic literary tradition. The *Encyclopaedia Britannica* informs that as a genre the ghazal developed in Arabia in the late 7th century from another poetic form called *nasib*, which was an amorous prelude to the *qasidah*. Qasidah is a form of poetry that is close to an ode, and it still exists in the Arabic poetic tradition. These forms of poetry were transported to other cultures through the Arab Muslim expansion. There were two major types of *ghazal*: one native to Hejaz in present-day Saudi Arabia, and the other developed in Iraq. Ghazal is mostly an invention by ancient male writers in the Arab tongue. It is perhaps those of Umar ibn Abi Rabi'ah (eighth century) of the Quraysh tribe of Mecca that are considered as the oldest of ghazals. His *ghazals* are based largely on his own life and are realistic in nature. He recorded his experiences in them and for their liveliness, they continue to be popular with modern readers. However, love, and especially the pangs of hopeless, idealistic lovers, developed as a more popular theme in later ghazals. Jamil al-Udhri, a late seventh-century Arab poet from Hejaz, introduced this theme. His poems were imitated by others in Arabic tradition and by many in Persian, Turkish and Urdu. It was popular till the eighteenth century. The most popular and modernized ghazal was perhaps those of Hafiz, who brought the poetic form to perfection in Persian literature. Interestingly, in Arabic 'ghazal' means praising women, talking to women, philandering, narrating about youth and love-making. This short history shows that both ruba'i and ghazal are components of male literary tradition.

What then could have been Zeb-un-Nissa's reasons for writing in that tradition? Do her writings to fall under the category of women's self-fashioning aimed at complementing the Mughal empire, as Afshan Bokhari claims Jahanara's writings to be? Or did she write to express her feelings that protested

---

[21] Omar Khayyam (1048–1131) was a Persian mathematician, astronomer, philosopher, and poet. He is popularly considered to be the originator of the quatrain or ruba'i. See note 58.

the many tortures her soul was suffering in the empire. Aurangzeb, her father, the mightiest and the cruelest of the Mughal rulers, was indifferent to the family members and especially to his wife and daughters, as far as history informs. Ruchir Gupta shows Zeb-un-Nissa in *Mistress of the Throne* as a little girl complaining to her paternal aunt Jahanara that her father does not like her writing poetry. Why did she write then? Was her poetic society called 'Makhfi' formed to dethrone her father, and later to support her brother Akbar as a culmination of her long-term plan, as Gupta shows in *The Hidden One*? Such questions cannot be answered directly through her poetry, though her poetry itself is a symbol of rebellion. That she was naturally inclined to producing poetry is claimed by her critics. She could instantly produce poetic lines on occasions, and as it was ingrained in her persona, whenever she needed to express herself, she would often do that through poetry. As the few poems that survived beyond her death bear witness, she would often openly declare her rebellious spirit and the pangs of imprisonment through poetry. All the same, one cannot say in an unqualified manner that her dictator father did not like her poetic faculty at all, for Aurangzeb's patronage of contemporary poets and allowing for poetic meets would not then be possible. However, it can be said with some certainty that he feared his daughter's discursive talent, and tried to dissuade her from writing in shrewd ways. Paul Smith refers to Emperor Aurangzeb's inviting Nasir Ali to have a kind of war of wits with her at a poetry tournament arranged by the emperor. Nasir Ali was a poet from Sirhind, famous for his Sufi poetry and was regarded as Zeb-un-Nissa's rival. In the poetry contests of the time, usually one poet would propose a line, usually in the fashion of asking something; and the other poet would answer, contradict, qualify, or expand it by a line or lines in the same meter, rhyming with the proposed line. Aurangzeb invited Nasir Ali to compete with her daughter, and his condition for Zeb-un-Nissa was that if she failed to respond to Nasir Ali's challenge, she would have to renounce poetry forever. Nasir Ali proposed a line like this, "Rare it is to find a black and white pearl." Zeb-un-Nissa spent three remorseful days in search of what to reply with, and finally decided to commit suicide by eating her own diamond ring. Before doing that, she called Imami, a beautiful Hindu woman, her servant and best friend. Imami came and when she found Zeb-un-Nissa in that state she held her in embrace and started crying. Seeing this, Zeb-un-Nissa exclaimed that she found her lines and completed Nasir Ali's proposition with "Except a mingled tear of a beautiful dark girl." Poetry was her retinue in that sense of which she had full command, and it was for this strength and resoluteness that her emperor father felt threatened.

Zeb-un-Nissa's poetry follows the Persian tradition of Hafiz, and hence steadily derives from his Sufi philosophy. He blended the mystical movement of Zoroastrianism, Christianity, Neoplatonism, and Buddhism. At times Hafiz heavily dotes on pantheism that shares the idea that the soul is part of the

Divine and a Sufi is a seeker of complete union with the Divine. Ultimately, the knowledge that Sufism circulates is that a human being himself or herself is that Divine that he or she seeks. This sometimes touches the point of blasphemy, because Sufism often claims the existence of God inside human beings. The Persian poet Husayn Mansur Hallaj (859-922)[22] was prosecuted as a heretic for writing so. Sufi poetry of Hafiz also referred to a divine existence in the poet speaker, which accordingly, was blasphemous to an orthodox emperor like Aurangzeb. Not only had he banned the reading of Hafiz in educational institutions for boys, even private reading in the harem was proscribed. Dara Shikoh was another great influence in Zeb-un-Nissa's life and she started writing poetry under his guidance. Aurangzeb allegedly put his own elder brother to death on the ground that he was blasphemous, even though a war of succession was the real reason behind it. So, poetry, for numerous reasons, was Zeb-ub-Nissa's way of opposing the powerful. Mundane love and love expressed for the divine must have been problematic for Aurangzeb, and Zeb-un-Nissa probably tested his patience on many occasions. Debamitra Kar writes that Zeb-un-Nissa's pen name 'Makhfi' represents her struggle to survive in a restricted life full of negation (my translation, Kar 2011, 83). She refers to the contradictions in Zeb-un-Nissa's life that gave birth to her poetry, and as women's writings originate from "herding contradictions into a single battlefield" (Cixous 2012, 248), Kar labels her a feminist. It is quite difficult to make a definitive statement at that, because many a time her revolt culminates in a bitter surrender to destiny, and hence misses the edge usually found in feminist writings. Sufi stoicism and volcanic rebellion are mingled proportionately in her poetry that give it a unique position in the genre.

As in Hafiz's poetry, Zeb-un-Nissa's poetry also basically talks about 'love'; a recurrent utterance in the ghazals and ruba'is is love in its infinite variety. The first of her ghazals begins in this way,

---

[22] Husayn Mansur Hallaj was born near Siraz (Bayda) in Persia and though was of Persian descent, wrote mostly in Arabic. He was a mystic and was an anomaly among other Sufi poets. Many of the other poets of the time felt it inappropriate to share the inner experiences with the masses that Hallaj used to do regularly through his writings and teachings. He would fall into trances and would attribute those to being in the presence of God. In one of those trances, he uttered "Anal haqq" meaning "I am the absolute Truth" that was taken to mean that he was claiming to be God. He also uttered other controversial statements like "There is nothing wrapped in my turban but God" and "There is nothing inside my cloak except God". Paul Smith in his introduction to the translated volume of Mansur Hallaj's poetry gives a detail of this. For further studies please check the 2016 edition of *I am the Truth (Anal Haqq): Diwan of Mansur Al-Hallaj*, translations and introduction by Paul Smith, published by New Humanity Books, Book Heaven, Australia.

> First, to You, Whose merciful clouds birth's my garden's rose, I
> See:
> lets praise of Your Love, beautify the first couplet of my Divan,
> 						purposely.
> 						(Zeb-un-Nissa, 2012, 63)[23]

The first couplet or the *Matlaa*[24] opens in an invocative tone, in which she praises the Divine love that beautifies her verse, but soon the self of the speaker turns into the Divine when she writes,

> My body and soul thirst for Your Love and like Mansur every
> Grain of this dusty body cries, "We are a part, You're all, we're
> Divinity!
> 						(Zeb-un-Nissa, 2012, 63)

This is some daring expression in a culture dominated by a strong Sunni Muslim like Aurangzeb, and she seems to be aware of this, and writes of the Persian poet Husayn Mansur Hallaj who claimed, "I am the Truth" (Smith, 2012, 7). Hallaj was prosecuted as heretic and was sentenced to death. Zeb-un-Nissa wrote many poems since her adolescence and the first fifty ghazals included in Westbrook's volume are not absolutely her first poems of this kind. These are writings discovered posthumously, and probably she wrote these in her years of imprisonment. It is evident that the first poem in this volume is produced by a mature poet whose life's experiences have taught her to restrict emotions publicly that comes in the fifth couplet,

> And now, not so easily do tears begin like cries off my tongue,
> for drops of blood from my heart as pearls on my lashes all can
> See.

The last couplet or the *Maqtaa*[25] brings the resolution of the poet, who reveals here her identity too,

> Makhfi, bear with patience your pain that is endless and your
> Night of passion...only then Khizer spring of joy with you will be.

---

[23] In this book all quotations from ghazals of *Diwan-i-Makhfi* are chosen from two volumes translated into English, one by Jessi Duncan Westbrook and the other by Paul Smith. The ruba'is are solely from Smith, because Westbrook did not include those.

[24] *Matlaa* is the first *sher* or couplet in a ghazal. It usually sets the tone of the ghazal with its rhyming and refrain pattern.

[25] The last couplet of the ghazal is called the *maqtaa*. It is common in ghazals that the poet's pen name for the poet's pen-name or *nom de plume*, known in Persian as *takhallus* comes in the last couplet. The *maqtaa* is typically a personal statement in a ghazal.

The final couplet of ghazals usually carry the poet's name, and Zeb-un-Nissa uses her pen-name here, and admits the 'pain' that is 'endless', ultimate truth of an imprisoned life. However, the poem ends with a hope of recompense; Khizer is the name of the prophet/saint Khwaja Khizer mentioned in Surah Kahf in the *Quran*, who lives in water and took Musa or Moses (the prophet of Judaism) during one of his strange journeys that the *Quran* describes. Moses got the permission to accompany Khizer on the condition that he would be patient and not ask Khizer any questions on the way. Moses failed to abide by this injunction and was eventually dismissed by Khizer. In the myths deriving from the Indus Valley[26] civilization, there is a Khwaja Khizer whose sanctum is situated in a small islet called Haji ka Tau in River Indus, between Rohri and Sukkur in modern day Pakistan. This shrine was built around the tenth century and is still revered by Hindus and Muslims alike. Khawaja Khizer is called by many other names: Zinda Pir, Darya Laal, Jhoolay Laal, Udero Laal. In popular imagination, he is depicted as a turbaned saint wearing a green robe, white-bearded and riding a fish. The green turban is common in Sufi symbology. So, Zeb-un-Nissa's final resort is Sufism.

It is not strange that she does not lack the wish for retribution even though her specialty is love. Love as a passion and love as spirituality are blended in most of her poems, and she mingles a religious fervor with mundane desires and uses direct Islamic references. For example, in the second ghazal she praises God for being the creator of everything, and then draws a reference to the Prophet of Islam and the holy pilgrimage to Qaba[27] at Mecca. She then negates the importance of specific places for worshipping, and writes, "You will remain my God, no matter where God someone is worshipping" (Zeb-un-Nissa, 2012, 64).

Bold and unorthodox views of religion are significant in her poetry. God is the Beloved in her poetry; and no intermediary is needed between the lover and beloved. This robust negation is either ingrained in her Sufi temperament, or it comes as an adjustment with her imprisoned life in which there was no hope of visiting the places of worship anymore. The second possibility, however, is

---

[26] In the middle of the third millennium BCE an urban culture developed in the Indus Valley spanning an area stretching from today's northeast Afghanistan, through a large area of Pakistan, and into western and northwestern India. Harappa and Mahenjo Daro were two large cities of this civilization.

[27] The *Qaba* or *Kaaba* is the most sacred site in Islam. It is referred to as *Al-Kabah al-Musharrafah* or the "Honored Kabah". It is a cubic structure at the center of the most important mosque in Islam, the Masjid al-Haram in Mecca, Saudi Arabia. One must not confuse it with another Qaba, which is a village in Al Madinah Province (Medina), in western Saudi Arabia.

stronger because the final couplets of most of her poems reveal the pain residing in her heart, as in the second ghazal it appears thus,

> Makhfi, drop your tears here...their quenching torrents rain
> on my heart burning with pain so hot...flames flare as I am
>     sighing!
>
> (Zeb-un-Nissa, 2012, 64)

It is obvious that the flames flaring within are drenched by the tears outside. Even so, the heart's desires do not remain unmentioned. She blatantly writes in the fourth couplet, "my desire's mirror burnishing!" (Zeb-un-Nissa, 2012, 64). The dauntless woman expresses her desires with such succinctness of language that one naturally wonders how it was possible for a woman in her time to write as she did. In ghazal 11 she asks her soul to wake up as spring has appeared. She refers to luscious flowers, wine and winebringer or *Saki*; she also mentions idol for worshipping, and the 'forbidden path' is encouraged. Her beloved is "tyrannical" whom she worships,

> Some pay their worship at the *Kaaba*,
> others in Temples apart are praying...
> Makhfi, think what secret joy is yours,
> always in your heart, your Idol having!
>
> (Zeb-un-Nissa, 2012, 76)

She calls the Beloved "tyrannical" whose indifference to the worshippers resonates in her proud negation of the chronotopes of religion in premodern India. Her denial of *Qaba* or the Temple as a place of worship shows that she was aware of major religious practices in the Empire, and she renounces both Muslim and Hindu places of worship because her Beloved resides in her heart, not in those. This is unimaginable for a woman in her time to utter such proud indifference to the normative values of religion. Her departure from the traditional ways of presenting her inner emotions put her in the position of a modernist. She was much ahead of her time.

Zeb-un-Nissa is even bolder when she addresses the Prophet in the third ghazal. She sets off with appraisal of the expansion of Islam as a religion and praises the Prophet's physical beauty: "Your lips open like rosebuds" (Zeb-un-Nissa, 2012, 65) that makes his wise words flow into hears of the creation. As such, nature never created a more beautiful object that gives happiness to her heart. However, in the fourth couplet of the same ghazal, she reverses the tone and writes that the beauty of the Prophet has trapped her, for which she can be off to the Prophet's trail that she calls "renunciation's path" (Zeb-un-Nissa, 2012, 65). The final couplets bring out the words of renunciation, in which she addresses herself and says if *Kaaba* shuts its doors on her, she would not regret it because she has a 'holier' place that is the beloved's face. The beloved's eyebrows are 'fairer' than Kaaba's gates. It is enough material to enrage a strict Muslim father like Aurangzeb.

Apart from the influence of her uncle Dara Shikoh, Zeb-un-Nisaa might also have drawn from Kabir Das (1398–1448/ 1440–1518)[28] too, who influenced Dara Shikoh in the first place. Kabir's Bhakti movement was largely to reconcile Islam and Hinduism. In his poetry, Kabir renounced the importance of holy places to reach the creator, because the creator lives in all creations,

> O SERVANT, where dost thou seek Me?
> Lo ! I am beside thee.
> I am neither in temple nor in mosque:
> I am neither in Kaaba nor in
> Kailash:
> Neither am I in rites and ceremonies,
> nor in Yoga and renunciation.
> If thou art a true seeker,
> thou shalt at once see Me: thou shalt meet Me
> in a moment of time.
> Kabir says, "O Sadhu ! God is the
>                        breath of all breath".
>
> - (Kabir in Tagore's translation, "Tagoreweb", Accessed on 12 October 2020)

The renunciation of Qaba as the holiest place was such a daunting expression for Zeb-un-Nissa that could bring adverse consequences upon her, were she not already imprisoned. The questioning and denial of authoritarian institutions is always risky, and the executions of William Tyndale (1494-1536) and Joan of Arc (1412-1431) from European history can be referred to here. Tyndale was accused of translating the *Bible* though the unuttered reason for his execution was his dissent to the royal decisions of the time. The same happened with Joan who became a hindrance for the authority of the French church as she claimed to have direct contact with God without any mediation. Zeb-un-Nissa was a graver sinner in that respect. Her bold utterances must have unsettled Aurangzeb, and to stop her progress in collaboration with Dara and Sulaiman

---

[28] Nirmal Das in his volume of Kabir's poetry in translation mentions the controversy regarding Kabir's date of birth. Some historians believe he was born in 1398 while the *Encyclopedia Britannica* records 1440 as his year of birth. He is an Indian mystic poet and saint who initiated the Bhakti movement of Hinduism. Kabir's was an open kind of religious philosophy, which goes against both orthodox Hinduism and Islam.

he must have felt compelled to kill both men. However, he could not stop her pen, and she continued to write within the boundaries of the Salimgarh fort. She challenges the monarch even in confinement, in ghazal 28,[29]

> Uselessly and long I struggled with you, O enemy: from fight nothing
> I won...I guard my treacherous heart, forever from you I am turning.
>
> (Zeb-un-Nissa, 2012, 97).

The following lines show that she believes her complains will reach high heavens. She believes that even though she has lost her life's dreams, her desires still thrive. She comments that she cannot reveal what treasures lie in her purses, but she knows she is richer than the king, who is her father in this case. Her pride is exposed in lines like "Dervish's rags will be more regal than king's majestic clothing" (Zeb-un-Nissa, 2012, 97).

The first couplet of this ghazal may have a connotation of her long struggle as a poet in a monarch's harem, where her poetic faculty was suppressed. Her determination to turn away from the enemy forever comes as her only retribution; fire burns in her, but the next moment she mentions the smoke of sighs that takes away the wrath and leaves her with heartache, not a wish for revenge. The second last couplet's reference to "purse" holding her "treasure" can have a specific meaning of confiscation of all her wealth, which is nullified in the last couplet that reveals her pride in her poor condition. She keeps deep faith in her Sufi life (dervish's rags), which is more important to her than monarchy. Here she voices against accumulation of wealth and expansion of empire because that leaves a monarch desolate in the long run. This idea is even clearer in ghazal 20 in which she discusses the fate of kings. The kings must taste defeat when stronger enemies meet them, and refers to the Turks in the poem; and a philosophical utterance "Our struggles were useless, victories...nothing!" (Zeb-un-Nissa, 2012, 85) follows. She compares the kings with moths that die in the flame they worship; since the kings meet their desires in death. Evidently, she is looking back at the history of the Mughal advent in the Subcontinent; the Turks were their ancestors from Tamerlane's side who came and captured India from the kings. She admits the fragility of kingship, but her address of the conqueror as a "moth" that worships the flame is obviously a stronger metaphor that may have referred to Aurangzeb. The bitterness ends in a hope of Divine justice on the Day of Judgement when the Almighty will repay his

---

[29] The sequence no. is maintained in Westbrook's translation, Smith does not mention it.

tyranny. Her address to the king, "all that blameless blood that you've shed/ shall on your haughty head revenge be taking" is a direct accusation and curse. She describes the field of judgement too: a darkened place that she compares with Karbala[30] and there the sinners will remember their disgrace and 'dark' humiliation; and yet she asks for forgiveness, and asks God to show kindness and have pity for the sinners. This ghazal does not maintain the tradition of the last couplet that reveals the identity of the poet and she ends in a possible reconciliation between the destitute souls and their destination, "And though like Majnun in the wild they roam/ through toils and trials them, home is leading" (Zeb-un-Nissa, 2012, 85).

Islamic references as well as figures from Arabic and Persian literatures that Zeb-un-Nissa was conversant with are amply existent in her poetry; and Majnun[31] is a recurrent figure in her ghazals. That through this figure in some of the poems, she reminisces some fiancé or lover cannot be established, but she calls herself Majnun in many of her poems. In ghazal 24 she writes that she wanders like Majnun driven by love, and sheds tears eternally for Layla (2012, 91). This reminds that she is a true follower of Hafiz whose poetry propounds the idea that the knowledge and love of God is a prerequisite for the attainment of love. Hafiz wrote that humans are beggars of love and as God is the Absolute Beloved, they should gain the Grace of the Almighty. Majnun has different connotations in her poems, but all meanings lead to her own destitute position. In one ghazal, she comments that she will take the course the lover Majnun took when he decided to give up life for his love. She mentions a tiled roof or the dome that undoubtedly are references of the Mughal palaces and buildings where her soul remained captivated (2012, 129). She renounces those for a beggarly life who would sleep on the bare earth. This beggarly speaker talks of

---

[30] Karbala or Kerbala, as Smith spells it, is a town in Iraq where The Battle of Karbala was fought in 680 AD between the army of the second Umayyad caliph Yazid I and a small army led by Husayn ibn Ali, the grandson of the Prophet Muhammad. Husayn was killed in the battle and his suffering and death became a symbol of sacrifice for justice and truth, and especially the Shi'a Muslims mourn his death on the tenth of the Islamic month of Muharram known as the Day of *Ashura*.

[31] Majnun is the male protagonist of *Majnun Layla*, an old story of Arabic origin that describes the affair between 7th-century Arab poet Qays ibn al-Mullawah and his beloved Layla bint Mahdi. Qays and Layla fell in love with each other when they were young, but when they grow up Layla's father doesn't allow them to be together. Qays becomes obsessed with her and composes poetry in her name. People start calling him *Majnun*that literally means "crazy". Ultimately the lovers meet their untimely deaths. This tragic story passed from Arabic to many other languages.

wine and poison in the same breath, since her pangs of love have made those equal (2012, 129).

Wine is an important trope in Hafiz's poetry that functions as a means to bring about spiritual proximity to God. In one ghazal, Hafiz wants to beguile himself in eternal drunkenness, and writes,

> Hafiz, should you seize a cup when the Hour is nigh,
> From the tavern gate, they'll bear you right to the Sky.
>
> (Tr. Ali Salami, 109) [32]

Death in a state of drunkenness is welcomed, as the spirit would meet eternity without any effort. Wine paves the secret way to knowledge, as Hafiz writes on another occasion,

> Stain the prayer mat with wine if the Magian Pir tells you to
> for the traveler knows the rules of the road's stations
>
> (Tr. Ali Salami)

Zeb-un-Nissa's poetry uses wine in numerous ways. Wine and tears are even equated in her lines when she writes that wine flows and tears rain, but they are the same to her (Zeb-un-Nissa, 2012, 129) as none of them can release her pain. Wine and Saki (winebringer) are shelters to a desolate heart in another ghazal, in which she writes, "Wine bringer hurry, bring wine that my dead heart may be enlivening (line 1, ghazal 32 as in Westbrook, quoted in Zeb-un-Nissa, 2012, 101). This wine becomes useless since the speaker's heart is sad and she compares wine with blood (Zeb-un-Nissa, 2012, 109). Wine is part of the festivity, when she writes, "See feast, what better giving guest than wine, music, a party? / Of wines, best…wine of tears; one sad song led to continual singing!" (Zeb-un-Nissa, 2012, 115). Wine is freedom in "O rival, do not steal from my lips cup holding wine of my delight…" (Zeb-un-Nissa, 2012, 99). Conversely, wine is also an image of divinity when she renounces wine in its physical sense saying, "I drank a drink more divine, its fragrance day and night I possess" (Zeb-un-Nissa, 2012, 95). Zeb-un-Nissa is full of contradictions, as Debamitra Kar has remarked.

---

[32] Ali Salami's translations of Hafiz's ghazals are appended to the book *Translating Hafiz: Challenges and Strategies* jointly written by Ali Salami and Saman Rezaei. It was published by Peter Lang in 2019. The first quote is from the book, and the second is accessed from Ali Salami's translations uploaded on Harvard University's blog. Please consult https://blogs.harvard.edu/sulaymanibnqiddees/2016/03/30/ghazal-1-of-hafezs-divan/ .

Wine is sometimes replaced with sherbet, a sweet drink compared with the beloved's kiss, and it is sometimes the lovers' divine delight. In a ghazal, she refers to the love story of Shirin and Farhad and compares herself with Farhad whose acceptance of the Royal challenge made him toil on the mountains till his death. Thus, the poet's eternal thirst for the sweet lips of the beloved is equal to that of Farhad. Here wine is replaced by the 'sherbet of success' that is suggestive of love's culmination (Zeb-un-Nissa, 2012, 99). This Shirin-Farhad[33] pair created by Nizami Ganjavi is also popular in Arabic and Persian literature that recurrently reappears in her poetry. Zeb-un-Nissa never proposes to speak in the persona of the females of these stories, she is always the male lover and a worshipper of female beauty. For example, in "Beloved, from glance You gave beauty flows" she writes that life is rather too short to offer enough gratitude for the beloved's beauty. The beloved is proud of her possessions and she cannot feel the presence of the devoted lover (Zeb-un-Nissa, 2012, 71). She proudly pronounces herself as 'Majnun' at the end of the ghazal who would walk for the beloved's favor all her life. This is certainly a breaking away from the earlier Mughal women who wrote with a subdued gait of feminine modesty. Zeb-un-Nissa's style was traditionally a male style and she overthrew the veneer of feminine shyness when she described the physical beauty of the beloved. It was a rumor that she had a lesbian friendship with some of her maids. Smith refers to Imami, the beautiful dusky Hindu servant who has been mentioned earlier, was a lover of her mistress according to the rumors. Rumors apart, she had a certain sensuousness apparent in her poetry. In one of the ruba'is she writes that the beloved had enchained the lover's heart in her curls, and the "pit" of her "dimpled chin" the lover will find the "fountain Khizer searched for ages for…a mere upstart!"(Zeb-un-Nissa, 2012, 60). The capitalization of the addressed beloved in the ruba'i indicates that she was talking to God, but the pronounced maleness in the speaker's persona is unmistakably present. This may not be unusual for a Sufi poet who is deeply in love with God, but this is not really the usual trend of women's poetry of the time. Lalded[34] (ca. 1320-

---

[33] "Shirin and Farhad" is a story originally titled "Khosrow and Shirin", which is a famous tragic romance written by Nizami Ganjavi (1141–1209), a Persian writer who also created the famous love story "Layla and Majnun". Zeb-un-Nissa has used the image of the lover pairs in many of her ghazals.

[34] Lalded (1320–1392) was also known as Laleshwari and lived in the 14th century Kashmir. She was the originator of a special branch of mystic poetry called vatsun or *Vakhs*. Vakhs literally means "speech" (from Sanskrit *vaak*). She is further discussed in the following chapter.

1393), Mira Bai[35] (ca. 1498-1546) or Habba Khatoon (ca. 1554-1609) were quite known for their poetry before Zeb-un-Nissa, but in their poems and songs the feminine attributes never left them. Lalded considered her Guru or lover as male and also devotedly wrote about Shiva[36] or Sankara (Shiva's other name), and she remains a female devotee in her poetry while she claims that her body and mind are cleansed through the union with him. Submission to the male authority is visible even though Lalded's life is one of silent suffering.

It is to be noted Lalded's nemesis was not a cruel father; she suffered in the hands of a ruthless mother-in-law and perhaps her poetry is not an assertion against patriarchy. However, Lalded kept her mark as a rebel when she finally left home. It is believed that she left unclothed. She was asked whether she felt no shame in her nakedness in front of men, she posed a counter-question whether there was a man around. She wrote that being persuaded by her Guru's teaching she learned to turn within herself and that inspired her to "dance in naked abandon" (Mattoo, 2019, 16). She also learned to internalize abuses and criticism as her "crown", and even though slander followed her wherever she went, she was never deviated from her goals (Mattoo, 2019, 16). Therefore, her attachment with her God or Guru as well as her understanding of men as nincompoops emboldened her to defy man. The fourteenth-century Kashmiri poet's rhetorical question on man is explained by Neerja Mattoo who in her introduction to Lalded's poetry writes that the poet exposed herself to her elements neither out of desire to shock the onlookers, nor was she seeking self-mortification or self-flagellation. She had a 'fine madness' that made her completely unselfconscious and unaware of her physique. That was why she was able to transcend her biological and sexual identity that usually inhabits much of the mental space of women intellectuals, thinkers and writers today, according to Matoo (Mattoo, 2019, 15). So, being completely insensitive about the presence of man was Lalded's poetic culmination, while she remains within the tradition of Kashmiri poetry that uses the female voice in love lyrics.

Conversely, Mira Bai, the early-fifteenth century Bhakti poet, writes of Lord Krishna, for whose love her existence has gone disarray –

> I am pale with longing for my beloved;
> People believe I am ill.
> Seizing on every possible pretext,

---

[35] Mira Bai or Meera was an early 16th-century Rajput princess who was one of the important Bhakti poets of the time. Her poems are of so abound with love and devotion for Lord Krishna that went against the traditions and customs of her time.

[36] Shiva is one of the major deities in Hinduism, who creates, protects, and transforms the universe.

> I try to meet him 'by accident.'
> [...]
> The sweetness of his lips is a pot of nectar,
> That's the only curd for which I crave;
> Mira's Lord is GiridharNaagar.
> He will feed me nectar again and again.
>
> (Tr. Nita Ramaiya, https://allpoetry.com/poem/14327846-I-Am-Pale-With-Longing-For-My-Beloved--by-Mirabai)

Her poet speaker sings that the village doctor comes and feels her pulse but her only remedy is in union with her Lord. Such references to physical union with God are what make Mira Bai's Bhakti poetry exceptional. Habba Khatoon (taken up in the subsequent chapter) is a follower of this tradition and produces pure love lyrics that capture the nuances of feminine existence. She exposes the poet speaker in most of her songs, and her sensuousness and craving for a human lover is not mixed with divine emotion. Her poetry calls for physical union in a more straightforward way, "Every pore of my body aches/ He fills me with desire!" (Mattoo 2019, 101). In this vein, Zeb-un-Nissa writes some ghazals. In one she compares the beloved's physical charm as breath-taking. Her poignant glances, curly hair, eyebrows, eyes, all are weapons that kill the speaker. Extreme desire causes a strange disease in the lover's heart and the cure of her strange disease is death. She mentions a Hindu-beauty whose dark eyes and pouting lips are objects of the lover's worship. "Hindu-beauty" may or may not be a reference to Imami, the girl at her service with whom she could have had an erotic relationship, but she goes on praising the beloved's physical charm till in the final lines that disclose the divine form of the beloved. Her final act of masculine attempt to praise the beloved comes in a ghazal that goes beyond all limits of modesty. She starts in the usual way by praising the physical charms, the black curls and eyes and the dagger-like lashes of the beloved (Zeb-un-Nissa, 2012, 106). The way the earlier poets like Lalded, Mira Bai or Habba Khatoon revealed their poetic faculty is truly bold and went beyond supposed limits of modesty; what Zeb-un-Nissa does to this already advanced poetic tradition, is a daring act; she adopts the male persona to speak her mind, as in this example. This could have been a traditional lover speaking about the many ways the beloved's sensuous beauty appeals to the onlooker. Right after this, she declares that paradise is in the beloved. She addresses the reader as 'fanatic' that clearly has a cynical undertone. She is even bolder when she invites the reader to get drunk and relish the beauty of the beloved as God is here; and her call to forget the path of Kaaba is beyond all limits of expression (Zeb-un-Nissa, 2012, 106). She is a 'heretic' here when she refuses to accept the idea of afterlife, which is a basic principle of Islamic faith. In this ghazal she even rivals God when she asks the beloved to share her/his beauty with her first, while she is waiting for it, not God (Zeb-un-Nissa, 2012, 106). This is one of those instances where she reveals her female identify after speaking in her masculine voice of the male lover. In this way, she has fashioned her trope of gender neutrality to challenge patriarchy. This is her way of uniting many selves and many voices.

Zeb-un-Nissa's attempt at attaining masculinity is visible in her performativity, not only of a male lover, but in most cases of intertextual references from Persian and Arab literatures. She poses to be the male characters, for example, in ghazal 31 (as in Westbrook) she writes, "I am today's Rustom[37]" (Zeb-un-Nissa, 2012, 100). It was not new for a male poet, because ghazal originally comes from the male tradition in Arabic or Persian poetry that uses the male lover's perspective. In that respect, Zeb-un-Nissa treaded the forbidden path, and contributed a new style in Indian poetry.

Ghazal as a form of poetry has allowed Zeb-un-Nissa the freedom and existence necessary to fight the melancholy naturally comes with a long imprisonment. She admits this in a ghazal that she or Makhfi is blessed by God beyond favor as she has received poetry's pearl and can sing songs (Zeb-un-Nissa, 2012, 124). In another, she claims that heaven's secrets flow from her lips as she sings passionately, and the world's wealth is nothing compared to what she possesses (Zeb-un-Nissa, 2012, 125). Comparison of the wealth and 'heaven's secrets' flowing from a poet's mouth clearly shows her stand as a proud poet. This self-assessment and assurance of identity is significant for a woman of pre-modern India. Such assertion of the self was already initiated by Jahanara, but she was not ready to stand against the establishment; Zeb-un-Nissa is an iconoclast, even a rebel who took her position against monarchy and patriarchy. Even in her state of imprisonment, she does not give in, and stays firm in her faith. In a ghazal, her complaints seeing the open sky that seems to mock her captivity is heartbreaking. Each atom of her body cries as she sees the open sky from her imprisonment (Zeb-un-Nissa, 2012, 95), and she begs for a day of joy as she approaches death (Zeb-un-Nissa, 2012, 95). But then she strives again in pride saying, "I still possess my proud eagle soul and have courage under duress" (Zeb-un-Nissa, 2012, 95). Finally, she proudly asserts herself in the last lines in which she claims that her pride will guide all to love's realm (Zeb-un-Nissa, 2012, 96). Pride is forbidden in Islam, but she must have noticed the pride in her tyrannical father who boasted of being a true follower of Islam. She

---

[37] Rustom or Rostam is a protagonist of the tragic story of Rostam and Sohrab, which is a part of the Persian epic *Shahnameh* by the Ferdowsi.

has deified love and fate here, which again does not follow the strict Islamic faith that forbids any deification. Sufism gave her a certain openness of religious thought; it became for her an enabling provision to scrutinize the orthodoxy and severity of Aurangzeb's steadfast Islamism pitted against the multiple cultural existences in the empire. She achieved a deep understanding of the syncretic nature of Indianness (that loomed large in her vision of the future), and understood the necessity of tolerance and sympathy for a peaceful co-existence of diverse communities living in the large region under the Empire. Her poetry is full of images and references borrowed from Islam, Hinduism, Christianity, and Zoroastrianism, and she can be considered a true ambassador of secular thought. Unlike the European secularism that demands the state machinery to be completely free of any kind of religion, hers was embracing all religions, the kind of secularism Emperor Akbar initiated. That is considered to be the state-sponsored secularism in the Subcontinent, even though the negative impact of religion on state polity and public imagination is witnessed across South Asia in later ages.

It, therefore, goes without saying that modern South Asian states and their polity would do good to take a leaf out of Zeb-un-Nissa's book if they aim to consolidate regional progress in the age of globalization, for our histories still emerge from the same wellsprings of the salad-bowl and not the repressive melting pot. Zeb-un-Nissa could be an inspiration for the South Asian citizens in the present situation who are in need of a guiding light.

Sudden revisionary notions of ethnicity expressed by the Indian government reflected in Citizenship Amendment Act (2019) and National Register of Citizens in recent times have shown once again how flawed and fatal the division of the Indian Subcontinent was, and to what extent the seeds of hatred and mistrust has been ingrained in the millions of people divided by religious faith. Subversive perspective of history and covert secularism have become threatening issues in the comparatively new nation state of Pakistan, as Declan Walsh writes in his recent book *The Nine Lives of Pakistan: Dispatches form a Divided Nation*. Bangladesh has been suffering the same. So, conflict of religion that became the reason for such a devastating blow to the integrity of British India, which was world's largest empire in Aurangzeb's time, could be minimized if Zeb-un-Nissa's tolerance and syncretism had sustained existence and growth.

The ghazals show that the writer had a thorough understanding of different religion and their scriptures. She mentions *Kaaba* at Mecca or temple pilgrims visit in the same breath, and it does not matter where one worships since God is only one and the same (Zeb-un-Nissa, 2012, 64). She mentions Mohammed, Moses, David, Abraham, Jacob, Joseph, and in the same breath she writes that

*Dissenting Songbird in the Aviary* 131

hers is not less holy than Brahmin's faith (Zeb-un-Nissa, 2012, 83). The range of her knowledge is broad, and the way she blends several references is wonderful. In a ghazal, she compares her imprisonment with Jacob's blindness (Zeb-un-Nissa, 2012, 95) and elsewhere she refers to several mythical historical figures like Alexander[38], Hatim Tai[39], Rustom, Zulaikha[40], Jamshid[41], Huma[42], and many more, that shows that she was a richly educated woman who had command over available literatures of the age. The maturity of her writing came from a deep knowledge of world literature and the varied experiences of life.

What strikes one most is her sensuousness and melancholic mood that has given her poetry a Keatsian quality. The poets of the romantic revival period in England were her late contemporaries. There are striking similarities between her verses and the imagery used in the romantics. For instance, she writes of rays covering the mountain's skirts that touches the creeks (2012, 151). The beautiful image vividly portrays the Himalayan ranges where the creeks create a panorama of lights. In the same breath, she compares the lips of the beloved with rosebud and ruby that are wine red, and the beloved's laughter is compared with those creeks flowing down the mountains (Zeb-un-Nissa, 2012, 151). If someone reads these lines, one is perhaps reminded of these,

---

[38] Alexander III of Macedon (356 BC-323 BC), commonly known as Alexander the Great, was a conqueror and a great statesman.

[39] Hatim al-Tai (b. unknown- 578) or Ḥatim bin Abd Allah bin Saʻad aʻt-Ṭaiyy was an Arabian poet who belonged to the Ta'i tribe of Arabia, but he was more popular as a benevolent man famous for charity. There is a proverbial phrase "more generous than Hatim" that has emerged from the many stories about his charitable work.

[40] Julaikha or Zuleikha is the wife of Potiphar or Aziz (Islamic tradition), a captain of Pharaoh's guards during the time of Jacob and his twelve sons. She is a minor character in the Hebrew *Bible* and *Quran*. According to the Book of Genesis, she advanced towards Joseph for his beauty and falsely accused him of attempted rape after he had rejected her. This resulted in Joseph's imprisonment. In Islamic world, this story has many versions in many languages. Its most famous version was written in the Persian language by Jami (1414-1492) in his *Haft Awrang* (Seven Thrones). In Sufi tradition Zulaikha's longing for Yusuf is interpreted as the soul's quest for God. The epic love of Yusuf and Zulaikha has a classic literary example from East Bengal or present-day Bangladesh): the Banglaversion of *Yusuf-Zulekha* by Shah Muhammad Sagir.

[41] Jamshid was the legendary king of ancient Persia who had a magic cup in which one could the whole world.

[42] The Huma or Homa is a mythical bird like the Phoenix. It is found in Iranian legends and fables, and has been used as a motif in Sufi and Diwan poetry. It is said never to alight on the ground; it spends its entire life flying invisibly high above the earth.

> Tasting of Flora and the country green,
>   Dance, and Provencal song, and sunburnt mirth!
>     O for a beaker full of the warm South,
> Full of the true, the blushful Hippocrene,
> With beaded bubbles winking at the brim,
> And purple-stained mouth;
> 
>    ('Ode to a Nightingale' by John Keats, in Abrams, 2000, 849-850)

Surprisingly, both Keats and Zen-un-Nissa were writing of pain of life with death looming large in their vision; Keats fighting with tuberculosis, and Zeb-un-Nissa with a life sentence decreed by her father. What is even more evocative of the modern readers' fancy is the way they surpassed the idea of death: Keats longing to leave the real for the world of imagination with the help of poetry,

> Away! away! for I will fly to thee,
> 
>  Not charioted by Bacchus and his pards,
> 
> But on the viewless wings of Poesy,
> 
>   Though the dull brain perplexes and retards:
> 
>    Already with thee!
> 
>     ('Ode to a Nightingale' in Abrams, 2000, 850)

Zeb-un-Nissa's Bacchus has a different connotation in her ghazals, while she takes her prayers as her divine cup. She does neither need a mosque to pray, nor does she depend on a friend to drink wine. Her drink is poetry (Zeb-un-Nissa, 2012, 103). Therefore, poesy is a harbinger of rightful artistic pride with all its subtlety, and she sings the glory of love through it, and the sensuousness of the flora is brough in while she writes that hyacinth and jonquil pray with her while she chants her poem (Zeb-un-Nissa, 2012, 151). She used those expressions in her poetry for which the romantic poets of England were applauded for beauty and novelty, but she remained unknown because she is the subaltern in the world literary arena as both a Muslim and a woman from the East!

## How to appraise Zeb-un-Nissa's modernity

The boldness of expression and sensuousness Zeb-un-Nissa possessed and displayed in her poetry is unimaginable for a woman of the pre-modern period. It is a pity that Zeb-un-Nissa was born in a world that was not yet ready to accept her kind. A woman, a poet, a rebel - she was unique in her many hats, all the more because none of these were extraneous to her personality. As a Sufi poet, she must have faced a double-edged sword at Aurangzeb's court. He free spirit engaged in poetry was nourished by the Sufi belief system, and on the other hand, she was always threatened by the strict Sunni Aurangzeb's many prohibitions that demanded an end to her freedom. She was a woman, but could not submit to the society's injunctions that usually asks a woman to act a woman. She was a feminist, but could not become one in public, and so used her masculine voice in poetry borrowed from a masculine tradition. She was a rebel, but did not have the necessary support to raise a rebellion. Hence, she did what she could do; write poetry. Within the boundary of the Mughal harem in the first part of her life, she wrote in secret; and finally, when the boundary stretched to the length of a prison house, she continued to write in a plaintive temperament. She was a poet of love, hope and devotion, and these became her weapon to fight oppression. She must have known about Lalded, Mira Bai and Habba Khatoon, though she never mentions them. Perhaps, the poetry of those subaltern women poetry never crossed the threshold of Aurangzeb's palace, and as they were not collected in written form at that time, it was improbable that she read them. However, it would not be wrong to say that she unknowingly became their progeny. She defined her own poetic cult through a unique blend of all that was profound in the East, and simultaneously contributed to Indian women's writing. She borrowed ideas from different religious creeds and movements, and became a true spokesperson of syncretic Indian culture. If she is seen as part of the Mughal tradition today, and is unnecessarily exoticized by the writers of historical fiction, it must be part of a larger political scheme. Aurangzeb has already been vilified by the mainstream historians as a ruthless monarch. In traditional Hindu historiography he is the demonic ruler who unleashed his wrath upon the Hindus of the land, and embarked on a spree of destroying Hindu architecture and defiling Hindu culture; a claim that is not always substantiated with historical evidences. In today's public imagination that is pervaded by an ultra-right neo-nationalist discourse, the perception of Aurangzeb is as a sectarian Mughal ruler; hence, the profanity with which women of his harem are shown as lusty, unscrupulous, and revengeful, cannot be taken at face value. As a work of contemporary literary history, this analysis of the poetry of Zeb-un-Nissa is for one, testimony to the complex variety that the harem abounded with. We can continue to argue why Aurangzeb in the first place permitted Zeb-un-Nissa's poetic pursuits to flourish, but it is beyond debate that her life and work has systemically resisted the imposition of a merely objectified identity. If Zeb-un-Nissa signified for Aurangzeb a discursive entity challenging patriarchy with her knowledge, she also stands as a challenge to monolithic historiography that has on a protracted basis taken only a reductive view of the period.

# 5

# The Plaintive Songbird beyond the Aviary: Habba Khatoon's Lol[1]

> Before the moon I am, what a woman is, a woman of power, a woman's power, deeper than the roots of trees, deeper than the roots of islands, older than the Making, older than the moon.
>
> — (Le Guin, 1990, 61)[2]

Habba Khatoon was popularly known in 16th century Kashmir as 'Zoon' or 'Moon', a name her parents fondly gave on account of her extraordinary beauty; and like Zeb-un-Nissa, with all her beauty and talent, Khatoon too met a tragic end. Her poetry spurts from the depth of her womanhood, which again epitomized love and sacrifice, as we shall see in this chapter. As we go into the life and works of this extraordinary Kashmiri beauty, it would be worthwhile to keep in mind Neerja Mattoo's observation that, "there are nuances that only a woman can introduce, while describing the many shades of suffering which she has undergone" (2019, 85). In her analysis, Mattoo gives Habba Khatoon the credit of depicting "the pain of being a woman, whether as a tortured daughter-in-law or an abandoned wife" (2019, 85-86). Khatoon's first marriage was a disaster because it was a complete mismatch; and her second marriage with the king of Kashmir was but a phase of short-lived happiness, cut off as they were by the whirlwind of politics. Her poetry, which can be called life-writing, effuses Khatoon's pain; and her complaint against the torture she went through, cumulatively making her a true feminist voice of Kashmir in pre-modern India when feminism was still far from being a fad. The earlier chapters narrated how the Mughal empire became an aviary for upper-class women who enjoyed limited freedom under its surveillance. Khatoon was outside of this aviary since she was born in a modest rural family of Kashmir; and when she had entered

---

[1] Khatoon means 'lady'. Some writers spell it 'Khatun', as Neerja Mattoo does. Conversely, Shyam Lal Sadhu calls her Haba Khatoon. In this book the traditional spelling has been used. Lol is a specific genre of Kashmiri love poetry or song-lyric introduced by Habba Khatoon in the sixteenth century. Aarnimal also practiced this poetry in the late eighteenth century.

[2] The quote is from *Tehanu: The Last Book of Earthsea* by the American author Ursula K. Le Guin (Atheneum, 1990, p. 61)

the Kashmiri aristocracy through her marriage with Yusuf Shah Chak[3], Kashmir was not yet annexed with the Mughal empire. However, as the queen, she had to receive the blows of Mughal imperial ambitions both in independent Kashmir and later when the province was captured by the Mughals. Being separated from her loving husband, she met her death in penury and pain. Lifelong suffering inspired pure poetry from her lips, and she became known as 'the nightingale of Kashmir' who poured forth "her soul abroad in ecstasy" as John Keats in "Ode to a Nightingale" defined the bird's song.

It is not surprising that Khatoon's poetry has been reigning in the Kashmir valley for centuries, because there has neither been an end to pain and suffering for women, nor has poetry ceased to be the grail of holding human emotion. A good example of the continuity of such poetic expression from Kashmir, which has the adverse accolade of being the world's most militarized zone, could be poems by Rumuz E Bekhudi,[4] which are a poignant expression of grief and loss that people of the valley are beset with, especially after the abrogation of Article 370 from the Indian Constitution that hitherto conferred a special status to Kashmir. Her poem 'A Letter' addressed to "Dear friends from a free land", talks about living in gloom and despair, in which a woman's voice represents the grief of the whole community. Writing poetry is the only way out in such a situation,

> What else can be done here?
> We have lots of idle time and
> the ingredients are in abundance, skills as well.
> Phonecalls and the Internet are scarce.
> Grief isn't.
> What else can be done
> in a country without a post office
> the privileged, left way back
> carrying their gods in their arms
> like babies?
> Will write back soon.
> Yours,
> "Call me Ishmael tonight"
>                     (Lines extracted from 'A Letter' by Rumuz E Bekhudi)

---

[3] Yusuf Shah Chak was the last independent ruler of Kashmir. It is claimed that he married Habba Khatoon after she had been divorced from her first husband. Indeed, it was he who arranged for the divorce, according to one section of the critics. On the other hand, it is also claimed that Khatoon entered his harem as a *tawaif* or courtesan, and remained his lifelong mistress.

[4] Rumuz E Bekhudi is a pen name of a living female poet of Kashmir whose poetry has attracted global readers via internet.

Be it the aggression of the Mughal empire or the aggression of a *Ramarajya*[5] in the present time, Kashmir's unending trysts are symbolized in "the country without a post office", Agha Shahid Ali's[6] famous coinage. Kashmir is now not only a 'country' without a post office, it is a 'country' where women need to learn living without their men who were either killed or abducted. Today's readers need to learn that the tradition of Kashmiri women forced to live without men began as early as with Khatoon, when the earliest colonial aggression of the Mughals affected the beautiful valley. Khatoon's poetry, therefore, still holds currency with its subjective feminine emotions, and recent poets also find her poetic diction and expressions unsurpassable. Rumuz-E-Bekhudi takes her pen name from Iqbal, but the influence of Khatoon's imagery is pervasive in her poetry. As a pioneer of Kashmiri resistance poetry therefore, Habba Khatoon's is a voice that needs to be reassessed at this juncture of history that can barely be confined within the political boundaries of India. This chapter reads through her poems at length, and tries to see how she became a representative voice of Kashmir through blending subjective emotion with the predicament of livelihood of a Kashmiri woman.

Habba Khatoon was no ordinary woman. In one of her poems, she comments,

> I read the Koran in one attempt
> I didn't make a single mistake
> But I could not read the text of love
> What will you gain from my death?
> 
> (Mattoo, 2019, 134)

The woman who dared to ask her creator this audacious question was not built in a day, nor was she molded from one single form. Habba Khatoon was more than a mystery, for which she was even thought to be just an imagined entity, a myth, physically non-existent. Her identity is still an enigma to many Kashmiris. There is hardly any extensive biography of her in English. Shyam Lal

---

[5] *Ramarajya* is a contested term that literally means "the rule of Rama". Mohandas Karamchand Gandhi defined it as a state where there would be democratic rule and equal rights for all. In a 1929 issue of the weekly *Young India*, which Gandhi published from 1919 to 1931, he wrote, "By *Ramarajya* I do not mean Hindu Raj. I mean by *Ramarajya*, Divine Raj, the Kingdom of God. For me, Rama and Rahim are one and the same deity. 1 acknowledge no other God but the one God of truth and righteousness." In the recent years, the concept of *Ramarajya* has become a tool of oppression for non-Hindu and Dalit citizens of India, as a result of the rise of rightwing politics in India, where the state promotes a majoritarian point of view.

[6] Agha Shahid Ali (1949-2001) was a Kashmiri born American poet who relentlessly wrote on Kashmir. His poems are pervaded with longing for home, memory and nostalgia were prominent themes. *The Country Without a Post Office* is a 1997 poetry collection and the titular poem in it has been referred to by Rumuz in her poem.

Sadhu's book is a well-researched one on her life and poetry, in which he has tried to relate her life with the history and culture of Kashmir. Som Nath Wakhlu (S. N. Wakhlu) wrote her biography in a fictional mode, and there he tries to establish her as a mystic, which she perhaps was. Many claimed her to be a mere courtesan, a singer, who became a favorite mistress of the king of Kashmir. Whatever she was, the apparent freedom of physique and spirit that marked her poetry signaled not only her personal progressiveness but also the openness of Kashmiri society in the sixteenth century.

### Habba Khatoon's life

Habba Khatoon is believed to have been born in 1554, ten years before Shakespeare was born and four years before Elizabeth I ascended the British throne. Wakhlu writes that she was born in August, 1551. There are all kinds of surmises about her date of birth. Some other writers claim that Khatoon was born between 1563 and 1569 during Hussein Shah's regime in Kashmir. Her father was Abdulla Rathar or Abdi Rathar, a young merchant from Srinagar who was at the service of a rich merchant Khawaja Amin. Her mother, a pretty woman without any name in Wakhlu's book, was a chieftain's daughter, who came from a noble descent of Gurez[7], a border district in Kashmir. Abdi Rathar came to Gurez with his master, married there and stayed back, when his master left for his new destination. Mattoo writes in her book that Khatoon's maternal grandfather was a 'Bota Raja'. Bota is a term used by the Kashmiris to identify the inhabitants of Ladakh, Baltistan and Gilgit who have Mongoloid features. Mattoo mentions the claim that Khatoon's mother was given to the Kashmiri trader for the money her father owed him. Whatever the case was, such a rumor reflects the miserable condition of women, who were treated as mere objects. After marriage, Abdi Rathar brought his beautiful wife to Srinagar. They moved to the village of Chandhara from Srinagar because Khatoon's father did not do well in the town, and wanted to lead a peaceful secluded life in the scenic countryside. Wakhlu's book informs that Khatoon's father had left Srinagar because of the corruption and riots taking place in the town. Perhaps Wakhlu reminds the readers of the decline of the Hussain Shah dynasty in Kashmir while the great Mughal Emperor Akbar was testing his military prowess to annex it. Around that time, Khatoon was born in a modest country house in Chandhara.

Wakhlu narrates a very long history of her birth, claiming that her parents had faced a lot of difficulties for the want of a child. Zoon was a late born child and

---

[7]Gurez lay on the trade route of Gilgit and the Northern Territories in present say Pakistan. (Mattoo 2012, 87)

as a girl she was, perhaps, not much welcome. Her parents tried all means and suggestions that came their way to have a child. In this connection, Wakhlu presents a very old syncretic Kashmiri culture that shows both Hindu and Muslim sages equally revered by both communities. Khatoon's parents went to their village doctor Kesho Pandit (a Hindu) who suggested them to visit Crar-i-Sheriff, a holy shrine dedicated to Sheikh Noor-ud-Din or Nund Rishi, who was an ancient sage in Kashmir. Khatoon's parents went to the shrine, prayed, and subsequently waited eagerly for the child's birth. Finally, when she was born, her father was upset because it was a girl child; he did not take her into his arms. Only when he learned from a fortune-teller that she was born with good signs and would become a queen, was he comforted. Hence, it is understandable that even though Kashmir was not politically as riotous as Delhi or Agra, and had a comparatively more peaceful living condition, women's lives were not much different from what has been witnessed in the cases of Gulbadan, Jahanara or Zeb-un-Nissa. Rather, as she was born in a modest merchant family, her education may not have been a serious concern for her parents. We are informed that she had the best available education, as Wakhlu puts it in his book,

> Zoon's parents gave her a good education as far as was possible in those times. By the time she grew up she learnt playing on several musical instruments from the apprentices in her father's workroom. The educational experience coupled with her growing beauty, charm and good humor gave her a reputation which very quickly spread to other villages. The city gallants visited her father's workroom to look at her but she kept them at a distance. Her grandfather began to take keen interest in her poetry. He used to admire and encourage her and he took her, off and on, to some of the good poets of Srinagar, whom he knew and they taught her prosody. On the advice of Sayyid Mubarak, a Sufi, she began to experiment with Persian metre. From childhood she delighted in reciting poems of the great poets of Persia. The exquisite of Saadi sharpened her wits and generated in her great zest for singing and composing rhymes. (Wakhlu, 2007, 61)

From this description, it is rather difficult to estimate exactly what kind of a grooming she had. It can be said that she was sent to a *maktab* or school near the village mosque where she would learn Arabic alphabets from a Moulvi[8]. She learned Arabic and Persian, and also learned to make ink from charcoal dust and write on paper. She was a brilliant student. Gradually she learned Persian poetry and started expressing herself in verses. She used to stay a major part of her days in her father's shop busying herself in embroidery and entertaining

---

[8] Moulvi or Mawlawi is a religious title given to Muslim religious scholars.

the ladies who visited the shop. She perhaps learned the air of good breeding form such interactions. She was good at singing, and Wakhlu records an event of an uncle of Khatoon visiting her house when she was a small child that is significant. Listening to her beautiful voice, he showed interest in training her in music under his guidance. Wakhlu refers to Ahmad, a son of this uncle who taught her to sing and play the *sarangi*[9], and with whom Khatoon had a very early intimacy.

From the first part of her biography, it becomes clear that a girl of Khatoon's time did not have much of choices in Kashmir. That she would be grown into a fine woman and go on to have a well-off groom was the expectation of parents, and one did not have any other option. Khatoon spent her days helping her parents in household chores, singing while she fetched water or picking vegetables or fruits in the orchard with girls of her age, and would have daydreams of a royal groom coming her way. Initially, she was in love with her cousin Ahmad, but the boy became limp forever after an accident, and lost all prospect of marrying her. Ahmad's untimely death in a few months came as a shock for Khatoon, and she had a pessimistic turn in her temperament since then.

The exquisite beauty and a blossoming poet that Khatoon was, it became very difficult for her parents to find her a 'proper' match. Not many scholarly books are written on Habba Khatoon's life. It is difficult to chronicle her actual history because the available information about her mostly came through oral records. It is evident that such oral records are usually tainted with rumors and speculations. Books are available on her life in Kashmiri language, but hardly there is any good one in English. Neerja Mattoo's *The Mystic and the Lyric: Four Women Poets from Kashmir* gives a brief account of her poetic career. S. N. Wakhlu's fictional biography makes it rather difficult to assess how much of the description is imaginary and what percentage of facts are there. The same has happened with books written on her in other languages. Wakhlu admits that Kashmiri poetry largely existed in oral tradition and the lives of poets are mostly wrapped in mystery (Wakhlu, 2007, v). Even though Khatoon became the queen of Kashmir, she did not receive any particular favor from the mainstream historians. Mattoo writes,

> It is almost as if her [Khatoon's] life was mapped by a team of surveyors, each of whom worked independently of the other, following the contours of their separate territories without consultation or coordination between them. Add to this liberal doses of imagination and the result is a life

---

[9] A Sarangi is a musical instrument with a skin-covered resonator. On it there are four playing strings made of goat gut accompanied by seventeen sympathetic strings made of steel.

shrouded in mystery and romance and in this, the truth is hard to find. (2019, 90)

These speculative and fictionalized biographical narratives bear witness to her helplessness when she was bound to marry an idler; and like the other great female poet of Kashmir, Lalleswari or Lalded (1335-1385), had an unhappy conjugal life. Her first husband was Aziz Lone, the idle and dull-brained son of a merchant in a neighboring village. That man never understood the value of Khatoon. To add to the angst of a gifted but unhappy woman, a rumor around Khatoon's mysterious spiritual power that scared her husband, was spread. Mattoo mentions that the specific version of Khatoon's life that presents her mother as a 'Bota' also presents her spiritual power, which shows some internal racial prejudice within the region. There have been several screen representations of Khatoon's life on India's national television network. A biopic in 13 episodes in 2017 titled *Habba Khatoon* shows that she discloses her strange power to her husband, and he takes fright and believes her to be a witch. He instantly informs his mother about this and refuses to live with her any further. Eventually, she gets divorced. This reminds of the demonizing of women that happened throughout the medieval ages in Europe and Asia. It was easy to declare a woman as a demon to ostracize or kill her. Wakhlu calls her marriage an unhappy one, and shows that a matchmaker name Mohamdoo was largely responsible for her marriage with the village brat. It happened in 1564, and Khatoon was thirteen in Wakhlu's speculation. Wakhlu does not mention anything about her spiritual power, rather blames the jealous mother of the groom for being instrumental in bringing about the dearth of happiness in Khatoon's conjugal life, if of course, there was a chance of any marital bliss. The old and jealous mother-in-law goes to a local sorcerer and takes help of his black magic to poison Aziz's mind against Khatoon. She uses a magic potion in his drink, for which he becomes hostile towards his wife. This interpretation by Wakhlu is less credible than the other interpretation he has about Aziz Lone's inferiority complex. Khatoon's excellence in beauty and brilliance of intellect worried her husband who literally found himself inadequate compared to her merits, and thus started bullying and beating her; but the blame went on his mother, a woman in the house and her connection with black magic. This episode of Khatoon's life is presented on silver screen as well. Bashir Budgami produced and directed the first full-length television feature film of Kashmir titled *Habba Khatoon* in 1976. In this film, Budgami does not show any use of magic, but pure logic of domestic repression and harassment. Being instigated by a jealous mother, Khatoon's slothful husband tortures her, and finally she jumps into a river to commit suicide. She is rescued by a villager and brought back to her parents. The village council arranges a meeting between the two families, and they decide to arrange a divorce between them. This film radically differs from Wakhlu, who does not mention the drowning episode at all, and also shows that the divorce is arranged by Yusuf Shah Chak who wants to marry Khatoon. The king threatens Aziz Lone, and additionally pays him a handsome amount to get her free. Wakhlu is, however, sympathetic towards Aziz and shows that the husband realizes his shortcomings and becomes remorseful after the divorce. Both Budgami and Wakhlu refer to Khatoon's meeting with Yusuf Shah in a field where she sings a song that the king of Kashmir overhears and proposes to marry her since she refuses to become his concubine or a courtesan. In 1988 the renowned film director of India Muzaffar Ali attempted *Zooni* in Hindi which could not be completed due to political turmoil in Kashmir. The Doordarshan TV drama serial on Khatoon aired in 2017 that has been mentioned earlier, was in 13 episodes. Directed by Ayash Arif, it is an interesting and more modernized take on her life. It begins in *medias res*, narrating Khatoon's attempt at suicide at a later stage in life when she was profoundly frustrated. She is eventually rescued by some courtiers of Yusuf Shah Chak. The king was visiting with his courtiers around the rural region of Kashmir at that time. They restored Khatoon with her parents. Put in a flashback technique, the narrative of this TV series coincides with Wakhlu's book. The only exception is the mysterious nature of Khatoon's character or her bouts of frenzy causing scare to her husband, that Wakhlu's narrative significantly does not hinge upon. While the TV drama shows Khatoon as a hysteric woman so much so that her husband stays away from nuptial union, Wakhlu's historicizing gives a more balanced portrayal, presumably drawing upon credible facts as might have been available in oral history. While the attempt at archiving the life and work of an important Kashmiri poet hitherto undocumented in literary history is appreciable, the problem of male gaze in presenting a talented woman as weird and frenzied can hardly be taken as oversight. As a popular medium, the screen representation of Khatoon walking in the fields by the River Jhelum where she meets the king of Kashmir, is romantic, but to a conscientious viewer, the patriarchal slant remains a challenge that this chapter interrogates at length.

There is a strong rumor that Khatoon was a courtesan at Yusuf Shah Chak's court, not actually his queen. Wakhlu opposes this view with his narration of how the marriage between the king and Khatoon took place. The king helps Abdi Rathar in all arrangements, including bearing all expenses for the wedding. Budgami supports the same view. However, Mattoo mentions the other possibility of Khatoon being a courtesan, which is explained to some detail in her book. She mentions that Khatoon created *Rast-e Kashmiri*, a popular composition in Sufi tradition, which enriched her own repertoire of songs. With this Mattoo also informs of the rumor that she was a professional singer, not the Kashmiri queen. The reason behind the existence of such rumors, according to Mattoo, might have been the difficulty for people to accept the fact that a moderately educated village girl like her became and remained the consort of a king; a fact not easy to grasp by the Kashmiri aristocrats. Some scholars even suggested that Khatoon's existence was a product of people's imagination to create a love lore that was quite popular and prolific in Kashmiri literature. This imagination needed a woman to connect with Yusuf Shah Chak to create a memorable love story. Obviously, this claim is very weak and Khatoon remains a real woman standing on the solid ground of her poetry, the footprints of which are ineradicable.

Kashmir is the northernmost geographical region of the Indian Subcontinent and it covers a large area today that includes the territories of Jammu, Kashmir and Ladakh under the administration of the Indian government. On the other side, it covers the Pakistani-administered territories of Azad Kashmir and Gilgit-Baltistan. China holds the territories of Aksai Chin and the Trans-Karakoram Tract. The Kashmir valley in Khatoon's time was a free state between the Himalayas and the group of mountains in the lesser Himalayan region called Pir Panjal Range. Till the mid-19th century, it remained so. Kashmir was an important center of Hinduism and Buddhism in the first half of the first millennium, and in the mid-ninth century, it was dominated by Kashmir Shaivism.[10] Around the first half of the 14th century, Kashmir came under Muslim rule, Shah Mir being its first Muslim ruler in 1339. It was the beginning of the *Salatin-i-Kashmir* or Shah Mir dynasty. Kashmir became a part of the Mughal Empire in 1586 under the rule of Akbar (1542-1605) and it remained so till 1751. The last ruler of this dynasty was Yusuf Shah Chak, Khatoon's husband, and the valley with its multicultural roots adds an interesting dimension to her life.

Akbar ascended the Mughal throne in 1556 and conquered Kashmir in the 30th year of his reign. Abul Fazl in the *Akbarnama* writes about Akbar, "The wise and far-sighted man is aware that in every period it is indispensable that there be a ruler who shall be strengthened by God's help and made fortunate by eternal blessings" (Fazl, 1902, 35). Though he called Emperor Akbar a 'ruby' preserved in 'the embryonic sac of the mine' to become fully matured to be fit for a 'royal diadem' (Fazl, 1902, 46), the annexation of Kashmir under the Mughal empire was not a smooth task even for the invincible Akbar. Though he

---

[10] Kashmiri Shaivism, also called Pratyabhijna that means "Recognition" in Sanskrit, is a religious and philosophical system of India originating in a group of several monistic and tantric religious traditions that flourished in Kashmir from the latter centuries of the first millennium CE. It worships the god Shiva as the supreme deity. These traditions have survived only in a reduced form among the Brahmans of Kashmir. There have been some efforts to revive them in India and globally. Further information can be accessed from https://www.britannica.com/topic/Kashmiri-Shaivism and https://iep.utm.edu/kashmiri/#H1.

was a great ruler, he had to wait for quite many years to finally capture Kashmir. Abul Fazl does not as elaborately describe Akbar's invasion in Kashmir as he does in the case of the former Mughals like Mirza Kamran or Mirza Haider Dughlat[11], but the way he tried to capture it was not fair. Ashraf Wani writes,

> Yet, the fact remains that notwithstanding having succeeded to cross the ring of mountains around Kashmir, none of these invaders (except for the latter [Akbar's invasion] which was supported by a disgruntled faction of nobility), could succeed to occupy Kashmir. In the absence of any local alliance, they faced united resistance from all sections of the society and were forced to leave. (Wani, 2012, 185)

This unity of people was declining for which Khatoon's father allegedly left Srinagar, as Wakhlu narrated in his book. Wani again writes, "no medieval empire builder who emerged on its borders could succeed to incorporate Kashmir in his empire even if all of them aspired and tried for it" (Wani, 2012, 185). If that was the case, it was not possible for Akbar to succeed without unfair means. According to Abul Fazl, Akbar had always cherished the idea of conquering Kashmir as it was situated close to the borders of the Mughal empire. Akbar's grandfather and father had shown great interest in having Kashmir as a part of their empire because apart from its geographical positioning, Kashmir had, and still has, natural beauty, economic potential, and a soothing healthy climate. Jahangir, the fourth Mughal emperor, used to recite Amir Khusrau's[12] lines –

> Agar firdaus bar roo-e zameen ast,
> Hameen ast-o hameen ast-o hameen ast.

The English translation goes like this:

> If there is a paradise on earth,
> It is this, it is this, it is this by
>
> (Tr. Habibuddin Ahmed)

---

[11] Mirza Haider Dughlat (1499-1551) was the son of Mohammed Hussain, a chieftain of the Dughlat tribe living in the territory of present-day Southern and Southeast Kazakhstan and Kashgar. His mother was Princess Khub Nigar, the third daughter of the ruler of Moghulistan, Yunus Khan. He was the representative of the first generation of Mughals in Kashmir who invaded Kashmir first in 1531 and again in 1540.

[12] Amir Khusrau or Ab'ul Hasan Yamin ud-Din khusrow (1253–1325 ) was a Sufi poet, musician, and scholar. He was a mystic and a spiritual disciple of Nizamuddin Auliya of Delhi. He is generally regarded as the father of the devotional form of the Sufi music called *Qawwali* in the Indian subcontinent. He also introduced a style of *ghazal*. These forms of music still exist widely in India and Pakistan.

Khusrau wrote this about Medina in Saudi Arabia, which city the Prophet of Islam took as his shelter when he was forced to leave his birthplace Mecca. The Mughals equally found Kashmir their shelter in the heat and dust of Hindustan. Abul Fazl mainly refers to Kashmir's beauty and its 'delightful climate' that made Akbar 'bear Kashmir always before his eyes' (Wani, 2012, 185), and adds to it Akbar's emotional agenda of fulfilling his father's "honored desires" (Wani, 2012, 185). Akbar sent his troops to Kashmir in 1573 and Ali Shah, the reigning king of the Shia Chak dynasty, surrendered immediately to the Mughals. Wakhlu writes that the *khutba* was read in Akbar's name and new coins with his image were struck. Ali Shah died in 1579, and his son Yusuf Shah declared himself king. In 1580 Yusuf Shah was overthrown by his cousin Lohar Chak and Yusuf sought help from the Mughals. Though he defeated his cousin and regained his throne without Akbar's help, Akbar demanded his allegiance. In 1585 Akbar ordered Yusuf Shah to come and meet him in Delhi. It is claimed by historians that though Yusuf Shah knew that Akbar's intention was to keep him as a hostage, he had to go to Delhi in 1586 to respond to the emperor's call. He was sent to Bihar and was kept imprisoned there till his death. Later, his son, Yaqub Shah, crowned himself as king and continued to resist the Mughal forces until 1989.

It is to be noted that earlier the Mughals had sent their forces seven times to Kashmir and several of those were to assist the factions of nobility who were trying to ascend the throne of Kashmir. Akbar learned that the conquest of Kashmir was not possible without a strong local alliance. The Mughal forces often succeeded to help the claimants to throne only when they had the support of the local leaders. The interesting fact was that though the Kashmiris were divided among themselves, they stood united against the uninvited invaders and the Mughals could not penetrate Kashmir. Factionalism in Kashmir made Akbar confident of getting an opportunity to divide the communities in Kashmir and around 1578 he found the situation ripe to strike. Thus, the Mughal conquest of Kashmir was preceded by a series of diplomatic initiatives – through extending patronage to the opponents of the ruling Chak rulers; and the leaders and the people of Kashmir were sensitized about the invincibility of the Mughal power. There remained no scope other than visualizing the Mughal emperor as the final arbitrator of local disputes. The charismatic personality of Akbar was propagated with the arson and massive killings in Kashmir, which was an interesting mix of coercive and soft diplomacy adopted by Akbar to finally annex Kashmir with his empire.

We must remember that Gulbadan Begam was watching over this expansion of empire sitting among the women of the Mughal zenana. The aviary was extended to the boundaries of Kashmir and even more towards Baltistan and Ladakh; but on the other side, the heaven of Kashmir became a hell for Habba

Khatoon. Wakhlu narrates a beautiful conjugality she had with Yusuf Shak Chak after her marriage. She became the center of the palace, as Ali Shah and his wife (Khatoon's in-laws) were also fond of her. After Ali Shah's death when Yusuf Shah became the king, she gradually became popular as a queen through her charitable work and beautiful poetry that reached every corner of the valley because of royal patronage. She was a very active queen and loved to listen to the people. Wakhlu writes that Khatoon decided not to remain idle like the other queens of Yusuf. She would wake up early and a bundle of petitions would come to her from the poor. She would help everyone. She would even plead to Yusuf on behalf of people who incurred the king's displeasure or his political offenders.

All this while, she would attend to her harem life and continue practicing music and poetry. She would also hunt on horseback, which seems not to be an exaggeration because riding was common for both men and women in Kashmir. She was quite fashionable and would design her own dresses and jewelry. Wakhlu also mentions a few rivals of Khatoon who tried to stop her poetry by instigating Yusuf Shah against her. Among these people, he especially mentions Baba Daud Khaki[13] and Shaikh Yaqub Sarfi[14], Akbar's allies, who argued that her poetry instigated sinful desires in the hearts of young men, and hypnotized the king too; and that she was the source of suffering Kashmir was facing. These arguments may have been only rumors that Wakhlu preferred to narrate to exoticize Khatoon's life and to scandalize Akbar, and it is equally doubtful that these rivals went to Delhi to report to Akbar against Khatoon. Wakhlu's narrative suggests that Akbar was furious against Khatoon and promised to punish her. Was it possible that the Mughal Emperor needed a woman to be the reason of his wrath and vengeance? Perhaps not.

When Akbar sent his call to Yusuf Shah, his son Yaqub and Habba Khatoon asked him not to go; and suggested they fight the Mughal invaders. Wakhlu writes that Yaqub had vested interests, and was violent in temper. Yusuf could not fully trust him. Khatoon, conversely, was a mere woman of pen and poetry, not an Amazon queen to spark enthusiasm and hope. Yusuf Shah chose to be

---

[13] A great Sufi saint of Kashmir in the sixteenth century. He was allegedly born in 1521 and died in 1585. e was 'Qazi-ul-Qaza', the Chief Justice of Kashmir, in his times. He was also called "Abu Haneefa Sani", second Abu Haneefa, because of his sagacity and profoundity in Islamic-legal matters.

[14] Shaikh Yaqub Sarfi was the most prominent Sufi saints of sixteenth century belonging to the Kubarwiya order. The Kubarwiya order had its remarkable influence on the different aspects of the life of Kashmiris. He was a man of international reputation for his piety, scholarship and learning. He had occupied an important place in the history of Kashmir and during the time Akbar he was given the title 'Haji Sani'.

diplomatic and yielding; and his intention was to maintain good relation with Akbar by accepting him as an overlord. He wanted to avoid bloodshed in his beautiful country. When he was treacherously imprisoned and Yaqub Shah declared himself king, Khatoon had to leave the palace. She chose to live at Panda Chok; and as Wakhlu writes, she spent her life in a small cottage on the bank of Jhelum. Yusuf Shah was kept imprisoned in Agra till 1587, and then he was taken to Patna in Bihar. Wakhlu informs that Khatoon was offered an opportunity to reunite with her husband in secret. Other historians do not say anything in this regard, but she refused to do that for Yusuf's safety. He also mentions that she burned all written copies of her poetry and renounced worldly life. Finally, she breathed her last in 1605 at Panda Chok.

### Habba Khatoon and our poetic understanding

Khatoon's poetry has survived through centuries in Kashmiri oral tradition. Her poetry is part of the collective memory of all Kashmiris. Since much of her life is draped in mystery, readers attribute mystical qualities to her work. However, she was no saint; at least she never claimed to be one. The presence of Mullah Shah Badakhshi and his followers in Kashmir has been discussed in the chapter on Jahanara, and we know that Kashmir was the seat for many saints and mystics from foreign lands who chose to settle here for its climate. For the same reason, it also attracted the attention of kings, who could not avoid its natural beauty and preferred to live half of the year in this valley away from the bustles of court and heat of Delhi and Agra. Sadhu comments that there was never any dearth of saints and mystics in Kashmir. Apart from local saints, the Kashmiri people enjoyed close communion with Muslim divines from Central Asia and further west. Conversely, Kashmiri kings were great patrons of music, acting and dance, that continued till the Mughals annexed it. Sadhu connects this history with the literary history of Kashmiri language that places Habba Khatoon in an important position in the context of Kashmiri literature.

In the poetic tradition of Kashmir, Khatoon's poetry is linked with Lalded's, the other great female poet of Kashmir though she lived almost two hundred years earlier than Khatoon. Two events are usually counted as important for Kashmiri language and literature. One is the birth of Lalded who brought a new turn in Kashmiri literature through introducing the *vaakh*[15] quatrain. She was also a precursor of the use of vernacular Kashmiri language in poetry. The second event was perhaps the ascension of Shams-ud-Din or Shah Mir to the throne of Kashmir in 1339 as the founder of the *Shah Mir* dynasty, the beginning of the

---

[15] 'Vaakh' is the poetic form used by Lalded, which abounds in alliteration and various repetitive sounds create a kind of music.

Muslim rule in Kashmir. Though he ruled for three years only, the Shah Mir dynasty continued to rule Kashmir till 1561. The rulers were great patrons of music, poetry, dance and contributed much in the development of Kashmiri literature; the Chak rulers after them continued to follow this tradition. Lalded and her younger contemporary Sheikh Noor-ud-Din or Nund Rishi set the tradition of Kashmiri poetry. He chose the verse form *shrukh*[16] to express his feelings. Both Lalded and Nund Rishi were highly reputed among common people for their simplicity, purity and truth and their messages against falsehood that corrupted the population. Habba Khatoon found a solid poetic tradition and a developed language when she was born two hundred years later; and she added to it the mix of Persian that gave her poetry more vigor. Due to the Muslim invasion in 1339, many Persian-speaking scholars, poets, theologians, and mystics sought refuge in Kashmir, and Persian became the court language. Ghazals and Sufi poetry had permeated the fabric of poetic culture of Kashmir. Khatoon was a product of this composite culture. As she was talented, she became the originator of a newer pattern, *Rast-e-Kashmiri*.

Sadhu gives a short background of *Lol* or Kashmiri love songs. Songs were always part of the music-loving people of Kashmir. He traces the origin of it in the fifth century and writes,

> Echoes of teaching, enshrined in poetry, of Kabir, the Sikh Gurus, Tulsidas, Surdas, Mirabai, etc. also travelled to Kashmir, especially through pilgrims, and some people turned to the *vacan*, or song-lyric, to enshrine a deep personal attachment to a spiritual ideal. A fervent longing for God, the eternal Beloved, is projected in a few of these song-lyrics. It is, however, human love that infused life and vitality in *vacan*-songs. (Sadhu, 1983, 11)

Some of these *vacan*-songs were found in written in the sixth century, but most of it came through the oral tradition. These were usually songs containing the feelings of a female lover addressing her male beloved. Even after Persian poetry had its influence on it, it retained the female personality addressing the male beloved, not the exact variant of Persian poetic convention that it followed otherwise. The scope of describing feminine beauty was less in these songs, because they were mostly about the love-smitten female lover who would be waiting for her unresponsive male beloved. In Sadhu's view, these songs also

---

[16] The word 'shrukh' is derived from the word 'shloka' or verse. The lexical meaning of shrukh is 'knot'. In Kashmiri this specific genre includes the verse of the fourteenth century saint poet Sheik Noor-ud-Din, who used 'Nund' as his pen name, and is widely known as Nund Rishi. It was generally interpreted that though the Sheikh's verses were easy to understand, the advice given therein was difficult to practice; his verses were, hence, called 'shrukha'.

lacked intellectuality in concept and content; which is to say that these were simple and direct utterances of a woman "affected by the sting of love waiting for her lover in a world vibrating with love's message in the form of flowers, the turtle-dove, and the bumble-bee. Her *lol*, unrequited love and longing, is bound in his absence to dissolve into a wistful and plaintive utterance" (Sadhu, 1983, 12). The Kashmiri songs of the fifteenth and sixteenth centuries hardly show any gaiety, merriment, or overt passion. These are generally characterized by their simplicity and sincerity of lyric. Secular love being the subject matter, the tone is natural and human. Sadhu claims Habba Khatoon to be "the crowning glory of the age" (Sadhu, 1983, 12). She is a true representative of the *lol* tradition in Kashmir because she practically suffered the pain of the female lover. Her modest birth and an unhappy first marriage paved the way for her painful existence out of which she uttered her songs. The Mughal empire acted externally as a deciding factor in her life, as she found herself desolate a second time when she was breached from her loving husband, to that extent the metaphor of aviary as a system of hemming in a woman does apply to Khatoon, though not in the way Mughal women have been its mixed beneficiaries. In this chapter, some of her songs translated by Neerja Mattoo are discussed to show what kind of femininity she advocated in her situation under the surveillance of a patriarchy that was defined primarily by its own cultural lagging and by external antagonisms.

Poetry has become a complicated genre over time. Today we have a huge range of poetry across cultures floating on the web. This global proliferation of poetry has created a lot of option for us –read, translate, evaluate, promote poetry. Resistance is one of the major themes in poetry, and Mahmud Darvish, perhaps, is the greatest poet of resistance of our time. There are several poetic voices in India, including Rumuz today, but protest poetry in India had started long before: with Lalded, Habba Khatoon and Arnimal. The specific genre did not become visible though. Their poetry was lyrical and romantic, but at the same time expressed personal grief and complaints. These women need to have our attention for initiation of this kind of poetry. While analyzing their poetry, one meets several challenges. As this poetry was carried forward orally, it is very difficult to revive the earliest version, so one is always dealing with variants that can only be presumed to have retained the core of original thought. Everyday language in Kashmir changed much after the Mughal conquest as the local language mixed with Persian. For the global readers, English translation is necessary. These female authors hardly attracted the translators across the ages. Some translators in recent times have found Khatoon worthy of reading, but even then, there is no dedicated volume of her poetry translated into English. S. L. Sadhu's book *Haba Khatoon* in the "Makers of Indian Literature" series published by Sahitya Akademi in 1983 is a dedicated English text on her life and poetry. Her poetry translated by Neerja Mattoo has been mostly quoted here because Mattoo's translation has a lucidity and simplicity of language that Khatoon had in the original. An example may elucidate this. The poem that starts with "May kari tseyi kiti poshi dasavaanay" has some lines that Sadhu translates as,

> Laila lit a candle on a dark night,
> The poor darling became insensible,
> I am the moth to you the candle,
> Come, enjoy my blossoming!
>
> The summer of my life is slipping away,
> And the roses are likely to wither;
> O nightingale, wish you were here for a while!
> Come, enjoy my blossoming! (1983, 18)

The very lines are translated by Mattoo in this way,

> In secret, Laila lit a lamp in the dark
> Innocent, she knew not the ways of the world!
> You are my candle, I am your moth
> Come my love, revel in the blooms.
> My summer is slowly waning
> Its flowers will fade away
> Bulbul, find a reason to come to me
> Come my love, revel in the blooms.
>
> (2019, 108)

Compared to the concessionary note inherent in "poor darling" of Sadhu's text, the suavity of "Innocent" in Mattoo gives a whole new range of meanings to the romantic appeal of the poet speaker. Similarly, while "insensible" in Sadhu's translation has a dismissive note about it, her "being unaware of the ways of the world" in Mattoo gives an autonomy of existence to the poet speaker. Once these basic differences of attributing a position to the subject are grasped, it is obvious to note that Mattoo's translation registers an appeal that is more fervent in that the blend of throbbing passion and coyness or the unsure nature of the speaker's self vis-a-vis her social position foregrounding a crisis or tension between identities that are innately conjoined and yet seem to be faced with the apprehensions of societal censure. Translation brings a new twist to the whole discussion, and it is to be noted that Khatoon's love lyrics are in no way lesser in quality than her English contemporaries who reveled in fame and fortune. The rich literature she produced has not reached the wide variety of international readers due to the lack of translation.

The dominant theme in Khatoon's poetry is 'love'. Love creates desire, and when desire is not met with fulfillment, there is desolation and complaint. Her poetry is obviously a series of emotions extracted from personal experiences. This subjective poetry presents the female lover as sensuous, who is not afraid of admitting her physical desire for the lover. She adopts different strategies to bring him close to her. When the temptations of her exceptional physical beauty fail, she becomes plaintive and reproaches the beloved.

The first poem Mattoo includes in her book, shares the Horatian[17] idea of "seize the day"; a long narration of all the transient beauties of the world with repeated call to the lover –"Come back, my flower-decked lover!" (2019, 98). Beginning with a complaint, the poet speaker invites her companions to carry on their everyday household chores; while at the back of her mind, the anxiety connected with the absence of the male lover is obvious. The beautiful Kashmir valley is rich with its fauna and flora, and women are part of its natural landscape. Women's life in general is beheld in the lines, while the 'hordes' is enough indication of the disturbances they have to face. Towards the end, the poet speaker becomes bold and says "the world is not immortal", and finally, she reveals the poet's identity. One must not look for the identity of the flower-decked lover, because the imaginative mind of the speaker keeps the essential obscurity about it. There is no shyness or coyness in her. Around the time Khatoon wrote this, Queen Elizabeth I was writing in a totally different vein. She was showing the repercussion of the coy poet speaker in the poem 'When I Was Fair and Young',

> When I was fair and young, then favor graced me.
> Of many was I sought their mistress for to be.
> But I did scorn them all and answered them therefore:
> Go, go, go, seek some other where; importune me no more.
> […]
> As soon as he had said, such change grew in my breast
> That neither night nor day I could take any rest.
> Wherefore I did repent that I had said before:
> Go, go, go, seek some other where, importune me no more.
>
> (Elizabeth I, https://www.poetryfoundation.org/poems/45657/when-i-was-fair-and-young)

That repentance for coyness in Elizabeth I comes as a sharp contrast to the bold and sensuous woman in Khatoon, who is not taken aback by the thought of

---

[17] Horace (65-8 BCE) was a Roman poet who wrote *Odes* published in 23 BCE. These have the *carpe diem* as the major theme that has come to stand for Horace's entire injunction "carpe diem quam minimum credula postero," or "pluck the day, trusting as little as possible in the next one." This is more widely known as "seize the day."

being ostracized by the society. While English poetry of this time, at least the major poets who are canonized as upholding the cult of post-Renaissance love in their work, has stilted female figures as beloveds or muses, Khatoon's poetry comes across as a bold assertion of feminine thoughts and their codification in a poetic language. Oriental love poetry, that was influenced by Persian *ghazal* tradition as well as Indian *bhakti* movement, molded Khatoon's poetic sensibilities for which she dares to tread dangerous limits of openness. She boldly writes of her carnal desires in another poem – "Every pore of my body aches/ He fills me with desire!" and she is not shying away her desire. Her male lover looked at her from different corners, entered her house, spoke to her "like a song- bird", let her burn "like a flaming torch", and left her "long-necked beauty" yearning for consummation. At times she is bolder and even dares to write, "Like a trader, he entered my house/ Bit by bit he wasted me away" (Mattoo, 2019, 102).

The search for sexual satisfaction and the lover's eventual departure, a strong motif in another poem in which the poet-speaker complains of the lover's disgust for her, makes one ponder on the modesty of a sixteenth-century woman. Suspicion, grievance and bodily desires make her restless and she invites the lover at the dead of the night. The union of the bodies becomes equivalent to the unity of the souls as the poet speaker believes in it. The lines in the poem are immersed in romantic eroticism. The doors being "thrown open" and the invite to "come in" expresses the sexuality of a woman, which is not only bold and erotic, it seems to be scandalous to a listener if one imagines the social environment of Kashmir at that time. She was fully taking advantage of the song tradition of the valley to express her feminine sensuality. An open invitation to the lover to enjoy her body coming from the pen of a poet of the time comes as a shock. Mattoo's comments that there was no sense of 'womanly' modesty or shame in such demands of sexual fulfillment. She associates with this Khatoon's training as a professional musician or a courtesan, which also taught her the art of seduction. Even though Mattoo keeps the issue unresolved, as Khatoon's biographers did too, it is obvious that she was never free of this kind of scrutiny regarding her true identity. However, Khatoon's poetic vocation is never questioned, nor is her feminist approach in the poems. Mattoo uses the French term *demi-monde* to describe Khatoon's social stand, and assumes that as the poet lived outside of the 'pale social norms', she could "turn the rules of puritanical morality upside-down" (Mattoo, 2019, 91). The readers may completely agree that after five hundred years, it is impossible to comment on this. The way the poet speaker expresses her desires are sometimes baffling in character; a courtesan's trained art of seduction and a wife's natural flow of pure emotion must have an ocean's difference in the provocation of sexual desires. Whatever the speaker is, the woman who is showing such self-awareness, and can defy the importance of physical charm, is again falling in the trap of patriarchy. She craves appreciation for her youthful luster from her lover. Sadhu connects such expression with Khatoon's unhappy first marriage and claims that she was trying to get back her husband Aziz Lone. In the poem "May kari tseyi kiti poshi dasavaanay", the one which was illustrated earlier to compare Sadhu and Mattoo, Sadhu even imports Aziz's name, which is not there in the original version,

> I have for you garments of the choicest make,
> Beloved Aziz, don't be annoyed with Zoon,
> Haba Khatoon's dreams have remained unfulfilled,
> Come, enjoy my blossoming!
>
> (Sadhu, 1983, 18)

While translating "Tsareith animay phamba moyane/ Jaanaana me mo rosh", Mattoo uses "my love", not any proper name, which is more authentic. A male translator's intention to connect the poet speaker's desires to the man she physically had in her life, is to be noted here, even though the man was not able to live up to the woman's expectations. It is as if a woman's body and soul are bound to the man through the institution of marriage and nothing could change it. Conversely, a female translator remains faithful to the poet's original and believes in her imaginative power that creates an ideal male lover whose appreciation is highly valued by the poet speaker. In the poem "Why do you turn from me in disgust?" is repeatedly uttered, but the poem ends in a proud revelation, when the woman utters "I, Habba Khatun crave for ever/ But never did I bow my head" (Mattoo, 2019, 111).

Being born in a tradition that teaches a girl from her birth that women are born to become wives and mothers, she must have resolved to be someone's wife, but she was not yet ready to give up her freedom and self-respect. The more we read her poetry, the more we understand she was taking refuge in some phantom, some image, not in any human lover she knew. For example, in a poem "I trudged through the woods with complaint on my lips" (Mattoo, 2019, 113), she seems to be lost in her dreams, and the lover's image oscillates between the mundane and the divine that could be interchanged. The poet speaker says that her youth bloomed and withered without the lover's caress and attention. When she says that her cry never reached him, the translator uses 'he' and not 'He' that confirms that she considers only human lover, but there is a connotative meaning in this pronominal form since the speaker refers to the unalterable 'fate' that makes it unclear if she was trying to connect to a human or trying to knock fortune's door and attract the attention of a divine lover. Indeed, her mysticism sprouts from such obscurities. The mysticism is even more solidified when she utters that whatever she gathers is never enough and she can only pray to her Lord in "This pain of your separation is what I must bear" (Mattoo, 2019, 116). It looks like the poet-speaker has created the image of an ideal that embodies her idea of love and union, which is to remain ever-unfulfilled. Poetic vocation often creates such illusion and the poet remains in everlasting desire.

However, some poems do show her reaction to the world she lived in with concrete references to her married life and in-laws. In a series of poems, she complaints against her marriage in a family that does not suit her. Her narrative poems clearly differentiate between her own family and her husband's. She refers to a sister-in-law (brother's wife) in one poem who shatters her sense of security in her paternal home. She regrets her birth and expresses her desire for death. In another poem, "A smouldering fire consumes a tender shoot", (Mattoo, 2019, 122) the poet-speaker narrates the whole episode of marriage and the experience of leaving a father's home for the husband's in a palanquin that has silver bells. The sweet music of the bells serves as a passage from innocence to experience. And again, in another poem, "I'm so unhappy in my in-laws home", (Mattoo, 2019, 124) the speaker seeks help from her parents. She describes how she feels insecure while spending her days fetching water and doing domestic chores in her in-laws' place. The water pitcher breaks and she is forced to gather its shards. She says her child self was "powdered to vermillion" the day she was married, and now when she is friendless and forlorn, her parents should come to their senses. Despite all the rich attires and jewelry, she has received during her wedding, the grief-stricken girl does not look forward to life, and the same palanquin becomes a symbol of her wake. The reference to the broken pot directly connects with Khatoon's personal life, but the grief of a young bride is nothing new in the Indian or greater South Asian societies. The girls are married off and the parents are hardly able to ease their lives. The festivities of the wedding day turn into grey melancholic days for the girl and she does not get refuge in the parents' home anymore. The reference to the brother's wife concretizes the fact that Khatoon was thinking of all suffering brides. She did not have a brother, and so, the brother's wife is imported as a social machinery for further oppression of the girl. If a girl tries to come back to her ancestral home, the brother's wife would never accept her with open arms. This invites a complicated feminist approach that is specifically of South Asian construct where female relatives perpetrate patriarchal oppression, which one may also find in western patriarchy. Khatoon's speaker becomes a representative of all women in that sense and the poet appears to be one of the earliest feminist voices in the region.

The suffering woman fails to find a shelter in the natural beauty of the valley. The rivers, lakes, meadows, glens, lilacs, delicate beauties of Kashmir, its divine waters, Zaina Bridge,[18] Sopore,[19] Wullar,[20] waters of Sindh,[21] dancers ascending from Indra's courts[22] – all these once cherished by the young girl, are fading now because of her life's tantrums. This suffering life reaches its height when the ideal lover once sought, was found to be lost again. Perhaps when she was living a desolate life in her cottage when Yusuf Shah Chak was taken a prisoner, she composed a series of sad songs. In her lyrics she recalls her misery and comments that nothing but misery is permanent in life,

> I searched through the world
> But the trickster gave me nothing
> No friends, nor siblings, no one remains
> Nothing will last, not a memory.
>
> (Mattoo, 2019, 129)

This time her complaints are of a different sort. She has gradually become more philosophical and cynical, and she starts questioning her own existence. Questions like "Why did I come into this world?" or "Why was I even born?" shows how desperately she was revolting against the ways of the world. The Mughal aviary was gradually becoming a place full of insecurity for women, and Khatoon clearly records how it took away her only happiness in life. Chak was the gold flower of her life, but she failed to preserve it, since 'they' cut it down. The poem "Like a blossom of gold you lined the wild rose woods" (Matto, 2019, 132) that can have multiple interpretations, presents absolute nihilism. The person addressed as 'you' could possibly be Yusuf Shah Chak, and 'they' may refer to the Mughals. At one point, she mentions "signs" that she looked for to make his garland, which could be read as her speculations about the Mughal aviary itself. Khatoon asked Yusuf Shah not to go to Delhi to meet Akbar, because she possibly read "signs", but the day was not saved and Yusuf was dethroned. The "You" in the poem could equally be Kashmir valley on which the Mughals had their eyes since the beginning. They loved it for its moderate weather and beautiful natural landscape, and wanted to seize it to

---

[18] This is a reference to the Zaina Kadal Bridge on the Jhelum built by Sultan Zain-ul-Abideen in the fifteenth century.
[19] *Sopore* is an important town within the Baramulla districtin Kashmir. It is located 50 km north-west from Srinagar.
[20] Wullar or Wular Lake in Bandipora district in Jammu and Kashmiris one of the largest fresh water lakes in Asia.
[21] Reference to the Indus that flows northwest through the Ladakh and Gilgit-Baltistan regions of Kashmir.
[22] Indra, the ancient Vedic deity in Hinduism,who the god of thunder, lightning, storm, rain, river and war. He is the supreme god and the king of heavenand all othergods. Here his court in heaven is referred to.

complete their conquer in Hindustan. In Khatoon's consciousness, Kashmir looms large as a "blossom of gold". These metaphorical lines with their apt symbolism tell of Khatoon's wisdom. Gradually she moves away from worldly wisdom and adopts a life of seclusion. Her pain becomes her companion, and she begins to ask those existential questions that accompanied her in her earlier years of misery. The last poem Mattoo includes in her volume bears witness to her direct questions to her creator. "What will you gain from my death?", is a seriously asked metaphysical and existential question. She blames God for burning her heart with desire and leaving the desires unfulfilled. Her piety and faith could not save her. "Forgive me my faults, God" (Mattoo, 2019, 134-135) refers to her reading the *Quran* without a single mistake, which is juxtaposed with the inability to read the book of love that comes as an irony; since love and religion are interchangeable if divinity is nourished as a passion, as we find in Sufi poetry. In traditional divine poetry of Kashmir that is established by Lalded and Nund Rishi, wisdom comes as a natural yield. In Lalded's poetry, the voice of the mystic comes amalgamated with that of a practically wise person. The mystic is never devoid of or alienated from the ordinary life around her. She refers to epics (read divine texts) like the *Ramayana* and the *Mahabharata*[23] with a sense of humor, and thus, she entered the common Kashmiri ethical and moral codes easily. If Lalded entered the intellectual realm, Khatoon entered the emotional realm of the Kashmiris through her melancholic love songs.

At one point in his book Wakhlu wishes that if Emperor Akbar had come in direct contact with Khatoon, and would have heard her songs, her history could be different. Does anything really change in that way? Would state polity pay heed to poets? Plato wanted to banish poets from his ideal state. Akbar possibly knew about her poetic talent, as he used to closely observe Kashmir through the news coming from his informers. Khatoon as a woman was not expected to create any influence on the great expansionist Akbar, and she did not. Gulbadan Begum's influence at Akbar's court could not secure the rights of women in the capital; the princesses were stopped from marrying because their marriage would cause the birth of inheritors and would initiate more dispute over monarchy. How would a woman living in the peripheries of the empire influence the emperor? Her sufferings caused by the empire's expansion can be read as the essential suffering needed for the maturity of a poetic mind.

With the annexation of Kashmir in the offing, Khatoon fled from the bustle of court life, and chose to remain in a remote corner of Kashmir. She refused to accept the subjugated existence of a prisoner in the Mughal aviary. Her voice is

---

[23] The *Ramayana* and the *Mahabharata* are the two ancient epics originating in Hindustan in the 7th- 4th century BCE and 3rd century BCE- the 3rd century CE respectively. Lalded has referred to many episodes of these epics rather playfully in her *vaakh*s, a genre she innovated.

a voice of dissent in all senses. She started her poetic journey with innocence and love, and gradually matured into a voice of protest and grievance over time. Hers is a truly representative voice that could be referred to at this 'moment of arrival' in the history of Kashmir we are now. It is time to explore such neglected voices to see how poetry as a genre thrived in Kashmir and has become a tool for intellectual resistance.

# 6
# Where to Conclude?

> You may write me down in history
> With your bitter, twisted lies,
> You may trod me in the very dirt
> But still, like dust, I'll rise.
>
> (Angelou, 1978)[1]

History is warped by the political act of forgetting. So true! It becomes even more political when a sudden remembrance jerks the mind and intends one to wake up to a different 'reality'. On the temporal matrix, this reality lies beyond the chronological passage of time traced in mainstream historiography; spatially, it is located in the India of today, where a new-nationalist resurgence is in place. This is manifest, among other things, in the systemic interpretation of episodes of Mughal history as extraneous in terms of its religious roots, colonial nature and oppressive intent. This triadic of forces is supposedly to be countered tooth and nail in order to reinstate the 'ancient ethnic glory' of 'Hindu' Hindustan. Arjun Appadurai connects the 'high globalization' that began in the 1990s with 'ethnic cleansing' and 'extreme forms of political violence against civilian populations' through his understanding of 'national ethos' of the present time – "No modern nation, however benign its political system and however eloquent its public voices may be about the virtues of tolerance, multiculturalism, and inclusion, is free of the idea that its national sovereignty is built on some sort of ethnic genius" (Appadurai, 2006, 3). Of the present Indian context that shows neither tolerance nor inclusion, Appadurai in a recent interview to *The Wire* raises the question as to why the whopping majority should be in such fear of minorities that it tries to invisibilize them by subverting, among other things, their history as well. In answering his own question, he completely turns on its head the very understanding of majoritarianism by saying that,

> The category of Hindu and Hindu majority is itself fragile and of recent origin. You need to do a lot of things to stabilize that. Violence is one of the ways to fortify the foundation, which is perennially weak […] Like many national identities, it is produced by the lathi, not by the poetry

---

[1] Lines from "Still I Rise" by Maya Angelou (1928-2014), the titular poem *And Still I Rise: A Book of Poems*, Random House, 1978.

and prose. These majoritarian voices actually reflect a kind of underlying instability and therefore anxiety. (*The Wire*, August 5, 2021)

The subversion of history or attempts to obfuscate cultural geography, therefore, lie at the heart of the politics of history surrounding the Mughal period in India. In terms of Subcontinental literary historiography, we can relevantly interpret the lack of even a minimal existence of the women writers whose lives and works have been taken up in this volume. At this 'globalized' juncture of ethno-nationalism in India when powerful Mughal monarchs are being denigrated and obliterated from the annals of history, it is easily comprehensible that the work of these women with their 'always already subaltern' identity would never surface in literary history.

Gulbadan Begam's tomb lies desolate in Bagh-i-Babur in Kabul, as the country stands face to face with new political challenges. In a country where women in general are oppressed beyond description, hardly anyone notices the grave of 'the first woman historian' of the world. Today thousands of devotees visit the shrine of the 13th-century Sufi saint Hazrat Nizamuddin Auliya at Delhi every day, but not many people are even aware that the same complex also houses the grave of Mughal princess Jahanara Begam. Though under the tutelage of the Archaeological Survey of India, her mausoleum still lies bereft of attention. Jahanara had written a couplet in Persian which is inscribed on her grave, and it means, "Let grass grow on my grave, only grass is sufficient on a grave of a fakir". Historian Sohail Hashmi once claimed that Jahanara's grave has a hollow on its top which was meant to be filled with soil and grass, because the grave's marble covering was built according to her wish expressed in that couplet. Some locals from the nearby Nizamuddin Basti say that there used to be an emerald stone on the grave, which went missing 20 years back.[2] It is not the precious gem that is important; it is a matter of concern that she has been denied her true history. The confusion regarding Zeb-un-Nissa's tomb is interesting, but whether it is at Sikandra in India or at Nawa Kot in Pakistan is of a lesser issue, for her very existence faces obfuscation in the annals of literary history. Habba Khatoon lies ignored in her tomb near Athwajan on the *Jammu*-Srinagar national highway, where hardly any visitor comes to pay a tribute to this legendary poet.

These women were hardly ever in limelight in life, nor are they paid any attention posthumously. While the physical scenario is this, the emergence of historical novels and narratives of different sorts in media representation of

---

[2] Source: *The Hindustan Times*. https://www.hindustantimes.com/delhi/delhi-jahanara-s-tomb-in-nizamuddin-remains-unloved/story-84StZ7b3w21mv5lhWJnJ5L.html accessed on October 22, 2020.

these women tell a different tale. Generically, a heady mix of romantic exoticism and distorted history has been a major characteristic of these narratives. Johannes Fabian reminds us of the politics of mixing "elements of Enlightenment and Romantic thought" (Fabian, 2007, 60), the eclectic practices that anthropology adopts. The manuscripts and forgotten writings that have been discussed in this book are ethnographic objects that may help construct a postmodern 'alterity' in Fabian's vocabulary, in lieu of the fictional works that are digressive in many ways. These women's lives need attention because they offer an 'alterity' that has been ignored by mainstream historians of the past centuries. Now when pseudo-nationalist upheavals in actions like erasing a Mughal emperor's name from a central street in Delhi are taking place, the emergence of the exoticized narratives can hardly be taken as innocent. They obviously offer counter-positions, the cognizance of which is necessary for modernist reconstruction of identity, but their presence also "simplify[ies] matters if the story is to be told at all" (Fabian, 2007, 60). These narratives are part of the 'alterity' because their authors claim to recognize the forgotten history of these women. Fabian logically argues for such alterity when he writes,

> Nonetheless, we should keep the horns of the dilemma apart, if only to make it possible to perceive what is crucial about relations between modern constructions of identity and alterity: Though the two concepts should logically be complementary, historically and politically they are not. The more we get to know about their history, the clearer it becomes that modern constructions of alterity emerged when spatial and temporal distancing merged to form the basis of a denial of recognition (of contemporaneity, or modernity). Intellectually, politically, and economically, identity became identity at the expense of others.
>
> (Fabian, 2007, 60)

The women writers of pre-modern India are denied the recognition of possessing philosophical modernity, as the age they lived in denies their identity. At their expense, men of their time were constructing identities, and these women were also willy-nilly assisting in fashioning that identity. Abul Fazl, for example, never acknowledged the contribution of Gulbadan in his *Akbarnama*, though it is proven beyond reasonable doubt that his work was based largely upon the *Humayun-Nama*. Through ages, these women were more and more consigned to oblivion, because of the politics of Hindu historiography in India that has created a demonic image of the Mughal patriarchy under which the modernity of the Mughal women was eternally buried within tropes of male gaze. The way these women enjoyed limited autonomy or practiced power has sometimes surfaced in fictional writings, feature films and television serials, but their literary merit never gained attention in these. Literary practices of these women could clearly function as *facta probantia* for their progressiveness and maturity.

The period spanning from the mid-fifteenth to seventeenth centuries are ideally a time when modernity showed its early phase in Europe. Women like Mary Sidney, Aemilia Lanyer, Elizabeth Tanfield Cary, Lady Mary Wroth, Margaret Cavendish, and Katherine Philips were writing at that time. They exceled in translating from Latin, Greek, and French texts, especially in the fields of theological discourse; they produced romance and classical tragedy; practiced original meditations and prayers; wrote letters and diaries, poetry, closet drama, advice manuals, and prophecies and polemics. Europe advanced in navigation, trade and industrialization, while its women writers advanced in writing in different genres, to the effect of a concurrent progress. Patricia Demers writes *Women's Writing in English: Early Modern England,*

> The recent focus on early modern women has altered the field of early modern literature so substantially that an anthologist of their writing can refer to 'the blossoming of a subjective self-consciousness and a female specific cultural scrutiny,' while editors of a teaching manual devoted to this recuperated writing can acknowledge that 'we are just beginning to learn (and teach) the genres, topics and styles of half our heritage. (Demers, 2005, 4)

In the Indian subcontinent, Modernity was yet to come, as major historians opine, but the markers of European modernity were already trickling in. Indian ports and shipping had for centuries been tied to the global sea passages, and the Subcontinent retained a favorable balance of trade with the rest of the world throughout the sixteenth to eighteenth centuries, as witnessed in the histories of various colonizing agencies in India around that time. In terms of trade and commerce, India entered modernity with the rest of the globe. India grew to a large territory due to the Mughal force that brought almost the whole of the subcontinent under its rule: by 1690, the Mughal emperor was the acknowledged ruler over nearly the entire Subcontinent. In terms of population and wealth India was a big power at that time. Architecture, art and culture, crop cultivation, warfare – in all sectors India became part of global early modernity, though the period till 1757 is generally termed as late medieval period. The difference of terminology is interesting, because before the arrival of the colonial masters, India seems to have been mired in a backward and dark era, which was not the case in reality. Is this because Indian historians never took the care to bring out the modernity of the region and blindly followed what their western counterparts said? Kumkum Chatterjee mentions the problem with Indian historiography, for which the colonial historians used it as a "blank slate" upon which they kept their "unmediated impact" (Chatterjee, 2009). Sugata Bose and Ayesha Jalal also comment that Indian historiography has gained rapid development in the last twenty years. What about historiography before that? When we reject all earlier forms of historiography, are we not depreciating our indigenous abilities? Historians like Sanjay Subrahmanyam or Sheldon Pollock termed the pre-colonial South Asia as a "featureless terrain" (Chatterjee, 2009) whose main function seems to have been to serve as a foil and contrast to colonial period" (Chatterjee 2009). Literary and historical treatises of the period, naturally, never saw their heydays. Gulbadan Begam's memoir, for example, failed to gain adequate repute as the first historical treatise written by a woman because of lack of proper analysis and appreciation of Indian historiography. While the perception of her position as a daughter of a Muslim ruler in the post-Partition Indian state has caused obfuscation at a regional level; her identity as a woman and that too from the Subcontinent, has greatly affected her chance of making it to the halls of fame in academic discussions of world historians. This limbo state of being invisibilized needs to be addressed if South Asia is to take rightful cognizance of its veritably complex and varied strands of historiography. A similar negligence has been marked in the case of other women writers, which in turn explains the sheer absence of initiatives to get them translated for a wider circulation among global readership.

These women writers were born and lived under strict patriarchal guidance, but the way they exercised freedom and autonomy was unimaginable in western cultures. It is surprising that despite the limited autonomy and palace intrigues into which the lives of Mughal princesses were inextricably tied, they could still write, and express themselves in prose and poetry so skillfully. Habba Khatoon, who was born in a merchant's house in Kashmir, and whose sole ambition could be nothing but becoming a merchant's wife, brings a new dimension to this Mughal aviary image as her life was also hemmed by the Mughal panopticon. She was not nurtured but tortured by the powerful antagonists, the Mughals, who became her nemesis. The problem of the self with which the American educated housewives ended up at the psychologists' doors in the 1950s and 60s that Betty Friedan refers to in *The Feminine Mystique* could have been a destiny that all these women were born with. Their lifelong effort was to adjust their lives to roles the patriarchs laid out for them. The Mughal princesses, married or unmarried, knew what they were to end up with; life in the harem where, for most women, there was very little to do outside of womanly gossip and occasional visits to different provinces with the emperor's followers. Still, they claimed a relatively sovereign inner self. Gulbadan wrote *Humayun-Nama* being "commissioned" as she said, but if she was short of the power and potential, an intelligent man like emperor Akbar would never have asked her to write. Jahanara and Zeb-un-Nissa clearly posit themselves as autonomous females whose writings were modes of their self-fashioning. They entered the realms of knowledge and religion with the same zeal, as they connected to the Sufi movements. Jahanara's lifelong companionship with Mullah Shah culminated in two Sufi biographies, and Zeb-un-Nissa's passion for poetry is amalgamated with Sufi philosophy. Writing is character for them.

Despite thousands of challenges these women wrote and created a space for themselves. For Zeb-un-Nissa, writing is an act of resistance that culminates in rebellion. Her Emperor father did not approve of her writing, but she continued to write. When she was thrown into life-imprisonment, she wrote vigorously till the end. Habba Khatoon appeared in the scene not as an insider, but one from outside the aviary, who was also pushed towards the peripheries of existence by Mughal patriarchy. She chose not to submit, and continued to compose poetry in the vales of Kashmir to become immortalized as its nightingale. The touching stories of these women are not only to inspire and follow, but there is a fact in these that history never realized. These women were born at a time that could not grasp their appeal and advancement.

They were forerunners of modernity in innumerable ways: they were individualists and triumphed over obstacles that came their ways, they were humanists beyond religion and castes, they were usherers of new forms and path breakers in modulating new themes. Gulbadan's biographical treatise, for all her quietness and neutrality, did not have a single line of admiration for the living emperor Akbar, whereas Abul Fazl recurrently praised his decisions and decrees those as divine will. It was a woman's apolitical and unbiased vision of the period that came unfiltered to the readers. Even though she was not completely free of hero-worship tradition of memoir writing, her detailed description of the Mughal interaction with the others clarify certain historical events that may scar the 'invincibility' of the mighty Mughals. Babur's bartering of Khanzada with his enemy in exchange for his self-preservation, for example, remains a dark spot in his long persevering leadership, and Gulbadan's narrative highlights the episode with such pathos that strips the founder of Mughal dynasty of his superman image. Babur is thus downscaled into a human being from his prototypical image of a bloodthirsty conqueror. The Neo-Historicist approach to texts and contexts may find Gulbadan's memoir an intimate reading of contemporary period that helps triangulate events of history. Her text is a kind of people's narrative, written from a perspective that abounds in alterity. A woman's perspective to history brings this alterity and creates scope for the readers to look at events in a new light.

Jahanara's biographical treatises contribute to mainstream history in numerous ways. She presents the lives of the Muslim Sufi saints in a way that clarifies much of the establishment of Islamic rule in India. Her narrative complements the fact that Mughal dynasty was rooted in coercion as well as soft diplomacy, and refutes the recent claim of the political Hindutva in India that Muslim rulers of India established a sovereignty of bloodshed and hatred. The Sufi saints came to India and converted thousands of people through their teaching of love and compassion that brought new light to the common and low caste people who were waiting for an exit from the tyrannical and oppressive caste system. Aurangzeb's intolerance and cruelty gained a scandalous and disgraceful repute in Hindu historiography, the aftermath of which is seen in the removal of his name from a central street in Delhi. Recently Audrey Truschke in *Aurangzeb: The Man and the Myth* has shown the politics behind such misinterpretations of Aurangzeb's action and claims that the well-being of Hindu religious institutions and their leaders was in Aurangzeb's default state polity which he inherited from his forefathers. It is true that he issued some orders to destroy a few temples, but that had grave political reasons behind it. Instead of destroying Hindu properties on a large scale, he granted land to Hindu communities, provided stipends to Hindu spiritual figures, and protected temples from unwanted interferences. The problem with accruing specific agenda to history lies in the rationale of selective reading it employs; and the texts discussed in this book can actually claim importance as authentic and alternative sources of providing a lens of cultural history. Jahanara's *Sahibiya* brings a new understanding in this regard. She hints at sibling rivalry and Aurangzeb's bigotry in contrast to Dara Shikoh's tolerance that throws a new light to the character of the last mighty Mughal. Zeb-un-Nissa's life also proves that Aurangzeb sinned against his own kinsmen more than he did against his enemies.

Apart from being historical material for the sake of history if read in the proper light, the writings of these four women map the gradual development of the trend of Persian literature and poetic tradition in India, and Indian literature at large. Gulbadan and Jahanara contributed enormously to the genre of life writing. Zeb-un-Nissa adopted the male vocabulary to express the unabashed passion in woman; she used the male voice of the Ghazal tradition to vent her female emotions, and thus she was a tradition breaker using tradition. For Khatoon, it was both the task of developing theme and form. She wrote beautiful and bold poetry of love and physical union and innovated *Rast-i-Kashmiri*.

Islam binds these women in one common string, but their religious thoughts are diverse. A Sunni Muslim, Gulbadan did not approve of Akbar's experiments with religions, and always favored the devotional quality of her father and brother, which is reflected in her writing, but she never advocated bigotry. On the other hand, Jahanara's inclination towards Sufism came through her brother Dara Shikoh, and that brought to her life and writing the necessary dimension to fashion herself as a Sufi princess and writer of hagiographies. Taking this note further, Zeb-un-Nissa's Sufi, secular and tolerant bent of mind gave her the daunting expressions of defying the Qaba or temple in her poetry. She used Islamic, Hindu, Christian and Zoroastrian images at the same breath. Habba was born and brought up in a secular Kashmir in which she also learned to mix images of Hinduism and Islam. The teaching of religion never became an impediment for the literary growth of these women, rather their trajectories signal the possibility of peaceful cohabitation in a multicultural context. Translating and reading them today, and more importantly, contextualizing them in the overtly religionized nationalist moment in India in particular, and the Subcontinent in general, looks more insightful than ever.

# Bibliography

Abu-l-Fazl. *The Akbarnama*. Translated by H. Beveridge. Kolkata: Asiatic Society of Bengal, 1907. https://www.indianculture.gov.in/flipbook/83536. Accessed on 12 November 2020.

Ahmed, Suneela. "Mythology: Khawaja Khizr of the Indus". https://www.dawn.com/news/1527475, 12 Jan 2020. Accessed on 2 October, 2020.

Alam, Muzaffar. "The Pursuit of Persian: Language in Mughal Politics". In *Modern Asian Studies*, Vol. 32, No. 2, pp. 317-349. Cambridge: Cambridge University Press, 1998.

Ali, M. Athar. *The Mughal Nobility under Aurangzeb*. New Delhi: Asia Publishing House, 1970.

Andaya, Barbara Watson. *The Flaming Womb: Repositioning Women in Early Modern Southeast Asia*. Honolulu: University of Hawaii Press, 2006.

Andrea, Bernadette. *Women and Islam in Early Modern English Literature*. Cambridge: Cambridge University Press, 2007.

Angelou, Maya. *And Still I Rise*. New York: Random House, 1978.

Appadurai, Arjun. *Fear of Small Numbers: An Essay on the Geography of Anger*. Durham and London: Duke University Press, 2006.

Arif, Ayash (dir.). Habba Khatoon. Drama Serial in Doordarshan India, 2017. Prasar Bharati Archives. https://www.youtube.com/watch?v=Irviltoa2ak. Accessed on 12 June 2020.

Aurangzebe. *Ruka'at-i-Alamgiri or Letters of Aurangzebe*. Translated by Jamshid H. Bilimoria. Bombay: Cherag Printing Press, 1908.

Banerjee, Pompa. Burning Women: Widows, Witches, and Early Modern European Travelers in India. Hampshire: Palgrave Macmillan, 2003.

Beauvoir, Simone de. *The Second Sex*. Translated by H. M. Parshley. London: Vintage, 1997.

Begam, Gulbadan. *The History of Humayun: Humayun-Nama*. Translated by Annette S. Beveridge. New Delhi: Atlantic Publishers, 2018.

Beveridge, Annette S. "Introduction". In *The History of Humayun: Humayun-Nama*. Translated by Annette S. Beveridge. pp. 1-79. New Delhi: Atlantic Publishers, 2018.

Beveridge, Annette S. "Appendices". In *The History of Humayun: Humayun-Nama*. Translated by Annette S. Beveridge. pp. 203-324. New Delhi: Atlantic Publishers, 2018.

Bhattacharya, Sudip. *Unseen Enemy: The English, Disease, and Medicine in Colonial Bengal, 1617-1847*. United Kingdom: Cambridge Scholars Publishing, 2014.

Blake, Stephen P. *Shahjahanabad: The Sovereign City in Mughal India* 1639-1739. Cambridge: Cambridge University Press, 1990.

Bokhari, Afshan. "The "Light" of the Timuria: Jahan Ara Begum's Patronage, Piety, and Poetry in 17th-century Mughal India". 2008. https://cpbuse1.wpmucdn.com/sites.suffolk.edu/dist/f/335/files/2011/12/The- %E2%80%9CLight%E2%80%9D -of-the-Timuria-page-1.pdf. Accessed on 13 August 2020.

Bokhari, Afshan. "Gendered Landscapes: Jahan Ara Begum's (1614-1681) Patronage, Piety and Self-Representation in 17th C Mughal India." PhD Dissertation submitted at University of Vienna, 2009. http://othes.univie.ac.at/3290/1/2009-01-090503884.pdf. Accessed 13 August 2020.

Bokhari, Afshan. "Imperial Transgressions and Spiritual Investitures: A Begam's "Ascension" in Seventeenth Century Mughal India". In *Journal of Persianate Studies* 4, 2011. pp. 86- 108. https://cpb-us-e1.wpmucdn.com/sites.suffolk.edu/dist/f/335/files/2011/12/Imperial-Transgressions-and-Spiritual-Investitures-page-1.pdf. Accessed on 13 August 2020.

Bokhari, Afshan. *Imperial Women in Mughal India: The Piety and Patronage of Jahanara Begum*. London: Tauris Academic Studies, 2013.

Bokhari, Afshan. "Masculine Modes of Female Subjectivity: The Case of Jahanara Begam". In *Speaking of the Self: Gender, Performance, and Autobiography in South Asia*. Eds. Anshu Malhotra and Siobhan Lambert-Hurley. Durham and London: Duke University Press, 2015.

Bose, Sugata and Ayesha Jalal. *Modern South Asia: History, Culture, and Political Economy*, Second edition. London and New York: Routledge, 2004.

Butenschon, Andrea. *The Life of a Mogul Princess Jahanara Begum, Daughter of Shahjahan*. Delhi: Sang-e-Meel Publications, 2004.

Butler, Judith. *Gender Trouble: Feminism and the Subversion of Identity*. London and New York: Routledge, 2006.

Chakrabarti, Pratik. *Medicine and Empire: 1600-1960*. Basingstoke: Palgrave Macmillan, 2013.

Chandra, Satish. *Medieval India: From Sultanat to the Mughals- Mughal Empire 1526-1748*. New Delhi: Haranand Publications, 2007.

Chatterjee, Kumkum. *The Cultures of History in Early Modern India: Persianization and Mughal Culture in Bengal*. Kindle edition. India: Oxford University Press, 2009.

Chaudhury, Sushil. *Companies, Commerce and Merchants: Bengal in the Pre-Colonial Era*. London: Routledge, 2016.

Cixous, Helene. "The Laugh of the Medusa" (1975). Translated by Keith Kohen and Paula Cohen. In *Critical Theory: A Reader for Literary and Cultural Studies*. Edited by Robert Dale Parker (ed.). Oxford University Press, 2012. pp. 242-257.

Crawford, Dirom G. *A History of the Indian Medical Service 1600-1913*. London: W. Thacker, 1913.

Cuffel, Alexandra and Brian Britt. *Religion, Gender, and Culture in the Pre-Modern World*. Hampshire: Palgrave Macmillan, 2007.

Dale, Stephen F. "The Poetry and Autobiography of the *Babur-Nama*". In *The Journal of Asian Studies*, Vol. 55, No. 3, (1996), pp. 635-664. USA: Association for Asian Studies, 1996.

Dale, Stephen F. *Babur: Timurid Prince and Mughal Emperor, 1483-1530*. Cambridge: Cambridge University Press, 2018.

Dalrymple, William. *City of Djinns: A Year in Delhi*. NY: Penguin Books Limited, 2004.

Das, Kabir. *The Songs of Kabir from the Adi Granth*. Translated by Nirmal Das. Albany: SUNY Press, 1991.

Demers, Patricia. *Women's Writing in English: Early Modern England.* University of Toronto Press, 2005.

Dhawan. Ayushi. *European Doctors Caught between the Two Worlds: On the Reception of South and East Asian Medicine in Early Modern Europe, 1600-1800.* PhD Dissertation submitted at Leiden University, 2017.

Dowd, Michelle M. and Julie A. Eckerle. *Genre and Women's Life Writing in Early Modern England.* England and USA: Ashgate Publishing, 2007.

Dowd, Michelle M. *Women's Work in Early Modern Literature and Culture.* Hampshire: Palgrave Macmillan, 2009.

Dubrow, Heather and Frances E. Dolan. "The Term Early Modern". In PMLA, 109(5), 1994. pp. 1025-1027.

Dumas, Alexandre. *Queen Margot; Or, Marguerite de Valois.* USA: Pohl Press, 2014.

Edwards, Stephen M. and Herbert Leonard. O. Garrett. *Mughal Rule in India.* Delhi: Asian Publications Services, 1979.

Emerson, Ralph Waldo. *The Complete Works of Ralph Waldo Emerson: Miscellanies* [Vol. 11], https://quod.lib.umich.edu/e/emerson/4957107.0011.001/1:26?rgn=div1;view=fulltext.

Emerson, Ralph Waldo. *Society and Solitude.* In *The Collected Works of Ralph Waldo Emerson,* Volume VII. Edited by Ronald A. Bosco and Douglas Emory Wilson. Harvard University Press, 2008.

Eraly, Abraham. *Emperors of the Peacock Throne: The Saga of the Great Mughals.* New Delhi: Penguin Books, 2000.

Eraly, Abraham. *The Mughal World: Life in India's Last Golden Age.* New Delhi: Penguin Books, 2007.

Fabian, Johannes. *Memory Against Culture: Arguments and Reminders.* Durham and London: Duke University Press, 2007.

Fazl, Abul. *Ain i Akbari.* Translated by Colonel H. S. Jarrett. Vol III. Calcutta: Royal Asiatic Society, 1978.

Fazl, Abul. *Akbarnama.* Translated by H. Beveridge. Calcutta: Asiatic Society of Bengal, 1902. https://www.indianculture.gov.in/rarebooks/akbarnama-abu-l-fazl-history-reign-akbar- including-account-his-predecessors-vol 1,2,3. Accessed on 2 October 2020.

Findly, Ellison Banks. *Nur Jahan: Empress of Mughal India.* New York: Oxford University Press, 1993.

Foster, William. "Gabriel Boughton and the Grant of Trading Privileges to the English in Bengal." In *Indian Antiquary,* 1911, pp 247-257.

Friedan, Betty. *The Feminine Mystique.* W. W. Norton and Company, Inc., 1963.

Gandhi, Supriya. *The Emperor who Never Was: Dara Shukoh in Mughal India.* Harvard University Press, 2020.

Gashtili, Paria. "Is an "Islamic Feminism" Possible?: Gender Politics in the Contemporary Islamic Republic of Iran". In Philosophical Topics, 41 (2), pp. 121-140. USA: University of Arkansas Press, 2013.

Godden, Rumer. *Gulbadan: Portrait of a Rose Princess at the Mughal Court.* New York: The Viking Press, 1981.

Greenberg, Mitchell. "The Concept of "Early Modern"". In *Journal for Early Modern Cultural Studies*, Vol. 13, No. 2 (Spring 2013), pp. 75-79. USA: University of Pennsylvania Press, 2013.

Greville, Fulke. *The Tragedy of Mustapha*. EEBO Editions. MI: ProQuest, 2010.

Gupta, Ruchir. *The Mughal Intrigues: Mistress of the Throne*. New Delhi: Srishti Publishers and Distributors, 2014.

Gupta, Ruchir. *The Hidden One: The Untold Story of Aurangzeb's Daughter*. Mumbai: Leadstart Publishing, 2019.

Gupta, Subhadra S. *The Teenage Diary of Jahanara*. New Delhi: Speaking Tiger Publishing Pvt Ltd, 2019.

Habib, Irfan M. "Medieval Period". In *Proceedings of the Indian History Congress*. Vol 24, (1961), pp. 350-357. New Delhi: Indian History Congress, 1961.

Hadi, Nabi. *Dictionary of Indo-Persian Literature*. India: Abhinav Publications, 1995.

Hallaj, Mansur. *I am the Truth (Anal Haqq): Diwan of Mansur Al-Hallaj*. Translations and introduction by Paul Smith. Australia: New Humanity Books, Book Heaven, 2016.

Hansen, Waldemar. *The Peacock Throne: The Drama of Mogul India*. Delhi: Motilal Banarasi Das Publishers, 1986.

Harris, Jonathan Gil. *The First Firangis: Remarkable Stories of Heroes, Healers, Charlatans, Courtesans, & Other Foreigners Who Became Indian*. New Delhi: Aleph Books, 2015.

Irvine, William. *The Later Mughals 1707–1739*. Edited by Jadunath Sarkar. Lahore: Sang-i- Meel, 2007.

Jahanara. *The Master of Pure Souls*. Translated by Dr. Valiur Rahman and Dr. Mohammed Adil. Jaipur: Hamari Taquat Publication, 2015.

Jahanara. *Risala-i-Sahibiya*. Translated by Sunil Sharma. Unpublished translation, 2020.

Kar. Debamitra. "Zebunnissa: Itihash o Naribad" [Zeb-un-Nissa: History and Feminism]. In *Bhorai*, January issue, 2011.

Kaviraj, Sudipta. "Modernity and Politics in India". In *Daedalus*, Vol 129, No 1, 2000. pp 137- 162.

Khan, Inayat. *The Shah Jahan Nama of Inayat Khan: An Abridged History of the Mughal Emperor Shah Jahan, compiled by his Royal Librarian: the nineteenth-century manuscript translation of A.R. Fuller*. Translated by A. R. Fuller, W. E. Begley and Z. A. Desai. New Delhi: Oxford University Press, 1990.

Kochhar, Rajesh. "The Truth behind the Legend: European Doctors in Pre-Colonial India." *Journal of Bioscience*, 24 (1999), pp 259-268.

Krynicki, Annie Krieger. *Captive Princess: Zebunissa Daughter of Emperor Aurangzeb*. Translated by Enjum Hamid. Oxford University Press, 2005.

Kumin, Beat. *The European World, 1500-1800: An Introduction to Early Modern History*. London and New York: Routledge, 2018.

Lal, Kishori S. *The Mughal Harem*. New Delhi: Aditya Prakashan, 1988.

Lal, Mohal (Ed.). *Encyclopaedia of India Literature*. Vol. 5. New Delhi: Sahitya Akademi. 2001.

Lal, Ruby. "Historicizing the Harem: The Challenge of a Princess's Memoir". In *Feminist Studies*, 30 (3), 2004, pp. 590-616. Stable URL: https://www.jstor.org/stable/20458986.

Lal, Ruby. *Domesticity and Power in Early Mughal World*. Cambridge: Cambridge University Press, 2005.

Lal, Ruby. *Empress: The Astonishing Reign of Nur Jahan*. New Delhi: Penguin Viking, 2018.

Larson, Catherine R. *Early Modern Women in Conversation*. Hampshire: Palgrave Macmillan, 2011.

Lasky, Kathryn. *Princess of Princesses of India 1627*. New York: Scholastic Inc, 2002.

Le Guin, Ursula K. *Tehanu: The Last Book of Earthsea*. New York: Atheneum Books, 2001.

Loomba, Ania and Ritty A. Lukose (Eds.). *South Asian Feminisms*. Durham and London: Duke University Press, 2012.

Losty, Jeremiah P. and Malini Roy. *Mughal India: Art, Culture and Empire*. London: British Library, 2013.

Malhotra, Anshu and Siobhan Lambert-Hurley (Eds.). *Speaking of the Self: Gender, Performance, and Autobiography in South Asia*. Durham and London: Duke University Press, 2015.

Manucci, Niccolao. *Storia do Mogur, or Mogul India* (1653-1708). Translated by William Irvine. Indian text series, vol. I. London: John Murray, 1907.

Marlowe, Christopher. *Tamburlaine the Great*. J J Cunningham et al. (Eds.). Manchester: Manchester University Press, 1999.

Marsden, Jean I. "Parsing Early Modernity". In *Journal for Early Modern Cultural Studies*, Vol. 13, No. 4, 2013. pp. 69-71.

Marshall, Dara N. *Mughals in India, A Bibliographical Survey* I, Bombay: *Manuscripts*, 1967.

Mattoo, Neerja. *The Mystic and the Lyric: Four Women Poets from Kashmir*. New Delhi: Zubaan, 2019.

Mehta, Jaswant L. *Advanced Study in the History of Modern India* 1707-1813. Delhi: Sterling Publishers Pvt. Ltd, 2005.

Misra. Rekha. *Women in Mughal India: 1526-1748 A.D*. New Delhi: Munshiram Manoharlal, 1967.

Mukhoty, Ira. *Heroines*. New Delhi: Aleph Book Company, 2017.

Mukhoty, Ira. *Daughters of the Sun: Empresses, Queens and Begums of the Mughal Empire*. New Delhi: Aleph Book Company, 2018.

Nath, Ram. *Private Life of the Mughals of India (1526-1803 A.D.)*. New Delhi: Rupa Publications Pvt Ltd., 2013.

Nath, Ram and Ajay Nath (Eds.). *Monuments of Delhi: Architectural and Historical*. Ajmer and Jaipur: The Heritage, 2018.

Nath, Renuka. *Notable Mughal and Hindu Women in the 16$^{th}$ and 17$^{th}$ Centuries*. New Delhi: Inter-India Publications, 1990.

Nicoll, Fergus. *Shah-Jahan: The Rise and Fall of the Mughal Emperor*. New Delhi: Penguin India, 2018.

O'Hanlon, Rosalind. "Kingdom, Household and Body: History, Gender and Imperial Service under Akbar". In *Modern Asian Studies*, 41(5), (2007), pp. 889-923. doi: 10.1017/S0026749X06002654. Cambridge University Press, 2007.

Parker, Charles H. and Jerry H. Bentley (Eds.). *Between the Middle Ages and Modernity: Individual and Community in the Early Modern World*. Lanham, MD: Rowman & Littlefield Publishers, Inc., 2007.

Parker, Charles H. *Global Interactions in the Early Modern Age, 1400-1800*. Cambridge: Cambridge University Press, 2010.

Peirce, Leslie P. *The Imperial Harem: Women and Sovereignty in the Ottoman Empire*. NY and Oxford: Oxford University Press, 1993.

Pocock, John Greville A. "Perceptions of Modernity in Early Modern Historical Thinking". In *Intellectual History Review*, 17:1, 79-92, DOI: 10.1080/17496970601140246, 2007.

Raychaudhuri, Tapan. *Bengal under Akbar and Jahangir: An Introductory Study in Social History*. Delhi: Munshiram Manoharlal, 1969.

Rezaei, Saman and Ali Salami. *Translating Hafiz: Challenges and Strategies*. Peter Lang, 2019.

Ribner, Irving. *The English History Play in the Age of Shakespeare*. London and NY: Routledge, 1965.

Rowe, John C. *At Emerson's Tomb: The Politics of Classic American Literature*. NY: Columbia University Press, 1997.

Roy, Tirthankar. *The East India Company: The World's Most Powerful Corporation*. New Delhi: Allen Lane, 2012.

Sadhu, Shyam L. *Haba Khatoon*. New Delhi: Sahitya Akademi, 1983.

Said, Edward W. *Orientalism*. New York: Pantheon Books, 1978.

Salzman, Paul. *Reading Early Modern Women's Writing*. Oxford: Oxford University Press, 2006.

Sarkar, Jadunath. "Jahanara: the Indian Antigone". In *Studies in Aurangzib's Reign*. London. 1989. pp. 99-107.

Sarkar, Jadunath. *Anecdotes of Aurangzib and Historical Essays*. Calcutta: M. C. Sarkar and Sons, 1917.

Sarkar, Jadunath. *History of Aurangzib*, Vol 1. Calcutta: M.C. Sarkar & Sons, 1912.

Sarkar, Jadunath. *History of Aurangzib*, Vol 2. London: Longmans, Green and Co., 1920.

Scott, Hamish (Ed.). *The Oxford Handbook of Early Modern European History 1350-1750*, Vol II, Oxford: Oxford University Press, 2015.

Sehran, Sohil. "Delhi: Jahanara's tomb in Nizamuddin remains unloved." https://www.hindustantimes.com/delhi/delhi-jahanara-s-tomb-in-nizamuddin-remains- unloved/story-84StZ7b3w21mv5lhWJnJ5L.html. Accessed on 14 October 2020.

Sengupta, Subhadra. *The Teenage Diary of Jahanara*. New Delhi: Talking Cub, 2019.

Shakespeare, William. *The Arden Shakespeare: Complete Works*. Eds. Richard Proudfoot et al. London, New Delhi, NY, Sydney: Bloomsbury.

Sharma, Sunil. *The Mughal Arcadia: Persian Literature in an Indian Court*. Harvard University Press, 2017.

Sharma, Sunita. "The Exponential Role of the Women Protagonists in the Formative Years of Babur – linkages Revisited". In *Proceedings of the India History Congress*, Vol 73, 2012. pp 358-366.

Showalter, Elaine. *A Literature of Their Own: British Women Novelists from Bronte to Lessing*. Princeton: PUP, 1977.

Showalter, Elaine. *The New Feminist Criticism*. London: Virago, 1986.

Singh, Jyotsna G. "Boundary Crossings in the Islamic World: Princess Gulbadan as Traveler, Biographer, and Witness to History, 1523–1603". In *Early Modern Women: An Interdisciplinary Journal* vol. 7, pp 358-366, 2012. https://www.jstor.org/stable/44156225. Accessed on 27 June 2020.

Smith, Paul. "Life and Times and Poetry of Makhfi...Princess Zeb-un-Niss". In *Makhfi the Princess Sufi Poet Zeb-un-Nissa: A selection of Poems from her Divan*. pp. 7-28. Victoria: New Humanity Books- Book Heaven, 2012.

Strauss, Valerie. "Who is the most educated English queen?" In *The Washington Post*. April 29, 2011. https://www.washingtonpost.com/blogs/answer-sheet/post/who-is-the-most-educated-english-queen/011/04/28/AF78i49E_blog.html. Accessed on 24 April 2020.

Subrahmanyam, Sanjay. "Hearing Voices: Vignettes of Early Modernity in South Asia, 1400- 1750". In *Daedalus*, Vol. 127, No. 3, 1998. pp. 75-104.

Stuart, Charles. *The History of Bengal from the First Mohammedan Invasion until the Virtual Conquest of that Country by the English A.D. 1757*. Cambridge University Press, 2013.

Sundaresan, Indu. *The Feast of Roses*. New York: Washington Square Press, 2003.

Sundaresan, Indu. *The Shadow Princess*. New York: Atria Books, 2010.

Tharu, Susie J. and K. Lalita. *Women Writing in India: 600 BC to Early Twentieth Century*. CUNY: Feminist Press, 1991.

Thunberg, Charles P. *Travels in Europe, Africa, and Asia, performed between the years 1770 and 1779*. 3rd ed Vol. III. London: Gale Ecco, 2018.

Tirmizi, Sayyid A. I. *Edicts from the Mughal Harem*. Delhi: Mohammad Ahmad for Idarah-i- Adabiyat-I, 2009.

Truschke, Audrey. *Aurangzeb: The Life and Legacy of India's Most Controversial King*. California: Stanford University Press, 2017.

Turner, Catherine. "Women's Travel Writing 1750-1830". In *The History of British Women's Writing, 1750-1830*. Vol 5, Labbe, Jacqueline M. (ed.), Palgrave Macmillan, 2010. pp. 47-62.

Venuti, Lawrence. *The Translator's Invisibility: A History of Translation*. New York: Routledge, 1995.

Verma, Chob Singh. *Mughal Romances*. Agra: Y K Publishers, 1996.

Viswanathan, Gauri. *Masks of Conquest*. New York: Columbia University Press, 2014.

Wakhlu, Som Nath. *Habba Khatoon: The Nightingale of Kashmir*. Kashmir: South Asia Publications, 1994.

Waldemar Hansen, *The Peacock Throne: The Drama of Mogul India*. Delhi: Motilal Banarasi Das Publishers, 1986.

Walsh, Declan. *The Nine Lives of Pakistan: Dispatches form a Divided Nation*. Bloomsbury Publishing, 2020.

Wani, Ashraf. "Sectional President's Address: Akbar and Kashmir". In *Proceedings of the Indian History Congress*, Vol. 73 (2012), pp. 184-204.

Zeb-un-Nissa. *The Diwan of Zeb-un-Nissa: The First Fifty Ghazals Rendered from the Persian*. Translated by Magan Lal and Jessie Duncan Westbrook. London. John Murray, 1913. Reproduced by Hardpress publishing.

Zeb-un-Nissa. *Makhfi: The Princess Sufi Poet Zeb-un-Nissa*. Translated and edited by Paul Smith. Australia: New Humanity Books, 2012.

"In Right Wing Politics, Inevitably New Figures Emerge That are even more Extreme." *The Wire*. Interview with Arjun Appadurai on August 5, 2021. https://www.youtube.com/watch?v=Td3BJyVkXiQ

# Index

## A

Adil, Mohammed, 15, 72, 74, 75, 170
Aghacha, 25
Agrippa, Heinrich Cornelius, 5
Ahmad of Jam, 49
Ahmed, Habibuddin, 144
*Ain-i-Akbari*, 23, 169
Ajayameru, 81
Ajmer, xvii,75, 79, 81, 96, 171
Akbar, Jalaluddin, xiv, xv, xxii, xxiii, 1, 9, 10, 14, 17, 18, 23, 24, 25, 28, 29, 30, 31, 36, 39, 45, 48, 49, 54, 56, 57, 59, 60, 70, 71, 87, 88, 91, 110, 112, 113, 114, 115, 117, 130, 138, 143, 144, 145, 146, 147, 156, 163, 164, 165, 172, 174
*Akbarnama*, xiv, xvi, 1, 23, 143, 161, 167, 169
Akbar, Sultan Muhammad, 113
Alam, Muzaffar, 9, 168
Alamgir, 106
Alexander, 131
Ali, Muhammad, 42
Amin, Sonia Nishat, vi, vii, xi, xxiv, 42
Amuli, Talib, 70
Ana Sagar Lake, 81
Andrea, Bernadette, 11, 12, 14, 62, 63, 167
Angelou, Maya, 159, 167
Appadurai, Arjun, 159, 167
Aqiqa, 28, 46
Arnimal, 136, 149
*Arsh e Muallah*, 82

Article 370, 8, 136
Aurangzeb, xi, xiii, xvi, xix, xx, 17, 46, 51, 62,63, 64, 65, 67, 68, 69, 70, 71, 84, 92, 94, 103, 104, 105, 106, 107, 109, 110, 111, 112, 113, 114, 115, 117, 118, 119, 122, 123, 130, 132, 133, 165, 167, 170
Aurangzeb Road, 65
Autotopographical, 1
Aviary, xiii, xiv, xvii, xviii, xix, xxi, xxiii, 1, 8, 14, 16, 17, 18, 23, 35, 37, 40, 43, 45, 46, 50, 93, 103, 110, 135, 145, 149, 155, 156, 163, 164,
Ayodhya, 59

## B

Babur, xiv, xv, 9, 16, 17, 20, 24, 25, 26, 27, 28, 29, 30, 31, 32, 33, 34, 35, 36, 37, 38, 39, 40, 41, 42, 43, 50, 51, 52, 53, 54, 55, 57, 58, 59, 60, 61, 70, 77, 87, 89, 93, 168, 173
*Babur Nama*, xv, 9, 25, 29, 88, 168
Badakhshi, Mullah Shah, xiv, xvii, 1, 67, 69, 72, 73, 74, 81, 87, 89, 90, 91, 93, 94, 95, 96, 98, 99, 147, 163
Badakhshan, 25
Bagh, Anguri, Shalimar, Hayat Baksh, Mahtab, 63
Bagh-i-Babur, 160
Bagh, Qara, 52
Bagh, Ram, 41
Bahadur, Tegh, 65

Bai, Mira, 127, 128, 133
Bajaur, 25
Bakhsh, Muhammad Kam, 106
Bakhtiyar, Bakhtiar, Sayyid Muhammad, 84
Baksh, Muhammad Murad, 69
Baqi, Mir, 59
Bayaz, Ustad, 107
Bedil, 104
Begam, Jahanara, vii, viii, xii, xiv, xv, xvi, xvii, xviii, xix, xxi, 1, 10, 11, 12, 13, 14, 15, 16, 17, 19, 21, 26, 34, 43, 46, 60, 61, 62, 63, 64, 65, 66, 67, 68, 69, 70, 71, 72, 73, 74, 75, 76, 77, 78, 79, 80, 81, 82, 83, 84, 85, 86, 87, 88, 89, 90, 91, 92, 93, 94, 95, 96, 97, 98, 99, 100, 101, 102, 103, 105, 113, 114, 116, 117, 129, 139, 147, 160, 163, 164, 165, 168, 170
Begam, Dildar, 25, 26, 46, 51, 56, 57
Begam, Gulbadan, xii, xiv, xv, xvii, xviii, xix, xxi, xxii, xxiii, 1, 10, 11, 14, 15, 18, 19, 21, 23, 24, 25, 26, 27, 28, 29, 30, 31, 32, 33, 34, 35, 36, 37, 38, 39, 40, 41, 42, 43, 44, 45, 46, 47, 48, 49, 50, 51, 52, 53, 54, 55, 56, 57, 58, 59, 60, 76, 88, 89, 91, 93, 95, 103, 139, 145, 156, 160, 161, 163, 164, 165, 167, 169, 173
Begam, Gulbarg, 44, 45
Begam, Gulchihra, 25
Begam, Gulrang, 25
Begam, Hamida Banu, 1, 26, 45, 48, 49, 50, 60
Begam, Khanzada, 32, 34, 40, 44, 49, 50, 51, 56, 93, 164
Begam, Mah, 57
Begam, Mah Chuchak, 51
Begam, Maham, 25, 26, 28, 35, 39, 40, 41, 42, 43, 45, 55, 57, 61

Begam, Mihr Angez, 56
Behn, Aphra, xxi
Behraaz, 107
Bengali Renaissance, 4
Beveridge, Annette Akroyd, xv, 15, 16, 25, 30, 31, 37, 38, 40, 41, 44, 45, 47, 48, 51, 54, 56, 167, 169
Bhira, Bhera, 35, 53
Bigotry, 94, 165
Blake, Stephen P., 9, 167
Bokhari, Afshan, vii, viii, 1, 12, 13, 14, 15, 21, 30, 75, 77, 78, 84, 86, 87, 88, 89, 94, 95, 96, 116, 167, 168
Boughton, Gabriel, 66, 67, 72, 102, 169
Brahmaputra, 5
Buddhism, 13, 117, 143
Butenschon, Andrea, 63, 168
Butler, Judith, 17, 168

# C

Cary, Elizabeth Tanfield, 162
Cavendish, Margaret Lucas, xxi, 18, 162
Chak, Yusuf Shah, xxii, 25, 136, 142, 143, 145, 146, 147, 155
Champanir, Champaner, 45
Charikaran, 52
Chatterjee, Bankim Chandra, xix
Chatterjee, Kumkum, 162, 168
Chauhan, Prithwiraj, 81
Chausa, 46, 49, 51
Chirag-Dehlavi, Nasiruddin Mahmud, 85
Chishti, Khwaja Moinuddin, xiv, xvii, 15, 17, 60, 69, 72, 75, 76, 77, 78, 79, 80, 81, 82, 83, 84, 87
Chishtiyah, xvii, 62, 72, 76, 83, 85, 87, 98, 139
Christine de Pizan, xix, xxi
Civilizing mission, xi

Cixous, Hélène, 2, 118, 168
Coleridge, S. T., 11, 67

## D

Dale, Stephen F., 9, 168
Daulatabad, 106
Das, Nirmal, 122, 168
*Diwan-i-Aam*, 95
*Diwan-i- Makhfi*, 115, 116, 119
Donne, John, 5
Dumas, Alexandre, 103, 169

## E

*Écriture féminine*, 2
Elizabeth I, 4, 29, 64, 66, 138, 151
Elizabethan Age, xix
Emerson, Ralph Waldo, 61, 169

## F

Fantasy, xi, 2, 67
*Faqira*, 86, 89, 101
Farish, J., xi
Fazl, Abul, xv, 1, 23, 27, 31, 49, 54, 55, 143, 144, 145, 161, 164, 167, 169
Fazl, Nagul, 27
Findly, Ellison Bank, 10, 169
*Firdaus-makani*, 30, 31
Flirting Bazaar, 64
Fort William College, 4
Franco, Veronica, xxi
Friedan, Betty, 163, 169

## G

Ganj-i-Shakar, Ganjesakar, Farid al-Din Masud, 85
Gaur, 28, 45, 48
Gazi, Rustum, 107
Ghakkar, Adam, 53

Gibbon, Edward, 3
Gilani, Abdul Qadir, 62
Girri, Maheish, 65
Godden, Rumer, 25, 26, 27, 28, 29, 48, 54, 60, 169
Greville, Fulke, 20, 170
Gupta, Ruchir, vii, 67, 91, 99, 102, 115, 117,
Gurez, 18, 138
Gynocritics, gynocriticism, xii

## H

Habib, Irfan, 3, 4, 12, 170
*Hadith*, 92
Hafiz, Hafez, poet, 104, 107, 116, 117, 118, 124, 125, 172
*Hafiz*, 106, 107
Hallaj, Husayn Mansur, 118, 119, 170
*Haqiqa*, 92
Harem, vi, xi, xii, xiii, xv, xvi, 1, 5, 6, 8, 9, 10, 11, 14, 16, 25, 26, 28, 37, 39, 42, 43, 44, 45, 46, 50, 51, 55, 57, 60, 61, 62, 63, 64, 65, 66, 69, 70, 88, 93, 97, 98, 101, 104, 107, 110, 114, 118, 123, 133, 136, 146, 163, 170, 171, 172, 173
Harun at Nisapur, 78
Haruni, Uthman, 78, 79, 83, 84
Hindal, Abu-n-Nasir Muhammad,10, 25, 31, 34, 37, 42, 44, 46, 47, 48, 51, 52, 53, 54, 56, 57, 58
Horace, 151
Huma, Homa, 131
Humayun, xiv, 16, 23, 24, 26, 27, 28, 29, 30, 31, 33, 34, 35, 41, 42, 43, 44, 45, 46, 47, 48, 49, 50, 51, 52, 53, 54, 55, 56, 57, 58, 59, 60
*Humayun-Nama*, xii, xiv, xv, xix, 15, 16, 17, 23, 24, 25, 26, 27, 29,

30, 31, 32, 33, 38, 54, 59, 88, 89, 161, 163, 167
Humayun Road, 65

# I

Ibrahim, Hadhrat, 77, 78

# J

*Jabarut, Malakut, Lahoot*, 92
Jaffrey, Dr Yunus, 75
Jainism, 13
Jamshid, 131
*Jannat-ashyani*, 30
Julaikha, Zuleikha, 131

# K

Kabir, 122, 148, 168
Kabul, xv, 25, 27, 28, 29, 32, 33, 34, 36, 38, 40, 41, 46, 49, 50, 51, 52, 53, 54, 55, 56, 57, 60, 69, 91, 97, 114, 160
Kalima, 79
Kamran, Mirza, 28, 29, 35, 38, 46, 47, 48, 49, 50, 51, 52, 53, 54, 55, 56, 57, 58, 59, 144
Kar, Debamitra, viii, 118, 125, 170
Kashani, Kalim, 104
Kashmiri, Ghani, 104, 107
Khaki, Baba Daud, 146
Khan, Genghis, Chingiz, 26, 38
Khan, Khizr Khwaja, 28, 48, 53, 60
Khan, Kubla, 11
Khan, Naimatullah, 107
Khan, Sher, 28
Khan, Shir, 47, 53, 59
Khanam, Sati-al-Nisa, 70
Khatoon, Habba, vii, xiv, xxii, xxiii, 1, 7, 13, 15, 17, 18, 19, 127, 128, 133, 135, 136, 137, 138, 139, 140, 141, 142, 144, 146, 147, 148, 149, 150, 151, 152, 153, 154, 155, 156, 160, 163, 164, 165, 167, 172, 173
Khayyam, Omar, 64, 116,
Kilan, Khwaja, 36, 38
Kulab, 51
Kulabi, 16
Kumaon, 5
Kunduz, 25, 51
Kush-ab, 53
Krynicki, Annie Krieger, 113, 114, 115, 170

# L

Lal, Ruby, 8, 14, 37, 66, 171
Lalchand, xii
Lalded, 126, 127, 128, 133, 141, 147, 148, 149, 156
Lalleswari, 141
Lalita, K, xi, xii, xxiii, 16, 173
Lal, Magan, 15, 114, 174
Lambert-Hurley, Siobhan, xviii, 13, 168, 171
Lamghanat, 52
Lanyer, Aemilia, 162
Lapel, 1
Lasky, Kathryn, vii, 64, 65, 66, 171
Le Guin, Ursula K., 135, 171
Lodi, Ibrahim, Sultan, 29, 36, 39
Lol, 135, 148, 149
Loomba, Ania, 105, 171
Losty and Roy, xii, 171

# M

Ma a'zam a-sha'ni, 93
*Magun*, 69
*Mahabharata*, xvii, 156
Makhfi, xiv, xxi, 17, 104, 108, 115, 116, 117, 118, 119, 121, 129, 173, 174

Malhotra, Anshu, xviii, 13, 168, 171
Manley, Delarivier, 12
Manucci, Niccolao, 66, 113, 115, 171
Mansingh Road, Shahjahan Road, Humayun Road, Prithviraj Road, 65
*Maqtaa*, 119
Marguerite de Briet, xxi
Mariam, Hafiza, 106, 107
Marlowe, Christopher, 5, 20, 171
Mary I, Queen, 4
Mattoo, Neerja, xxiii, 127, 128, 135, 137, 138, 140, 141, 142, 149, 150, 151, 152, 153, 154, 155, 156, 171
Mawarau-n-Nahr, 34
Maywa-jan, 43
Milwat, 29
Mir, Shah, 143, 148
Miran-shahi, Sulaiman Mirza, 16, 56
Mirza, Bayasanghar, 32
Mirza, Haider Dughlat, 144
Mirza, Khan, 16, 56
Mirza, Najabat Khan, 68, 71
Mirza, Sulaiman, 35, 51, 57
Misra, Rekha, 9
Miyabai, 107
Mohamdoo, 141
*Monis-ul-Roh*, 115
Mughal, vi, xi, xii, xiii, xiv, xv, xvi, xvii, xviii, xix, xx, xxi, xxii, xxiii, xxiv, 1, 3, 4, 5, 6, 7, 9, 11, 12, 13, 14, 15, 17, 18, 19, 20, 21, 23, 25, 26, 27, 29, 32, 33, 34, 35, 37, 40, 41, 43, 44, 45, 46, 47, 48, 49, 50, 51, 52, 53, 54, 56, 57, 58, 59, 61, 62, 63, 65, 66, 67, 68, 69, 70, 71, 72, 73, 74, 75, 76, 77, 78, 79, 80, 81, 82, 84, 85, 86, 87, 88, 89, 90, 91, 93, 95, 96, 97, 98, 99, 100, 101, 102, 103, 104, 105, 106, 107, 108, 109, 110, 111, 112, 113, 116, 117, 123, 124, 126, 133, 135, 136, 137, 138, 143, 144, 145, 146, 147, 149, 155, 156, 159, 160, 161, 162, 163, 164, 165, 167, 168, 169
Muhammad, Sayyid, 54, 84
*Muhr Uzak*, 69
*Mujar e Manjil*, 82
Mukhoty, Ira, vii, 24, 25, 26, 27, 29, 74, 171
Mumtaz Mahal, xvi, 16, 62, 68, 69, 70
*Munis, Munis-ul-Arwah*, xvii, xviii, 69, 70, 72, 74, 75, 77, 78, 81, 89, 91, 101

## N

Nagori, Hadhrat Sheikh Hamiduddin Sufi, 84
Naqshabandi, 87
Nath, Renuka, 10, 171
*Navaratnas*, 23
Nawa Kot, 115
Nawaz, Khwaja Gharib, 75, 78
Neolithic, 4
Nur Jahan, 10, 11, 16, 61, 64, 169, 171

## O

O'Hanlon, Rosalind, 10, 172
Orientalist Gaze, xi, 14

## P

Padshah, Padishah, 19, 34, 44, 46, 61, 69
Pal, Ajay, 81, 82
Panda Chok, xxii, 147
Peirce, Leslie P., 10, 55, 56, 172

Philips, Katherine, 162
*Pir*, 87, 88, 94, 125
Pir Panjal Range, 143
Pir, Zinda, 120
Pocock, J.G.A., 3, 172
Pre-Modern, vii, viii, xiii, xix, xxiv, 1, 2, 4, 5, 7, 12, 14, 15, 19, 20, 21, 52, 56, 57, 60, 62, 69, 85, 102, 129, 132, 135, 161, 168
Puran, 99
*Purdah*, 26, 56, 65

## Q

Qaba, 77, 120, 121, 122, 165
Qadiriya, xvii, 3, 62, 68, 69, 72, 74, 81, 98, 100
Qandahar, 16, 25, 32, 35, 50, 51, 56
Qasim, Khwaja, 39, 40
Quibchaq, Sultan Wais Kulabi, 52
Qutb Minar, 84

## R

Rabi'a Basri, Rabi'a , xvii, 74, 90
Rahaman,Valiur, 15, 72, 74, 75, 170
*Ramarajya*, 137
*Rast-i-Kashmiri*, 142, 148, 165
Raychaudhuri,Tapan, 9, 172
Razi, Aqil Khan, xx, 107, 110, 111, 115
Roushanara, 62, 64, 68, 69
Roy, Ram Mohan, 4
Rumuz E Bekhudi, 136, 137
Rustom, Rostam, 129, 131

## S

Sadhu, Shyam Lal, xxiii, 122, 135, 138, 147, 148, 149, 150, 152, 153, 172
Sa'di, Shaikh, 87
*Safinat-ul-Aulia*, 77

*Sahibiya, Risala-i-Sahibiya*, viii, xvii, 15, 21, 68, 69, 70, 72, 73, 74, 75, 78, 81, 85, 86, 89, 90, 95, 96, 98, 99, 100, 101, 165, 170
Sahib-qiran, 38
Sahitya Akademi, xxiii, 149
Showalter, Elaine, xii, 173
Said, Edward, 12, 19
Sajastan, 77, 79
Salami, Ali, 125, 172
Samarqand, 32, 34, 78
Sarfi, Shaikh Yakub, 146
Sarkar, Jadunath, xix, xx, 70, 106, 111, 115, 170, 171, 172
Sayab, Nasir Ali, 107
Sazsi, Hadhrat Khwaja Moinuddin Hasan, 76
Shadi djinn, 82
Shah, Muhammad Azam, 106
Shah, Yaqub, 145, 146, 147
Shahjahanabad, 9, 65, 72, 167
Shakespeare, William, 5, 20, 138, 172
Shariat, 92
Sharma, Sunil, viii, 15, 72, 74, 75, 90, 101, 170
Shikoh, Dara, xvii, 10, 34, 69, 70, 71, 72, 73, 77, 71, 81, 88, 92, 95, 97, 100, 103, 109, 112, 118, 122, 165
Shikoh, Sulaiman, 109
Shir Khan, 46, 47, 53, 59
Shirin-Farhad, 126
Shuja, Shah, 69
Sidney, Mary, 162
Sikandra, 114, 160
Smith, Paul, xxi, 15, 108, 109, 110, 111, 117, 118, 119, 123, 124, 126, 170, 173, 174
Subalternity, xiv, 17
Sufi, ix, xiii, xiv, xv, xix, 17, 19, 22, 34, 58, 68, 69, 70, 72, 73, 74, 75, 76, 77, 78, 79, 80, 81, 82, 83, 84,

85, 86, 87, 88, 89, 90, 92, 93, 94,
  96, 97, 100, 101, 102, 104, 107,
  108, 110, 112, 117, 118, 120,
  123, 126, 131, 132, 133, 139,
  142, 144, 146, 148, 156, 160,
  163, 164, 165
Sufism, 62, 67, 68, 74, 80, 83, 84,
  87, 88, 102, 118, 120, 130, 165
Sufi ideology, Jabarut, Malakut,
  Lahoot, 92
Sultan, Qasim, 40
Sundaresan, Indu, 67, 68, 173
Sunni, xix, xx, 19, 36, 58, 60, 62, 87,
  92, 93, 98, 119, 133, 165
Swat, 25
*Swayamvara*, 109

## T

Tabrizi, Saa'eb, 104
Tagore, Abanindranath, xv
Tai, Hatim, 131
Tamerlane, Timur, 6, 26, 87, 123
Tahmas, Shah, 58
*Tariqat*, 92
Tarkalankar, Madan Mohan, 4
Terrible Elephant, 48, 49
Tharu, Susie J., xi, xii, xxiii, 16, 173
*The Feminine Mystique*, 163
*The Laugh of the Medusa*, 2, 168
The Passing of Shah Jahan, xv
The pleasure principle, 9
Timurid, 6, 19, 20, 26, 27, 37, 38,
  40, 44, 52, 54, 55, 57, 58, 59, 72,
  77, 81, 87, 88, 96, 98, 99, 168
Tirmizi, S. A. I., 1, 5, 6, 16, 173
Transoxania, 34
Trope, xii, 18, 81, 102, 125, 129, 161
Truschke, Audrey, 165, 173
Tsang, Hiuen, 5
Tyndale, William, 122

## U

Udaipuri Mahal, 106
Ullah, Shams Wali, 107
Umarkot, 49
Uthman-i-Haruni, Uthman
  Haruni, 78, 79, 83, 84
Uzbegs, 33, 35, 58

## V

Vahdat, 93
Venuti, Lawrence, 15, 173
Verma, Chob Singh, 71, 173
Vidyasagar, Ishwar Chandra, 4
Viswanathan, Gauri, xi, 173

## W

Wahdat al-Wujud, 93
Wakhlu, S. N., vii, xxii, 138, 139,
  140, 141, 142, 144, 145, 146,
  147, 156, 173
Wellesley, Lord, 4
Westbrook, Jessie Duncan, 15, 108,
  112, 113, 115, 119, 123, 125,
  129, 174
Wollstonecraft, Mary, xix
Wroth, Mary, 12, 162

## Y

Yousufzai, Malik Mansur, 34

## Z

Zaina Bridge, 155
Zeb-un-Nissa, viii, xiv, xix, xx, xxi,
  10, 11, 13, 14, 15, 17, 19, 35, 46,
  51, 102, 103, 104, 105, 106, 107,
  108, 109, 110, 111, 112, 113,
  114, 115, 116, 117, 118, 119,
  120, 121, 122, 123, 124, 125,

126, 127, 128, 129, 130, 131, 132, 133, 135, 139, 160, 163, 164, 165, 170, 173, 174
Zenana, xiv, xxiii, 16, 17, 18, 24, 26, 44, 46, 96, 103, 145
Zinat-un-Nissa, 106
Zubdat-un-Nissa, 106
Zulaikha, 131

www.ingramcontent.com/pod-product-compliance
Lightning Source LLC
Chambersburg PA
CBHW052117300426
44116CB00010B/1696